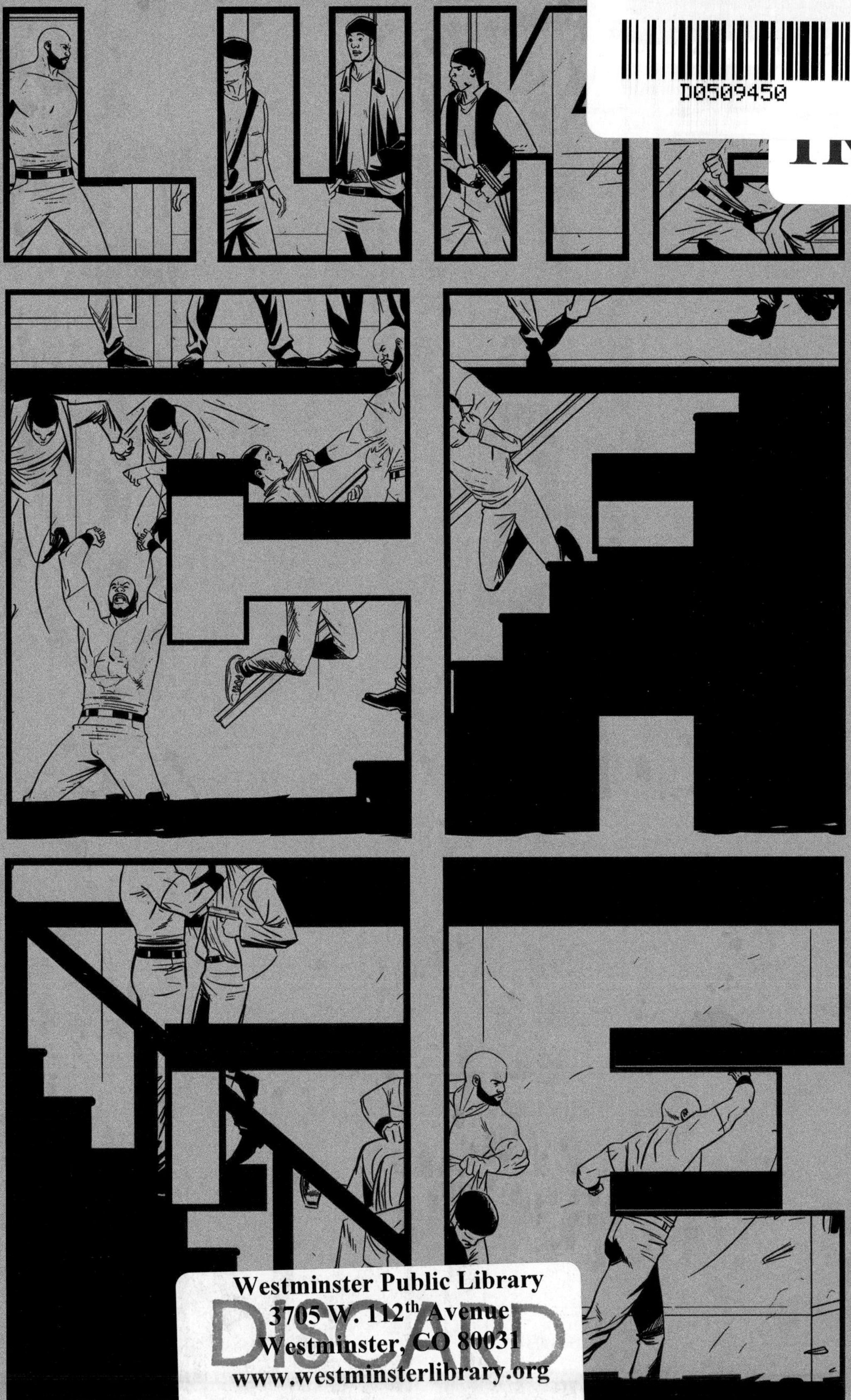

SINS OF THE FATHER

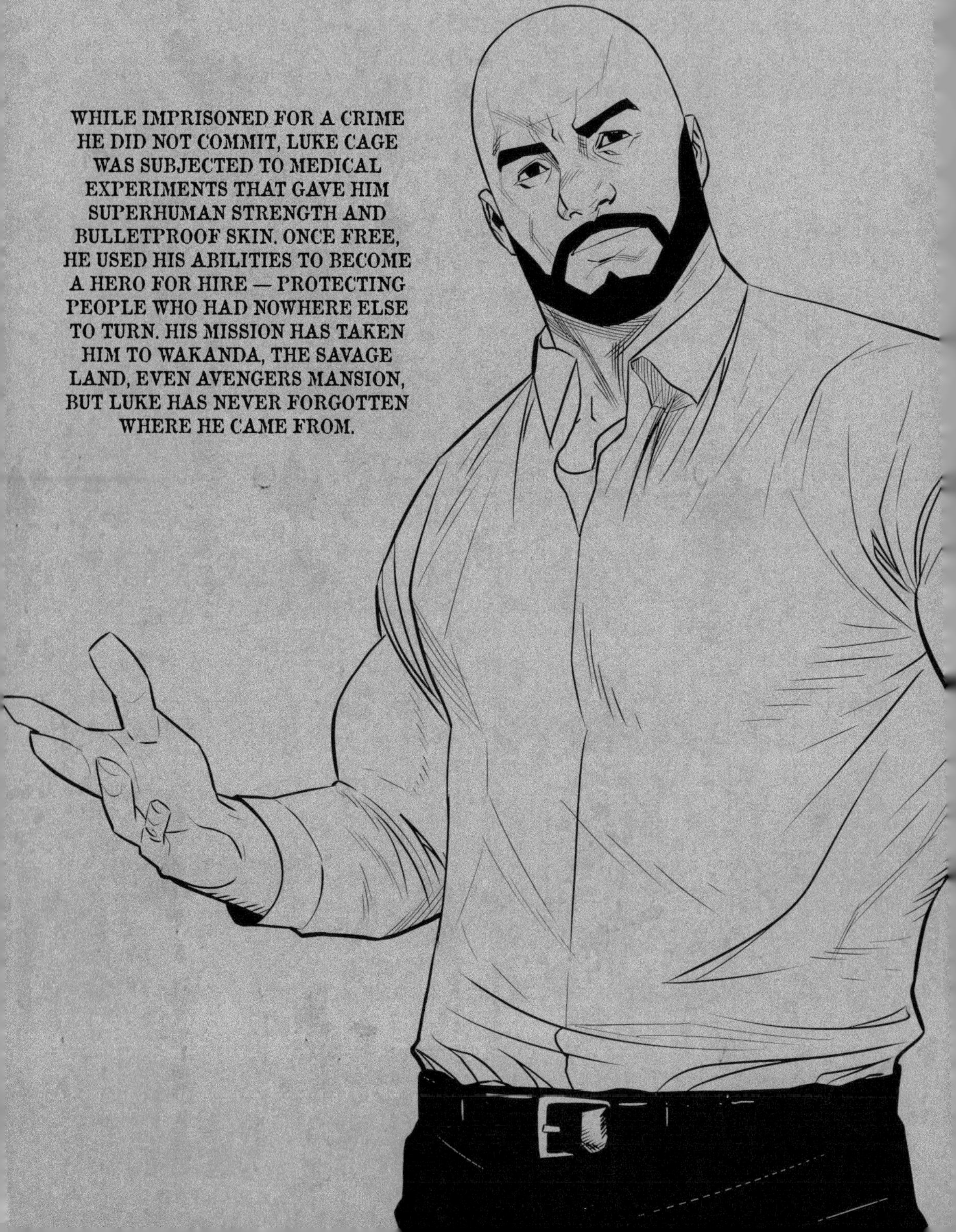
WHILE IMPRISONED FOR A CRIME HE DID NOT COMMIT, LUKE CAGE WAS SUBJECTED TO MEDICAL EXPERIMENTS THAT GAVE HIM SUPERHUMAN STRENGTH AND BULLETPROOF SKIN. ONCE FREE, HE USED HIS ABILITIES TO BECOME A HERO FOR HIRE — PROTECTING PEOPLE WHO HAD NOWHERE ELSE TO TURN. HIS MISSION HAS TAKEN HIM TO WAKANDA, THE SAVAGE LAND, EVEN AVENGERS MANSION, BUT LUKE HAS NEVER FORGOTTEN WHERE HE CAME FROM.

LUKE CAGE

SINS OF THE FATHER

DAVID F. WALKER
WRITER

NELSON BLAKE II
ARTIST

MARCIO MENYZ
COLOR ARTIST

RAHZZAH
COVER ARTIST

VC's JOE SABINO
LETTERER

KATHLEEN WISNESKI
ASSISTANT EDITOR

JAKE THOMAS
EDITOR

COLLECTION EDITOR **MARK D. BEAZLEY**
ASSISTANT EDITOR **CAITLIN O'CONNELL**
ASSOCIATE MANAGING EDITOR **KATERI WOODY**
SENIOR EDITOR, SPECIAL PROJECTS **JENNIFER GRÜNWALD**
VP PRODUCTION & SPECIAL PROJECTS **JEFF YOUNGQUIST**
SVP PRINT, SALES & MARKETING **DAVID GABRIEL**
BOOK DESIGNER **ADAM DEL RE**

EDITOR IN CHIEF **AXEL ALONSO**
CHIEF CREATIVE OFFICER **JOE QUESADA**
PRESIDENT **DAN BUCKLEY**
EXECUTIVE PRODUCER **ALAN FINE**

LUKE CAGE VOL. 1: SINS OF THE FATHER. Contains material originally published in magazine form as LUKE CAGE #1-5. First printing 2017. ISBN# 978-1-302-90778-5. Published by MARVEL WORLDWIDE, INC., a subsidiary of MARVEL ENTERTAINMENT, LLC. OFFICE OF PUBLICATION: 135 West 50th Street, New York, NY 10020. **Printed in the U.S.A.** DAN BUCKLEY, President, Marvel Entertainment; JOE QUESADA, Chief Creative Officer; TOM BREVOORT, SVP of Publishing; DAVID BOGART, SVP of Business Affairs & Operations, Publishing & Partnership; C.B. CEBULSKI, VP of Brand Management & Development, Asia; DAVID GABRIEL, SVP of Sales & Marketing, Publishing; JEFF YOUNGQUIST, VP of Production & Special Projects; DAN CARR, Executive Director of Publishing Technology; ALEX MORALES, Director of Publishing Operations; SUSAN CRESPI, Production Manager; STAN LEE, Chairman Emeritus. For information regarding advertising in Marvel Comics or on Marvel.com, please contact Vit DeBellis, Integrated Sales Manager, at vdebellis@marvel.com. For Marvel subscription inquiries, please call 888-511-5480. **Manufactured between 9/22/2017 and 10/24/2017 by QUAD/GRAPHICS WASECA, WASECA, MN, USA.**

10 9 8 7 6 5 4 3 2 1

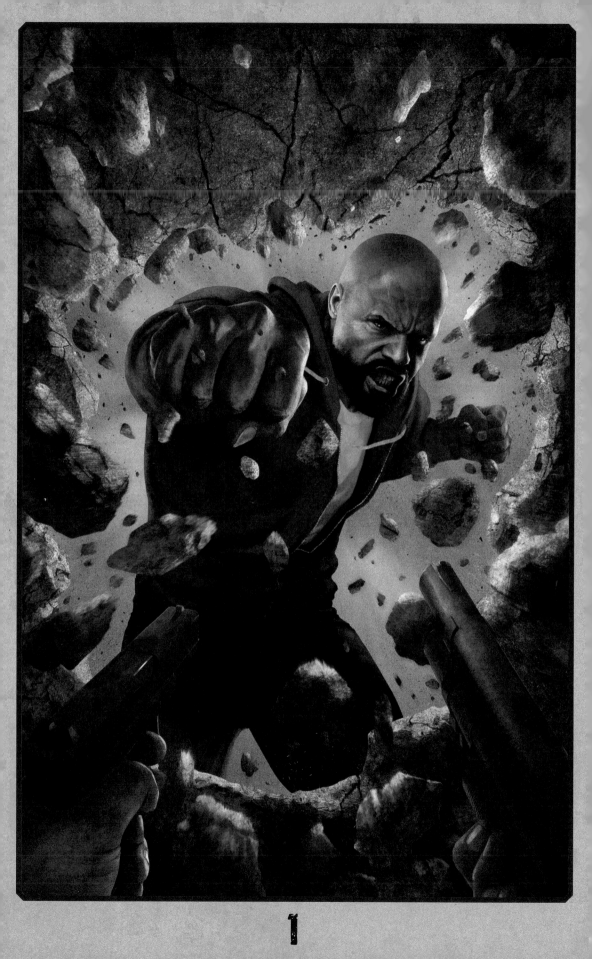

1

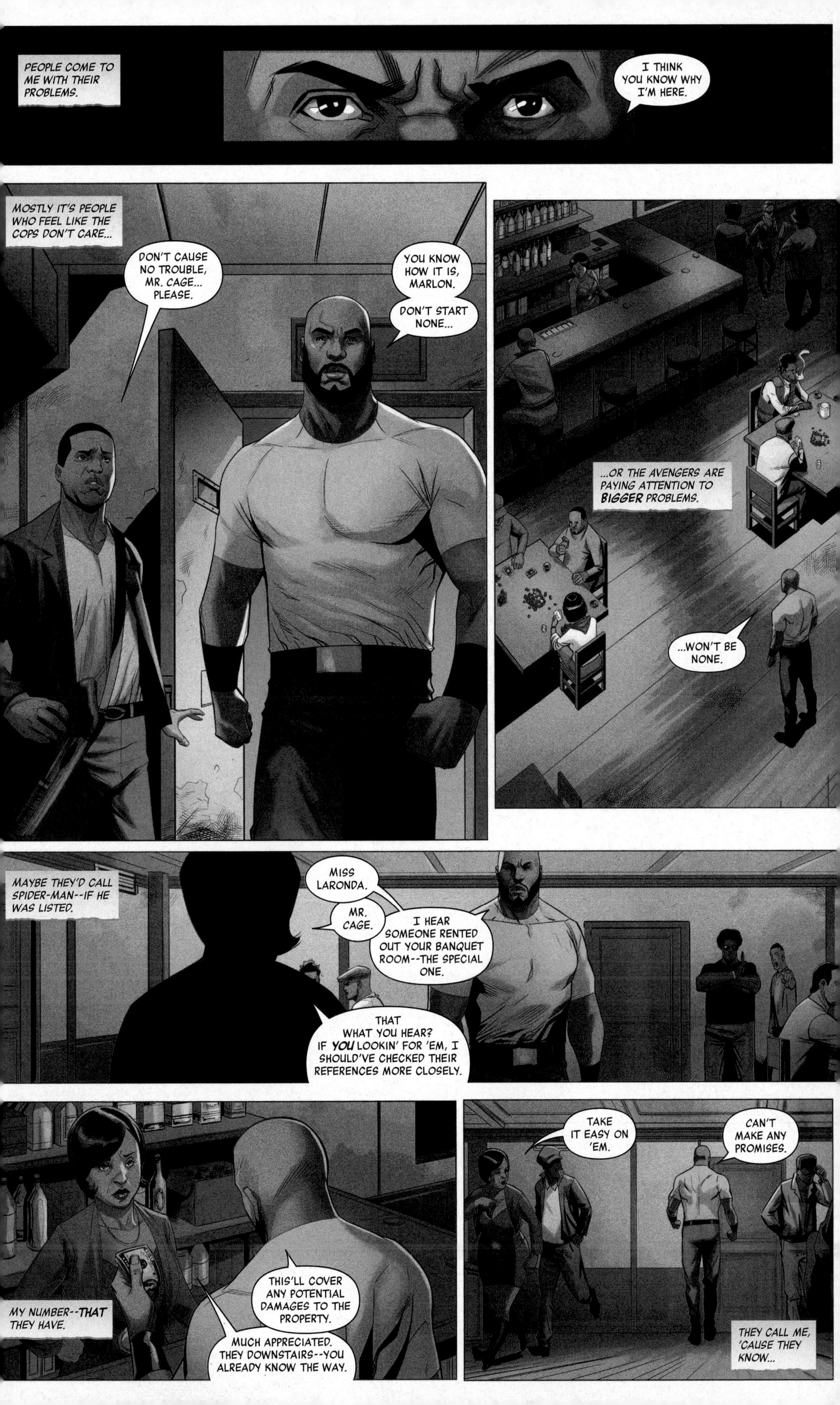
PEOPLE COME TO ME WITH THEIR PROBLEMS.
I THINK YOU KNOW WHY I'M HERE.
MOSTLY IT'S PEOPLE WHO FEEL LIKE THE COPS DON'T CARE...
DON'T CAUSE NO TROUBLE, MR. CAGE... PLEASE.
YOU KNOW HOW IT IS, MARLON.
DON'T START NONE...
...OR THE AVENGERS ARE PAYING ATTENTION TO BIGGER PROBLEMS.
...WON'T BE NONE.
MAYBE THEY'D CALL SPIDER-MAN--IF HE WAS LISTED.
MISS LARONDA.
MR. CAGE.
I HEAR SOMEONE RENTED OUT YOUR BANQUET ROOM--THE SPECIAL ONE.
THAT WHAT YOU HEAR? IF YOU LOOKIN' FOR 'EM, I SHOULD'VE CHECKED THEIR REFERENCES MORE CLOSELY.
MY NUMBER--THAT THEY HAVE.
THIS'LL COVER ANY POTENTIAL DAMAGES TO THE PROPERTY.
MUCH APPRECIATED. THEY DOWNSTAIRS--YOU ALREADY KNOW THE WAY.
TAKE IT EASY ON 'EM.
CAN'T MAKE ANY PROMISES.
THEY CALL ME, 'CAUSE THEY KNOW...

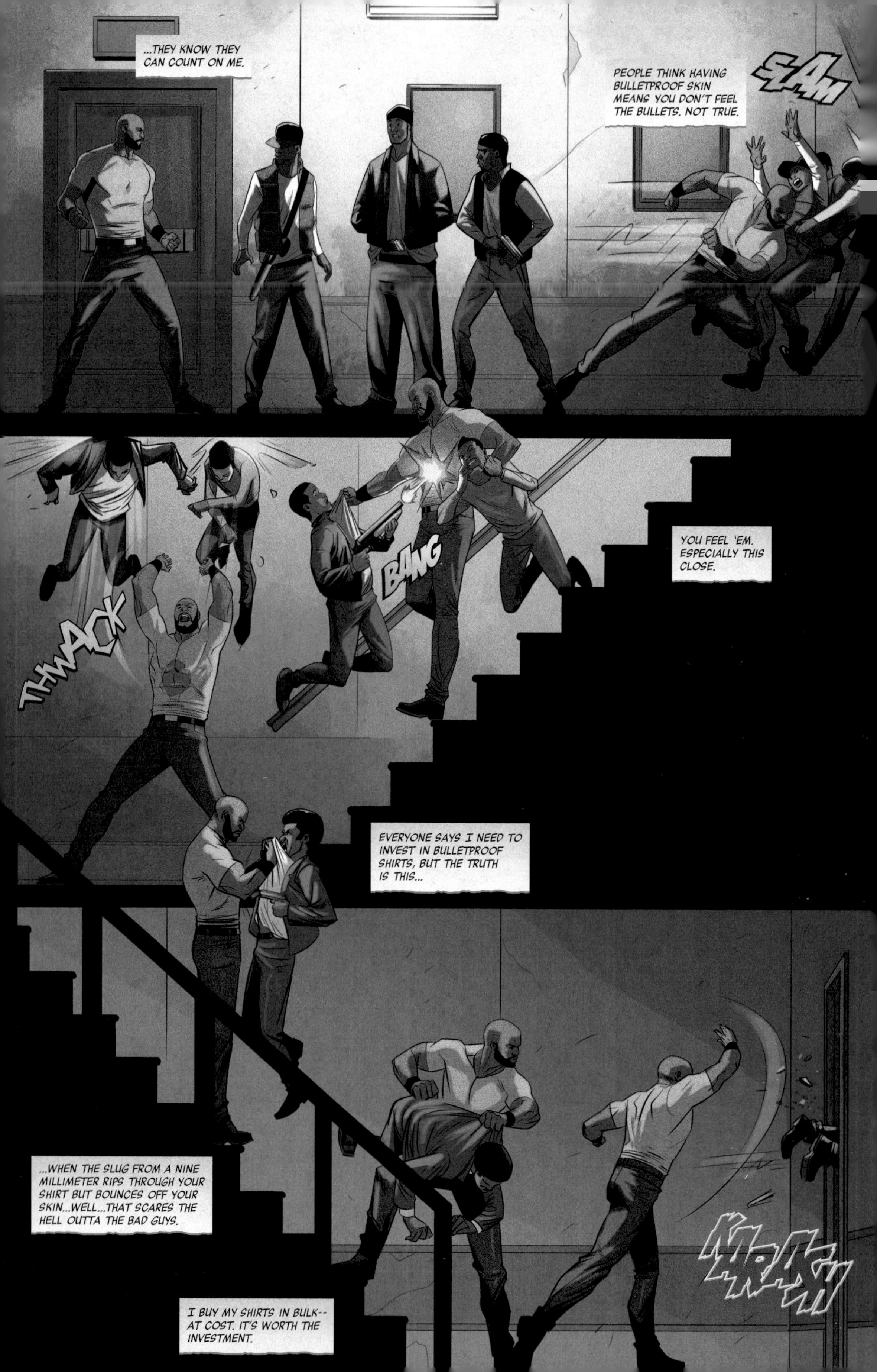
...THEY KNOW THEY CAN COUNT ON ME.
PEOPLE THINK HAVING BULLETPROOF SKIN MEANS YOU DON'T FEEL THE BULLETS. NOT TRUE.
SLAM
BANG
THWACK
YOU FEEL 'EM. ESPECIALLY THIS CLOSE.
EVERYONE SAYS I NEED TO INVEST IN BULLETPROOF SHIRTS, BUT THE TRUTH IS THIS...
...WHEN THE SLUG FROM A NINE MILLIMETER RIPS THROUGH YOUR SHIRT BUT BOUNCES OFF YOUR SKIN...WELL...THAT SCARES THE HELL OUTTA THE BAD GUYS.
I BUY MY SHIRTS IN BULK-- AT COST. IT'S WORTH THE INVESTMENT.

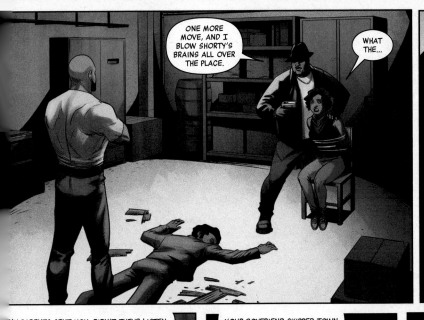

ONE MORE MOVE, AND I BLOW SHORTY'S BRAINS ALL OVER THE PLACE.

WHAT THE...

...WHAT'RE YOU DOIN' HERE?!

COME TO TAKE YOU HOME.

MY PARENTS SENT YOU, DIDN'T THEY? LISTEN, MY BOYFRIEND AND I ARE *GROWN-UPS,* AND WE DON'T NEED HELP.

HE'LL BE HERE ANY MINUTE TO PAY THESE FOOLS THE MONEY HE OWES THEM, THEN *WE'RE* GOIN' HOME!

YOUR BOYFRIEND SKIPPED TOWN AFTER HE TOLD YOUR PARENTS YOU WERE BEING HELD FOR RANSOM.

THEY CALLED ME.

NOW I'M HERE.

WHAT?! YOU LYIN'-- MARKEESE WOULDN'T DO ME LIKE THAT! HE LOVES ME!

WHAT ABOUT THE MONEY HE OWES ME?! I WANT MY FIVE GRAND!

HOLD UP THERE, BIG WORM... YOU TELLIN' ME YOU WENT THROUGH ALL THIS TROUBLE--KIDNAPPING, SENDING A RANSOM NOTE--ALL OF THAT, FOR *FIVE GRAND?*

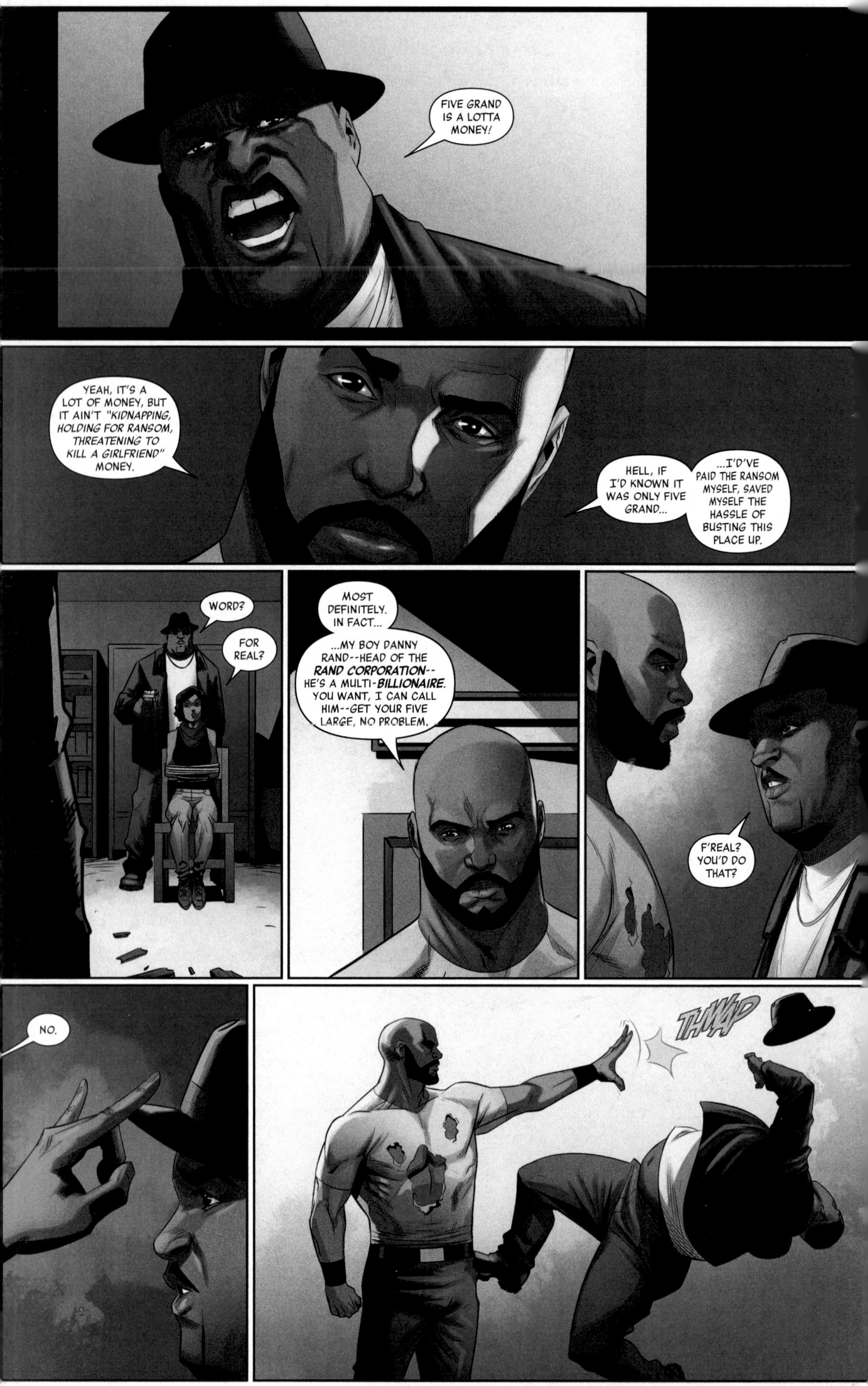
FIVE GRAND IS A LOTTA MONEY!
YEAH, IT'S A LOT OF MONEY, BUT IT AIN'T "KIDNAPPING, HOLDING FOR RANSOM, THREATENING TO KILL A GIRLFRIEND" MONEY.
HELL, IF I'D KNOWN IT WAS ONLY FIVE GRAND...
...I'D'VE PAID THE RANSOM MYSELF, SAVED MYSELF THE HASSLE OF BUSTING THIS PLACE UP.
WORD?
FOR REAL?
MOST DEFINITELY. IN FACT...
...MY BOY DANNY RAND--HEAD OF THE RAND CORPORATION--HE'S A MULTI-BILLIONAIRE. YOU WANT, I CAN CALL HIM--GET YOUR FIVE LARGE, NO PROBLEM.
F'REAL? YOU'D DO THAT?
NO.
THWAP

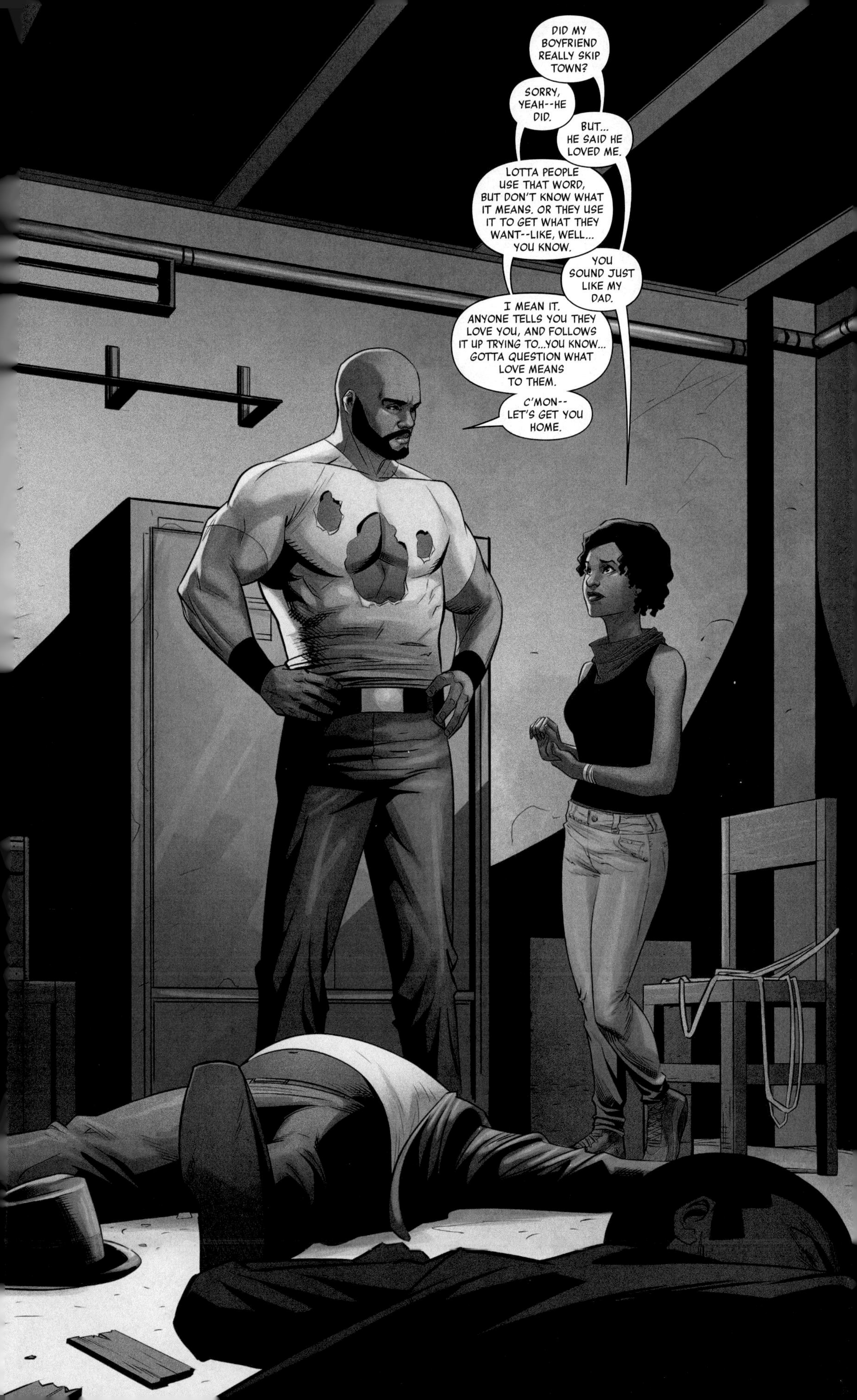

DID MY BOYFRIEND REALLY SKIP TOWN?
SORRY, YEAH--HE DID.
BUT... HE SAID HE LOVED ME.
LOTTA PEOPLE USE THAT WORD, BUT DON'T KNOW WHAT IT MEANS. OR THEY USE IT TO GET WHAT THEY WANT--LIKE, WELL... YOU KNOW.
YOU SOUND JUST LIKE MY DAD.
I MEAN IT. ANYONE TELLS YOU THEY LOVE YOU, AND FOLLOWS IT UP TRYING TO...YOU KNOW... GOTTA QUESTION WHAT LOVE MEANS TO THEM.
C'MON-- LET'S GET YOU HOME.

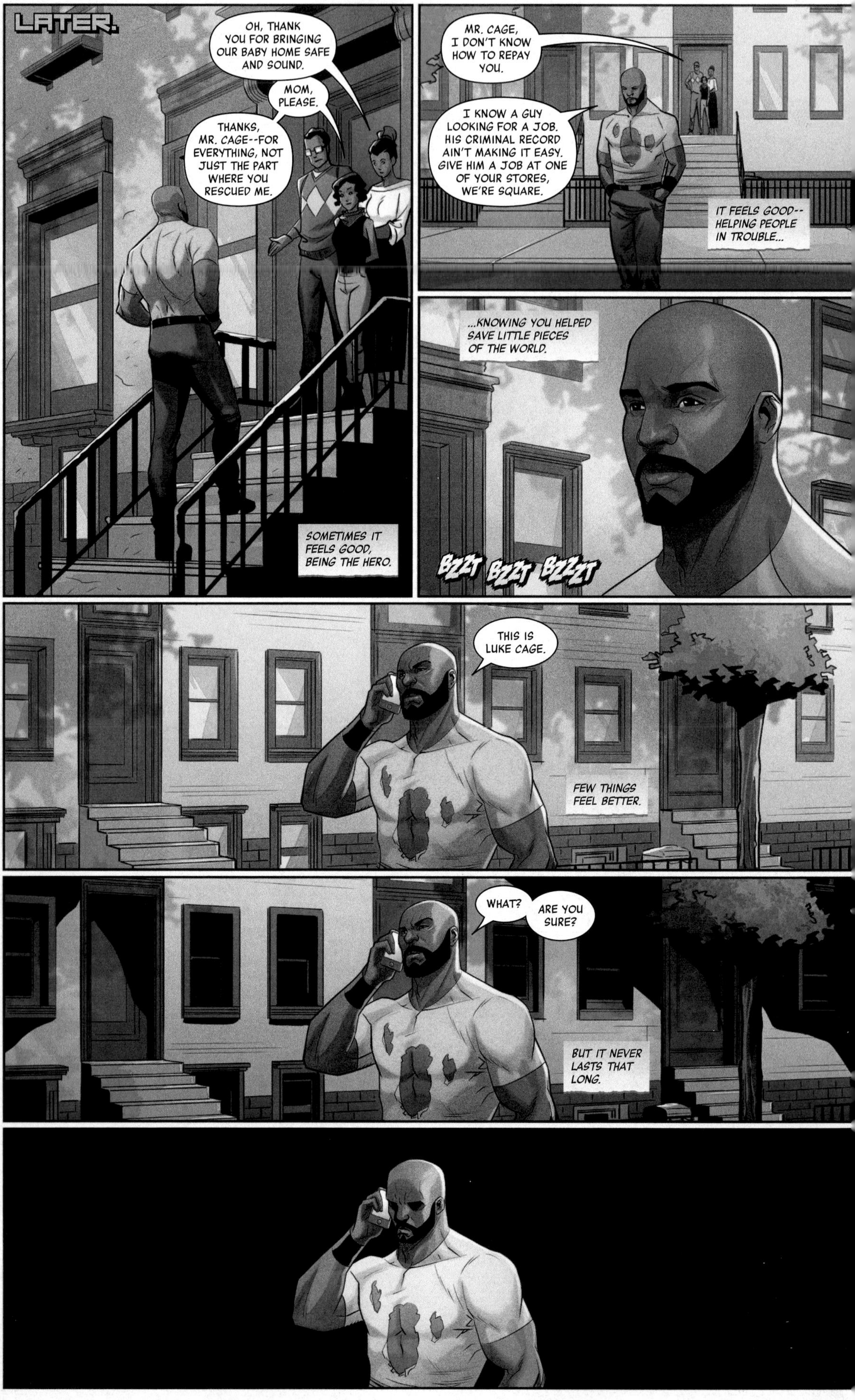

LATER.
OH, THANK YOU FOR BRINGING OUR BABY HOME SAFE AND SOUND.
MOM, PLEASE.
THANKS, MR. CAGE--FOR EVERYTHING, NOT JUST THE PART WHERE YOU RESCUED ME.
SOMETIMES IT FEELS GOOD, BEING THE HERO.
MR. CAGE, I DON'T KNOW HOW TO REPAY YOU.
I KNOW A GUY LOOKING FOR A JOB. HIS CRIMINAL RECORD AIN'T MAKING IT EASY. GIVE HIM A JOB AT ONE OF YOUR STORES, WE'RE SQUARE.
IT FEELS GOOD--HELPING PEOPLE IN TROUBLE...
...KNOWING YOU HELPED SAVE LITTLE PIECES OF THE WORLD.
BZZT BZZT BZZZT
THIS IS LUKE CAGE.
FEW THINGS FEEL BETTER.
WHAT?
ARE YOU SURE?
BUT IT NEVER LASTS THAT LONG.

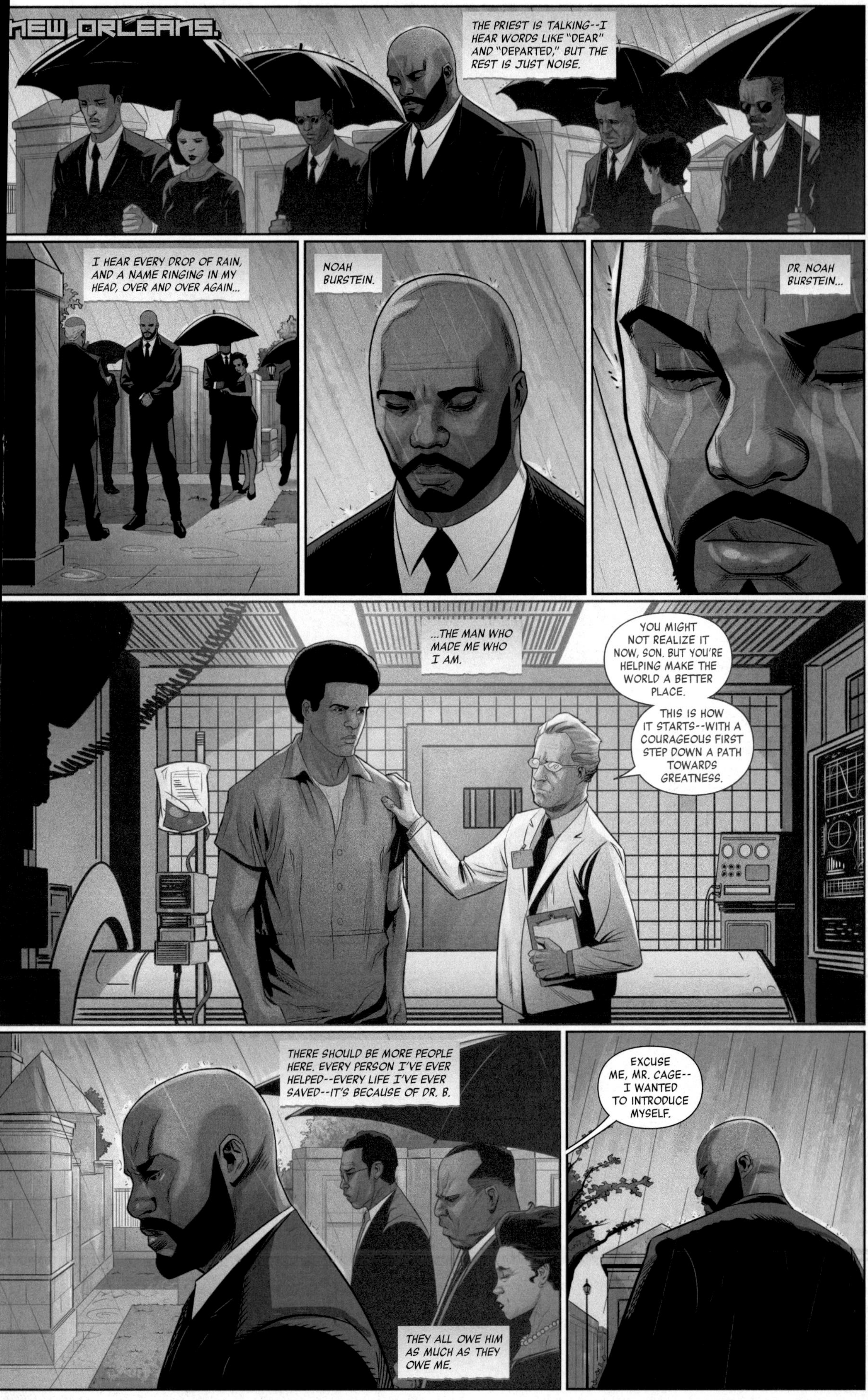
NEW ORLEANS.
THE PRIEST IS TALKING--I HEAR WORDS LIKE "DEAR" AND "DEPARTED," BUT THE REST IS JUST NOISE.
I HEAR EVERY DROP OF RAIN, AND A NAME RINGING IN MY HEAD, OVER AND OVER AGAIN...
NOAH BURSTEIN.
DR. NOAH BURSTEIN...
...THE MAN WHO MADE ME WHO I AM.
YOU MIGHT NOT REALIZE IT NOW, SON. BUT YOU'RE HELPING MAKE THE WORLD A BETTER PLACE.
THIS IS HOW IT STARTS--WITH A COURAGEOUS FIRST STEP DOWN A PATH TOWARDS GREATNESS.
THERE SHOULD BE MORE PEOPLE HERE. EVERY PERSON I'VE EVER HELPED--EVERY LIFE I'VE EVER SAVED--IT'S BECAUSE OF DR. B.
THEY ALL OWE HIM AS MUCH AS THEY OWE ME.
EXCUSE ME, MR. CAGE--I WANTED TO INTRODUCE MYSELF.

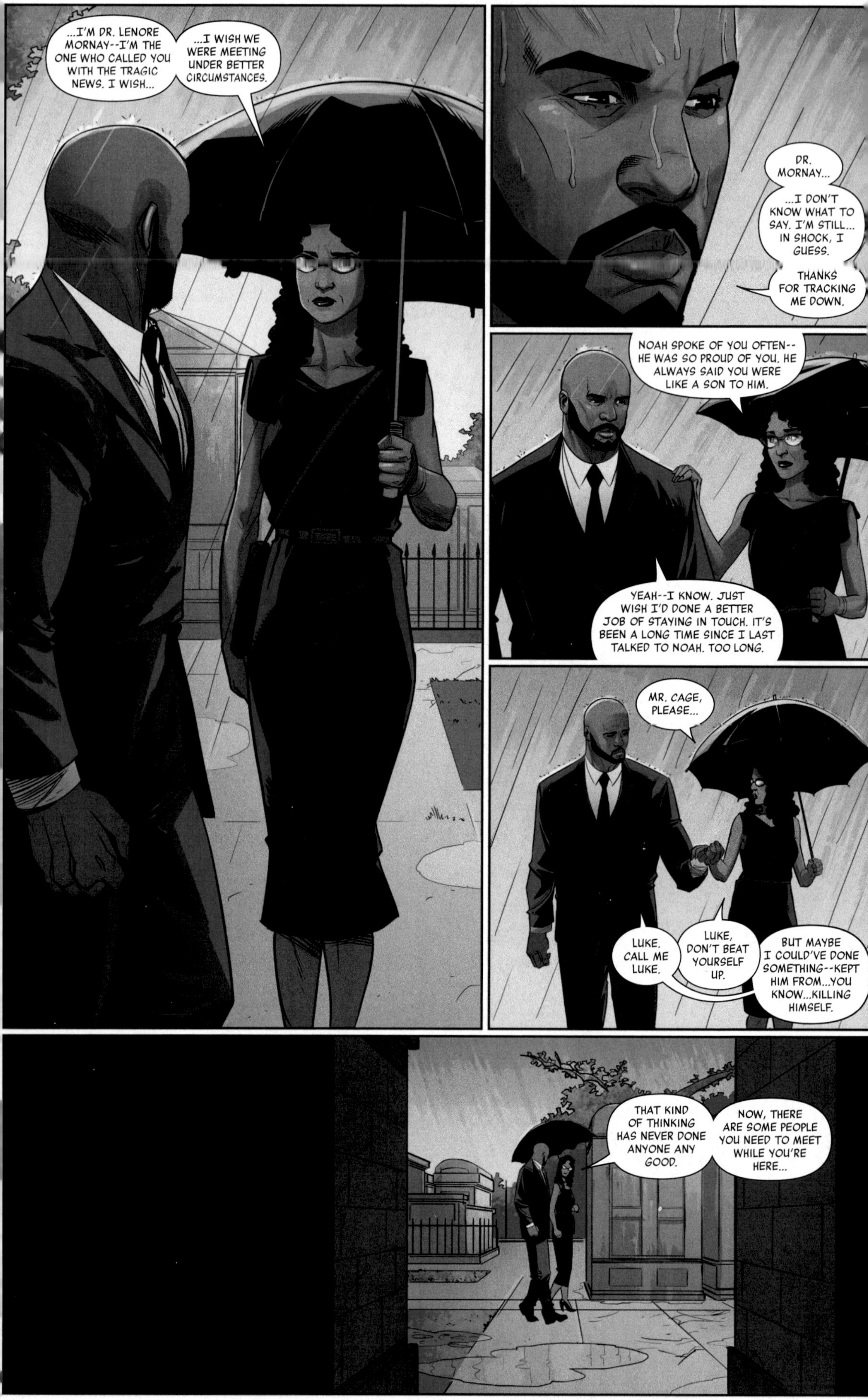
...I'M DR. LENORE MORNAY--I'M THE ONE WHO CALLED YOU WITH THE TRAGIC NEWS. I WISH...
...I WISH WE WERE MEETING UNDER BETTER CIRCUMSTANCES.
DR. MORNAY...
...I DON'T KNOW WHAT TO SAY. I'M STILL... IN SHOCK, I GUESS.
THANKS FOR TRACKING ME DOWN.
NOAH SPOKE OF YOU OFTEN--HE WAS SO PROUD OF YOU. HE ALWAYS SAID YOU WERE LIKE A SON TO HIM.
YEAH--I KNOW. JUST WISH I'D DONE A BETTER JOB OF STAYING IN TOUCH. IT'S BEEN A LONG TIME SINCE I LAST TALKED TO NOAH. TOO LONG.
MR. CAGE, PLEASE...
LUKE. CALL ME LUKE.
LUKE, DON'T BEAT YOURSELF UP.
BUT MAYBE I COULD'VE DONE SOMETHING--KEPT HIM FROM...YOU KNOW...KILLING HIMSELF.
THAT KIND OF THINKING HAS NEVER DONE ANYONE ANY GOOD.
NOW, THERE ARE SOME PEOPLE YOU NEED TO MEET WHILE YOU'RE HERE...

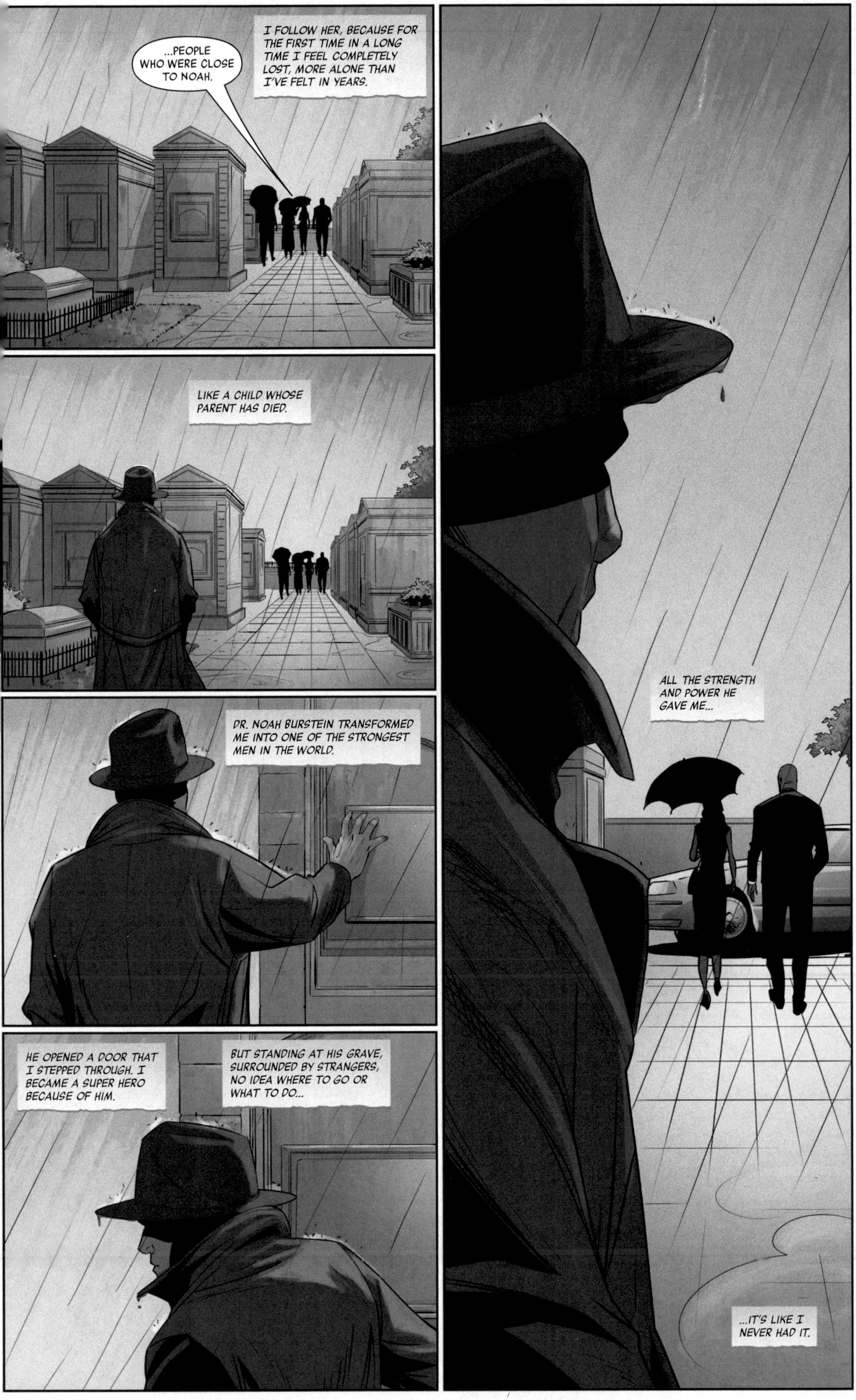
...PEOPLE WHO WERE CLOSE TO NOAH.
I FOLLOW HER, BECAUSE FOR THE FIRST TIME IN A LONG TIME I FEEL COMPLETELY LOST, MORE ALONE THAN I'VE FELT IN YEARS.
LIKE A CHILD WHOSE PARENT HAS DIED.
DR. NOAH BURSTEIN TRANSFORMED ME INTO ONE OF THE STRONGEST MEN IN THE WORLD.
HE OPENED A DOOR THAT I STEPPED THROUGH. I BECAME A SUPER HERO BECAUSE OF HIM.
BUT STANDING AT HIS GRAVE, SURROUNDED BY STRANGERS, NO IDEA WHERE TO GO OR WHAT TO DO...
ALL THE STRENGTH AND POWER HE GAVE ME...
...IT'S LIKE I NEVER HAD IT.

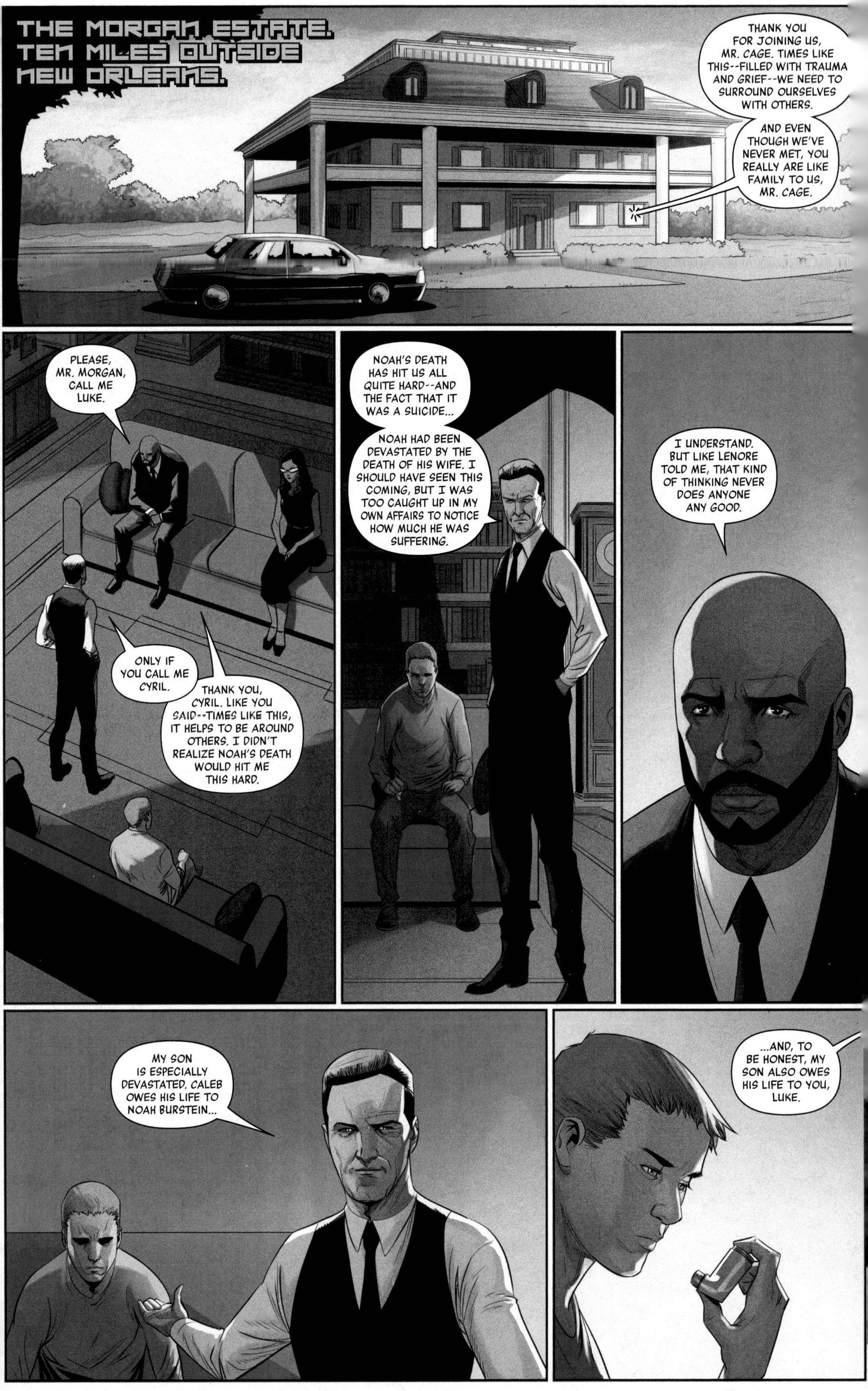
THE MORGAN ESTATE. TEN MILES OUTSIDE NEW ORLEANS.
THANK YOU FOR JOINING US, MR. CAGE. TIMES LIKE THIS--FILLED WITH TRAUMA AND GRIEF--WE NEED TO SURROUND OURSELVES WITH OTHERS.
AND EVEN THOUGH WE'VE NEVER MET, YOU REALLY ARE LIKE FAMILY TO US, MR. CAGE.
PLEASE, MR. MORGAN, CALL ME LUKE.
ONLY IF YOU CALL ME CYRIL.
THANK YOU, CYRIL. LIKE YOU SAID--TIMES LIKE THIS, IT HELPS TO BE AROUND OTHERS. I DIDN'T REALIZE NOAH'S DEATH WOULD HIT ME THIS HARD.
NOAH'S DEATH HAS HIT US ALL QUITE HARD--AND THE FACT THAT IT WAS A SUICIDE...
NOAH HAD BEEN DEVASTATED BY THE DEATH OF HIS WIFE. I SHOULD HAVE SEEN THIS COMING, BUT I WAS TOO CAUGHT UP IN MY OWN AFFAIRS TO NOTICE HOW MUCH HE WAS SUFFERING.
I UNDERSTAND. BUT LIKE LENORE TOLD ME, THAT KIND OF THINKING NEVER DOES ANYONE ANY GOOD.
MY SON IS ESPECIALLY DEVASTATED. CALEB OWES HIS LIFE TO NOAH BURSTEIN...
...AND, TO BE HONEST, MY SON ALSO OWES HIS LIFE TO YOU, LUKE.

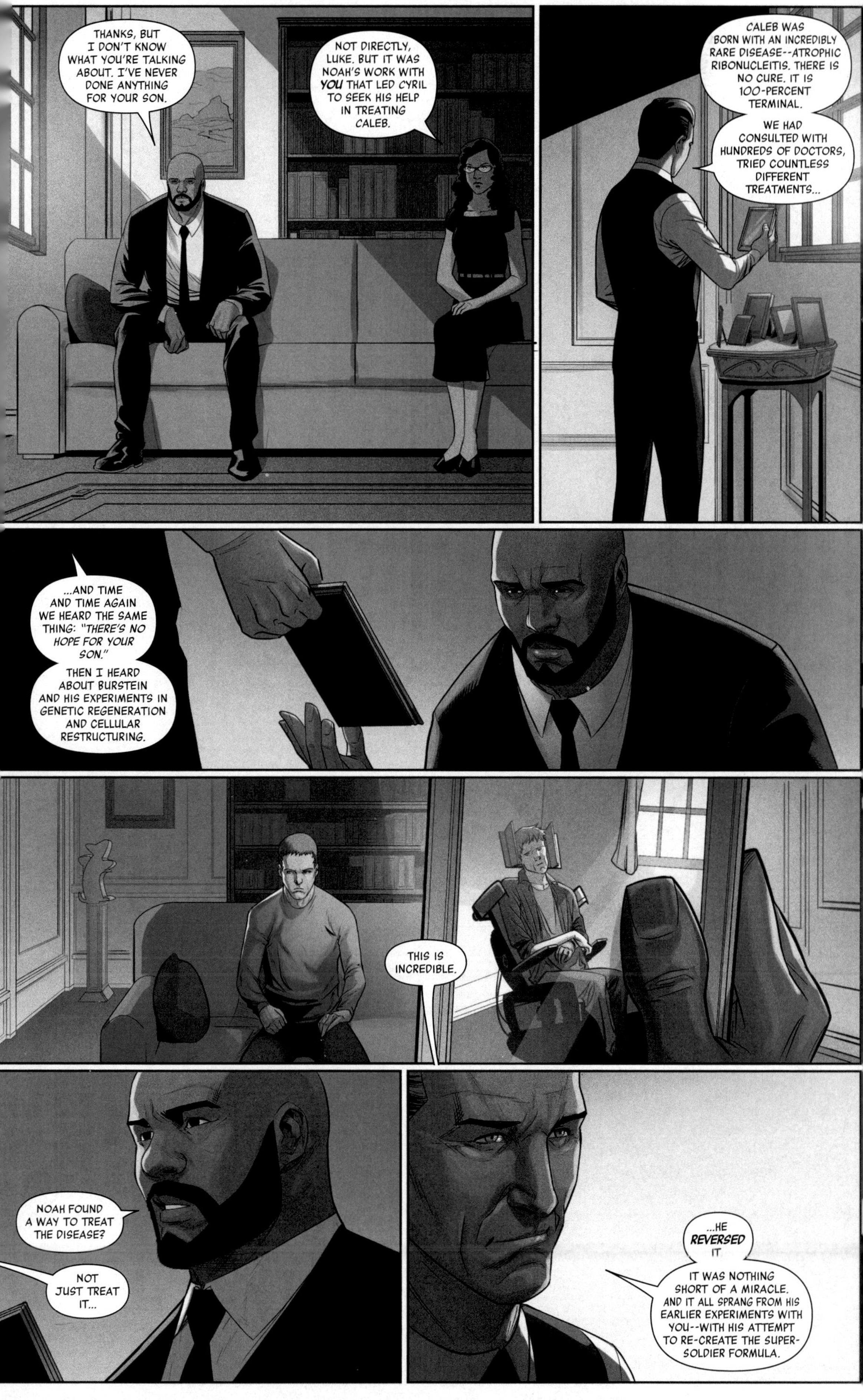
THANKS, BUT I DON'T KNOW WHAT YOU'RE TALKING ABOUT. I'VE NEVER DONE ANYTHING FOR YOUR SON.
NOT DIRECTLY, LUKE. BUT IT WAS NOAH'S WORK WITH *YOU* THAT LED CYRIL TO SEEK HIS HELP IN TREATING CALEB.
CALEB WAS BORN WITH AN INCREDIBLY RARE DISEASE--ATROPHIC RIBONUCLEITIS. THERE IS NO CURE. IT IS 100-PERCENT TERMINAL.
WE HAD CONSULTED WITH HUNDREDS OF DOCTORS, TRIED COUNTLESS DIFFERENT TREATMENTS...
...AND TIME AND TIME AGAIN WE HEARD THE SAME THING: *"THERE'S NO HOPE FOR YOUR SON."*
THEN I HEARD ABOUT BURSTEIN AND HIS EXPERIMENTS IN GENETIC REGENERATION AND CELLULAR RESTRUCTURING.
THIS IS INCREDIBLE.
NOAH FOUND A WAY TO TREAT THE DISEASE?
NOT JUST TREAT IT...
...HE ***REVERSED*** IT
IT WAS NOTHING SHORT OF A MIRACLE. AND IT ALL SPRANG FROM HIS EARLIER EXPERIMENTS WITH YOU--WITH HIS ATTEMPT TO RE-CREATE THE SUPER-SOLDIER FORMULA.

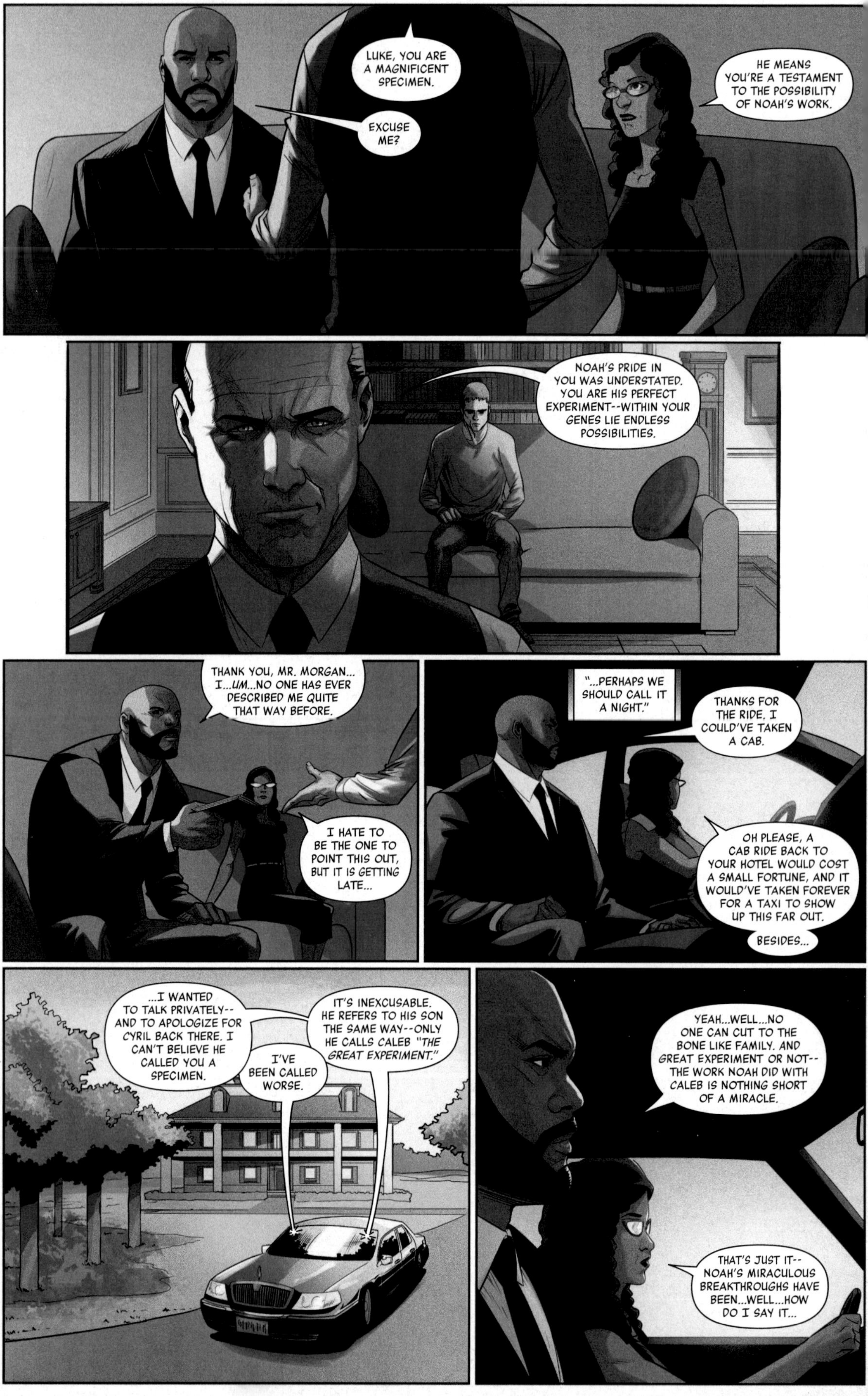

LUKE, YOU ARE A MAGNIFICENT SPECIMEN.
EXCUSE ME?
HE MEANS YOU'RE A TESTAMENT TO THE POSSIBILITY OF NOAH'S WORK.
NOAH'S PRIDE IN YOU WAS UNDERSTATED. YOU ARE HIS PERFECT EXPERIMENT--WITHIN YOUR GENES LIE ENDLESS POSSIBILITIES.
THANK YOU, MR. MORGAN... I...*UM*...NO ONE HAS EVER DESCRIBED ME QUITE THAT WAY BEFORE.
I HATE TO BE THE ONE TO POINT THIS OUT, BUT IT IS GETTING LATE...
"...PERHAPS WE SHOULD CALL IT A NIGHT."
THANKS FOR THE RIDE. I COULD'VE TAKEN A CAB.
OH PLEASE, A CAB RIDE BACK TO YOUR HOTEL WOULD COST A SMALL FORTUNE, AND IT WOULD'VE TAKEN FOREVER FOR A TAXI TO SHOW UP THIS FAR OUT.
BESIDES...
...I WANTED TO TALK PRIVATELY--AND TO APOLOGIZE FOR CYRIL BACK THERE. I CAN'T BELIEVE HE CALLED YOU A SPECIMEN.
I'VE BEEN CALLED WORSE.
IT'S INEXCUSABLE. HE REFERS TO HIS SON THE SAME WAY--ONLY HE CALLS CALEB *"THE GREAT EXPERIMENT."*
YEAH...WELL...NO ONE CAN CUT TO THE BONE LIKE FAMILY. AND GREAT EXPERIMENT OR NOT--THE WORK NOAH DID WITH CALEB IS NOTHING SHORT OF A MIRACLE.
THAT'S JUST IT--NOAH'S MIRACULOUS BREAKTHROUGHS HAVE BEEN...WELL...HOW DO I SAY IT...

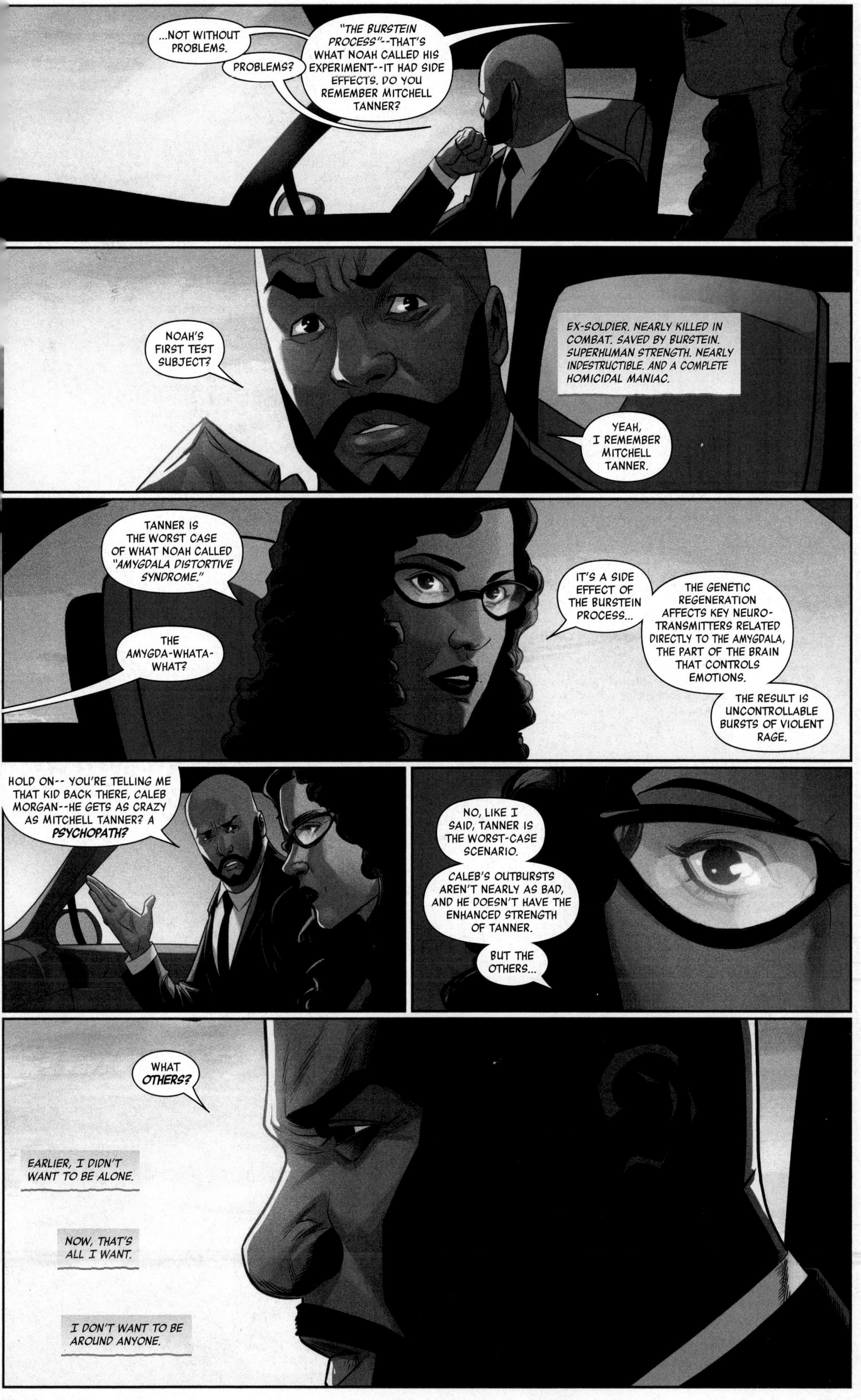
"THE BURSTEIN PROCESS"--THAT'S WHAT NOAH CALLED HIS EXPERIMENT--IT HAD SIDE EFFECTS. DO YOU REMEMBER MITCHELL TANNER?
...NOT WITHOUT PROBLEMS.
PROBLEMS?
NOAH'S FIRST TEST SUBJECT?
EX-SOLDIER. NEARLY KILLED IN COMBAT. SAVED BY BURSTEIN. SUPERHUMAN STRENGTH. NEARLY INDESTRUCTIBLE. AND A COMPLETE HOMICIDAL MANIAC.
YEAH, I REMEMBER MITCHELL TANNER.
TANNER IS THE WORST CASE OF WHAT NOAH CALLED "AMYGDALA DISTORTIVE SYNDROME."
THE AMYGDA-WHATA-WHAT?
IT'S A SIDE EFFECT OF THE BURSTEIN PROCESS...
THE GENETIC REGENERATION AFFECTS KEY NEURO-TRANSMITTERS RELATED DIRECTLY TO THE AMYGDALA, THE PART OF THE BRAIN THAT CONTROLS EMOTIONS.
THE RESULT IS UNCONTROLLABLE BURSTS OF VIOLENT RAGE.
HOLD ON-- YOU'RE TELLING ME THAT KID BACK THERE, CALEB MORGAN--HE GETS AS CRAZY AS MITCHELL TANNER? A PSYCHOPATH?
NO, LIKE I SAID, TANNER IS THE WORST-CASE SCENARIO.
CALEB'S OUTBURSTS AREN'T NEARLY AS BAD, AND HE DOESN'T HAVE THE ENHANCED STRENGTH OF TANNER.
BUT THE OTHERS...
WHAT OTHERS?
EARLIER, I DIDN'T WANT TO BE ALONE.
NOW, THAT'S ALL I WANT.
I DON'T WANT TO BE AROUND ANYONE.

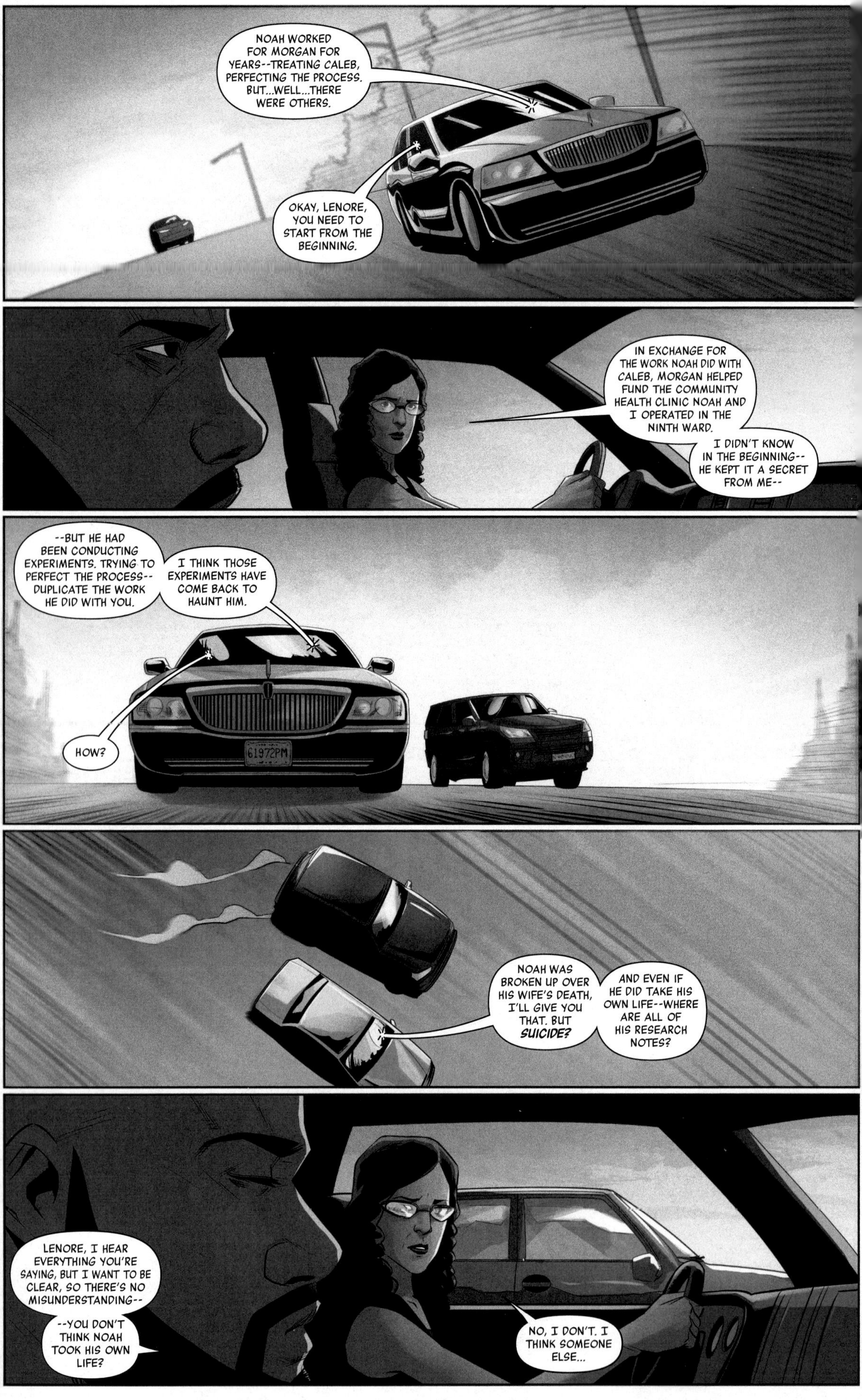

NOAH WORKED FOR MORGAN FOR YEARS--TREATING CALEB, PERFECTING THE PROCESS. BUT...WELL...THERE WERE OTHERS.
OKAY, LENORE, YOU NEED TO START FROM THE BEGINNING.
IN EXCHANGE FOR THE WORK NOAH DID WITH CALEB, MORGAN HELPED FUND THE COMMUNITY HEALTH CLINIC NOAH AND I OPERATED IN THE NINTH WARD.
I DIDN'T KNOW IN THE BEGINNING--HE KEPT IT A SECRET FROM ME--
--BUT HE HAD BEEN CONDUCTING EXPERIMENTS. TRYING TO PERFECT THE PROCESS--DUPLICATE THE WORK HE DID WITH YOU.
I THINK THOSE EXPERIMENTS HAVE COME BACK TO HAUNT HIM.
HOW?
61972PM
NOAH WAS BROKEN UP OVER HIS WIFE'S DEATH, I'LL GIVE YOU THAT. BUT *SUICIDE?*
AND EVEN IF HE DID TAKE HIS OWN LIFE--WHERE ARE ALL OF HIS RESEARCH NOTES?
LENORE, I HEAR EVERYTHING YOU'RE SAYING, BUT I WANT TO BE CLEAR, SO THERE'S NO MISUNDERSTANDING--
--YOU DON'T THINK NOAH TOOK HIS OWN LIFE?
NO, I DON'T. I THINK SOMEONE ELSE...

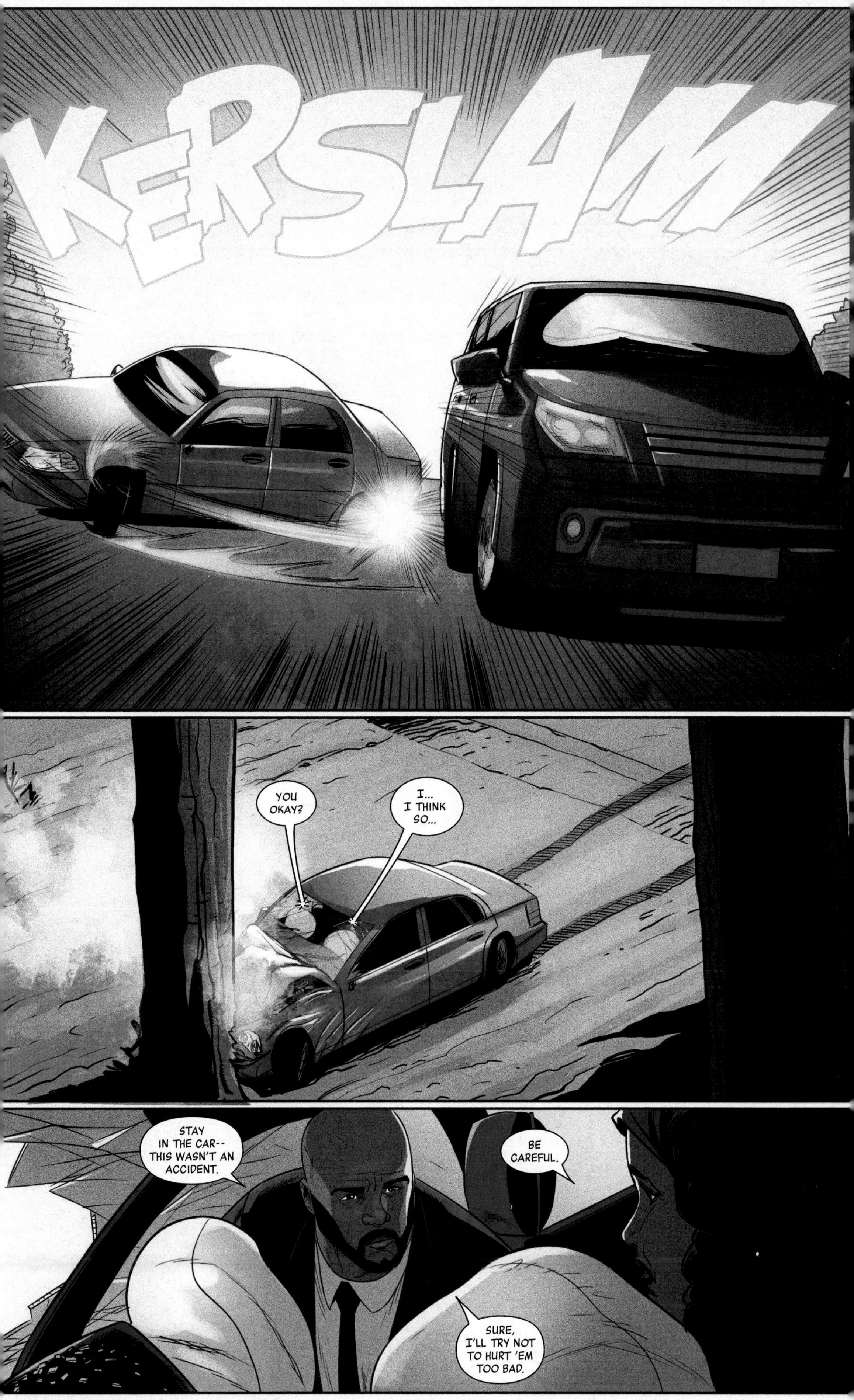
KERSLAM
YOU OKAY?
I... I THINK SO...
STAY IN THE CAR-- THIS WASN'T AN ACCIDENT.
BE CAREFUL.
SURE, I'LL TRY NOT TO HURT 'EM TOO BAD.

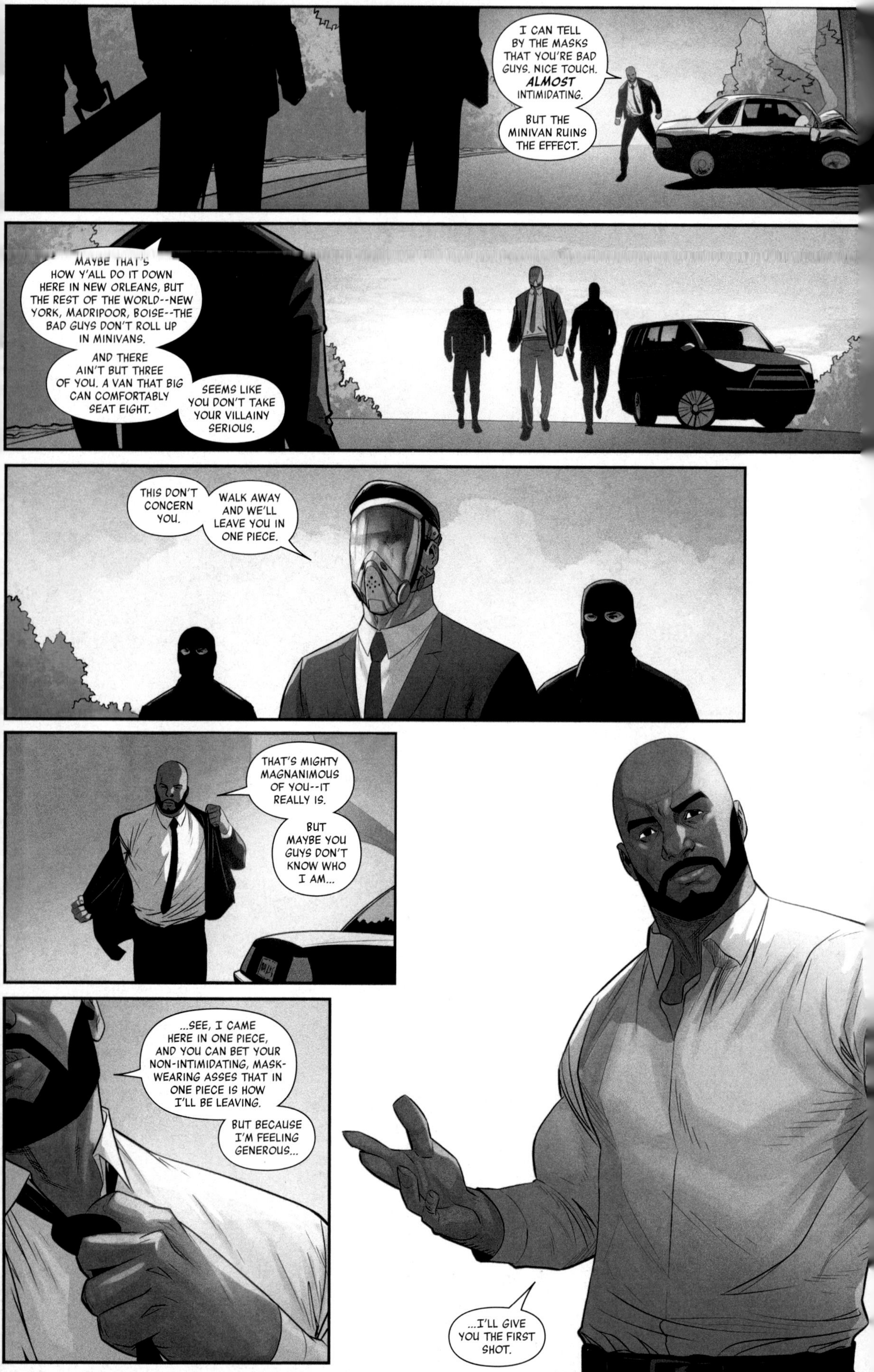
I CAN TELL BY THE MASKS THAT YOU'RE BAD GUYS. NICE TOUCH. ALMOST INTIMIDATING.
BUT THE MINIVAN RUINS THE EFFECT.
MAYBE THAT'S HOW Y'ALL DO IT DOWN HERE IN NEW ORLEANS, BUT THE REST OF THE WORLD--NEW YORK, MADRIPOOR, BOISE--THE BAD GUYS DON'T ROLL UP IN MINIVANS.
AND THERE AIN'T BUT THREE OF YOU. A VAN THAT BIG CAN COMFORTABLY SEAT EIGHT.
SEEMS LIKE YOU DON'T TAKE YOUR VILLAINY SERIOUS.
THIS DON'T CONCERN YOU.
WALK AWAY AND WE'LL LEAVE YOU IN ONE PIECE.
THAT'S MIGHTY MAGNANIMOUS OF YOU--IT REALLY IS.
BUT MAYBE YOU GUYS DON'T KNOW WHO I AM...
...SEE, I CAME HERE IN ONE PIECE, AND YOU CAN BET YOUR NON-INTIMIDATING, MASK-WEARING ASSES THAT IN ONE PIECE IS HOW I'LL BE LEAVING.
BUT BECAUSE I'M FEELING GENEROUS...
...I'LL GIVE YOU THE FIRST SHOT.

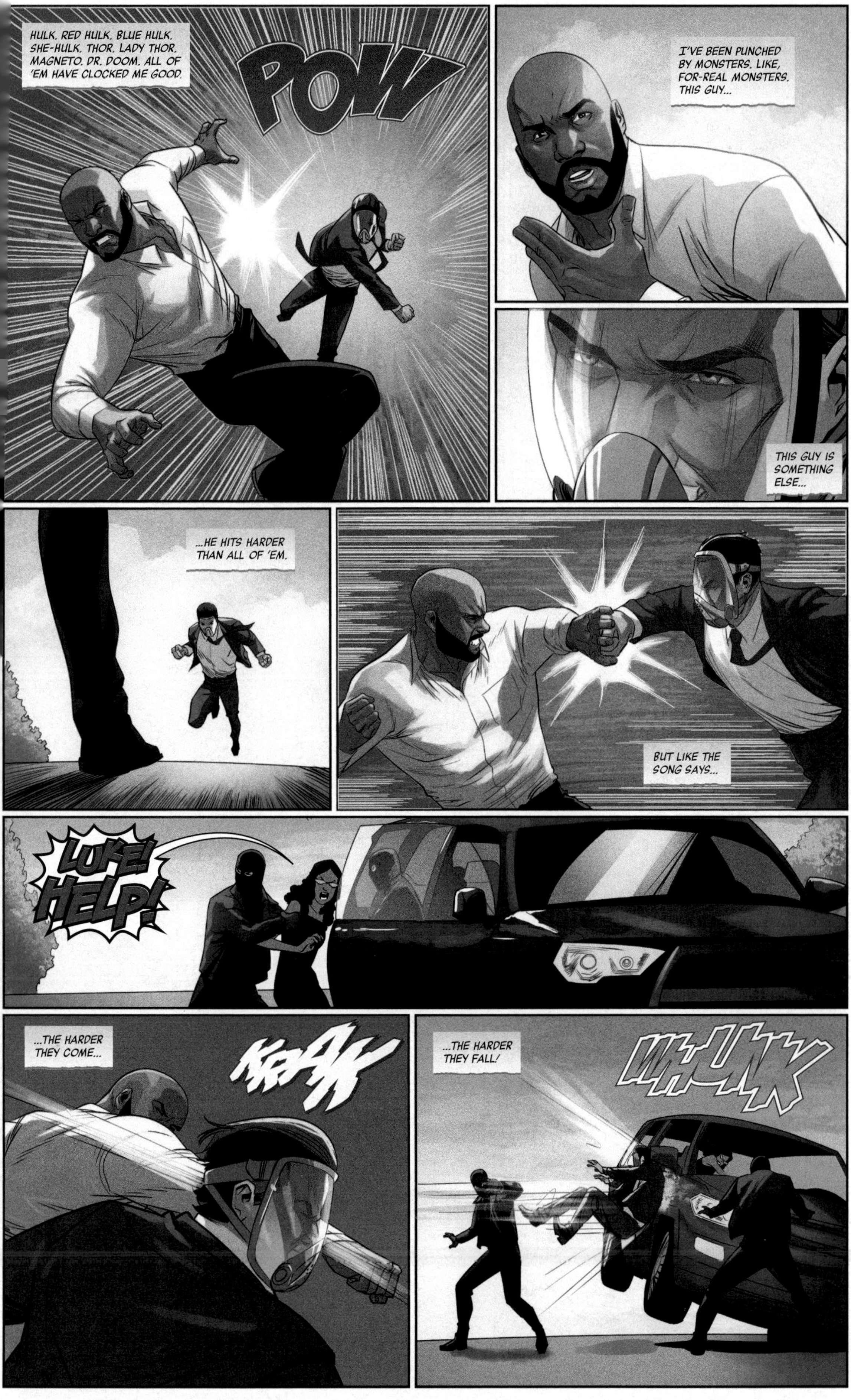
HULK. RED HULK. BLUE HULK. SHE-HULK. THOR. LADY THOR. MAGNETO. DR. DOOM. ALL OF 'EM HAVE CLOCKED ME GOOD.
POW
I'VE BEEN PUNCHED BY MONSTERS. LIKE, FOR-REAL MONSTERS. THIS GUY...
THIS GUY IS SOMETHING ELSE...
...HE HITS HARDER THAN ALL OF 'EM.
BUT LIKE THE SONG SAYS...
LUKE! HELP!
...THE HARDER THEY COME...
...THE HARDER THEY FALL!
WHUNK

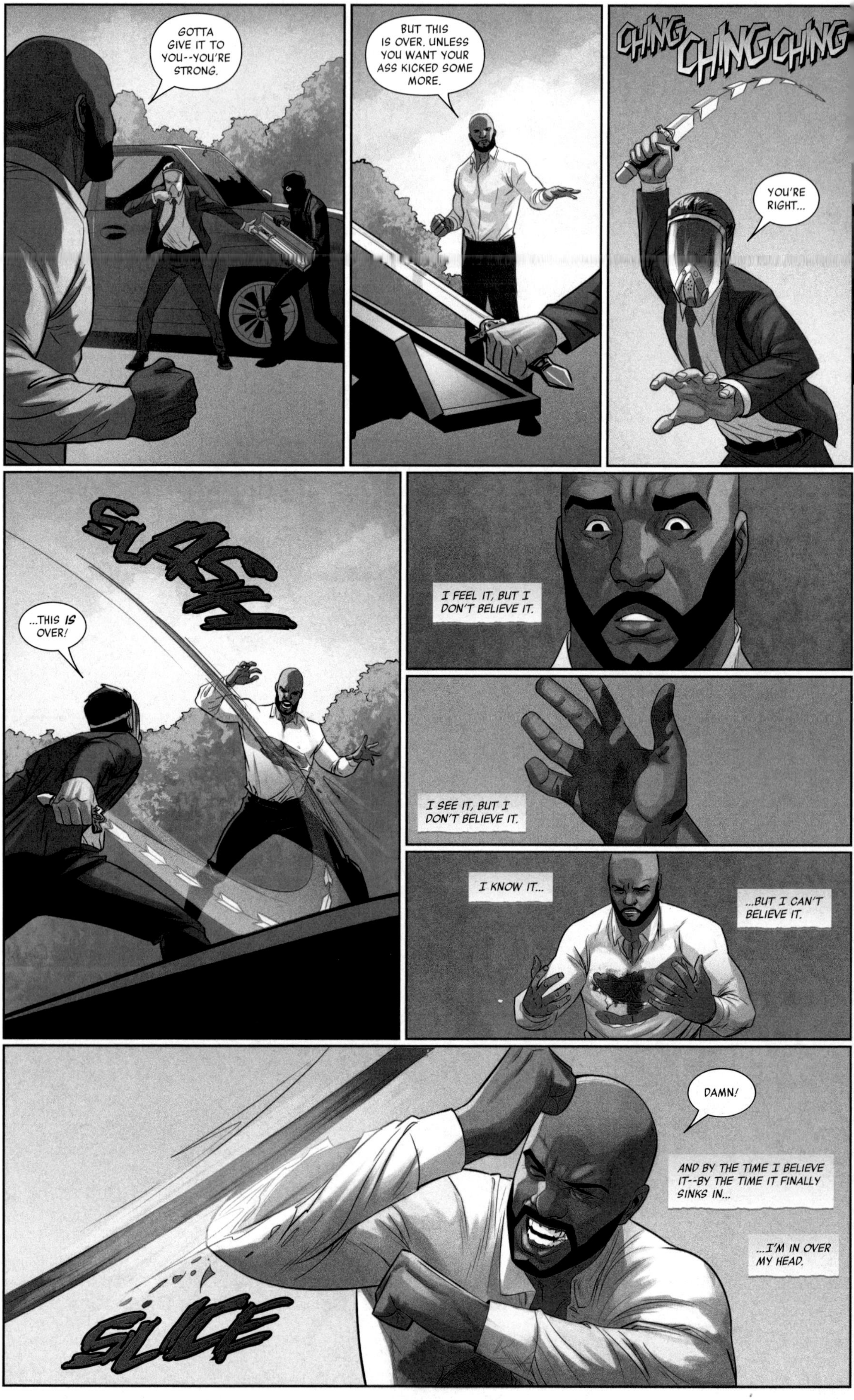
GOTTA GIVE IT TO YOU--YOU'RE STRONG.
BUT THIS IS OVER. UNLESS YOU WANT YOUR ASS KICKED SOME MORE.
CHING CHING CHING
YOU'RE RIGHT...
SLASH
...THIS IS OVER!
I FEEL IT, BUT I DON'T BELIEVE IT.
I SEE IT, BUT I DON'T BELIEVE IT.
I KNOW IT...
...BUT I CAN'T BELIEVE IT.
DAMN!
AND BY THE TIME I BELIEVE IT--BY THE TIME IT FINALLY SINKS IN...
...I'M IN OVER MY HEAD.
SLICE

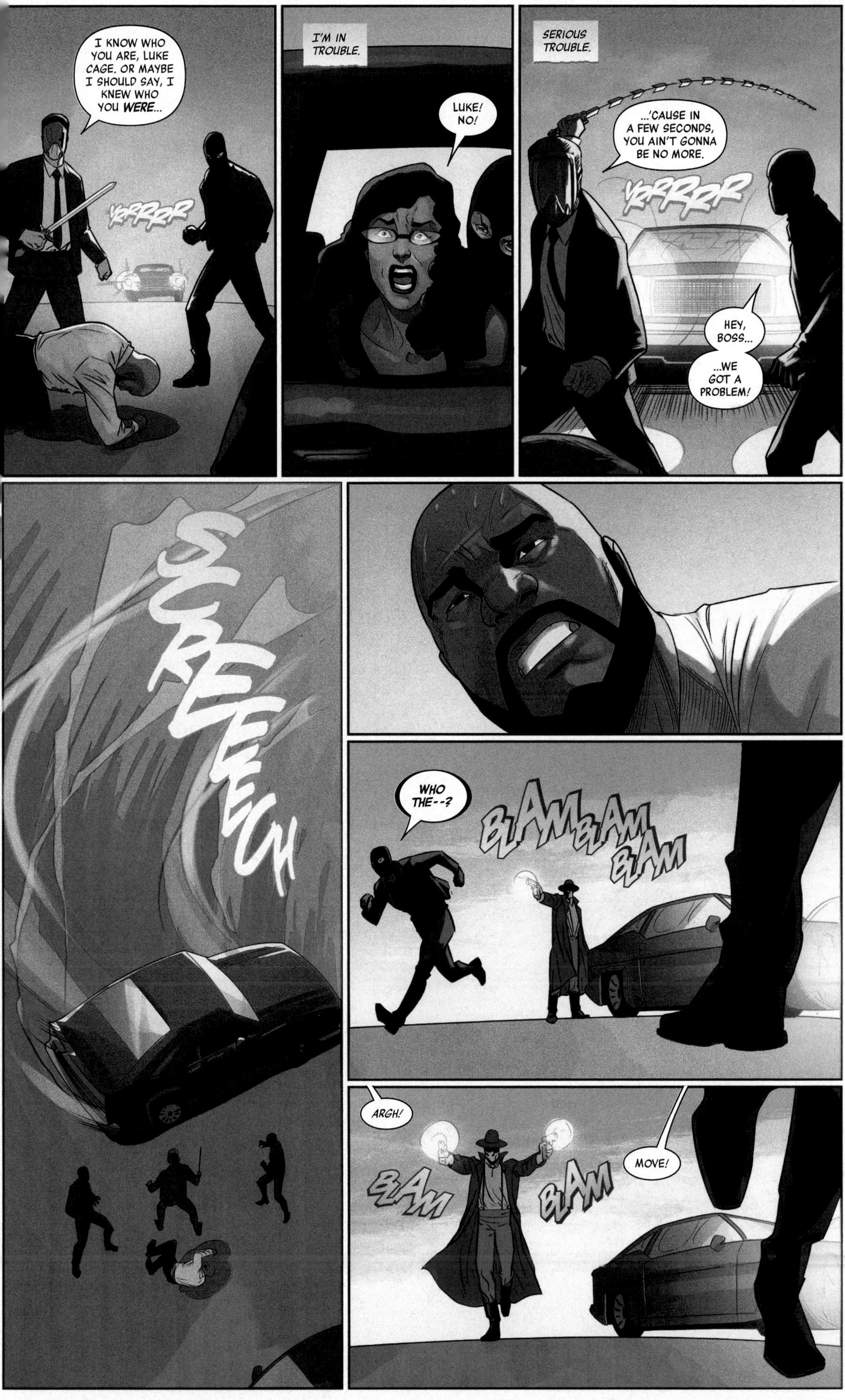
I KNOW WHO YOU ARE, LUKE CAGE. OR MAYBE I SHOULD SAY, I KNEW WHO YOU *WERE*...
VRRRRR
I'M IN TROUBLE.
LUKE! NO!
SERIOUS TROUBLE.
...'CAUSE IN A FEW SECONDS, YOU AIN'T GONNA BE NO MORE.
VRRRRR
HEY, BOSS...
...WE GOT A PROBLEM!
SCREEEECH
WHO THE--?
BLAM BLAM BLAM BLAM
ARGH!
MOVE!
BLAM
BLAM

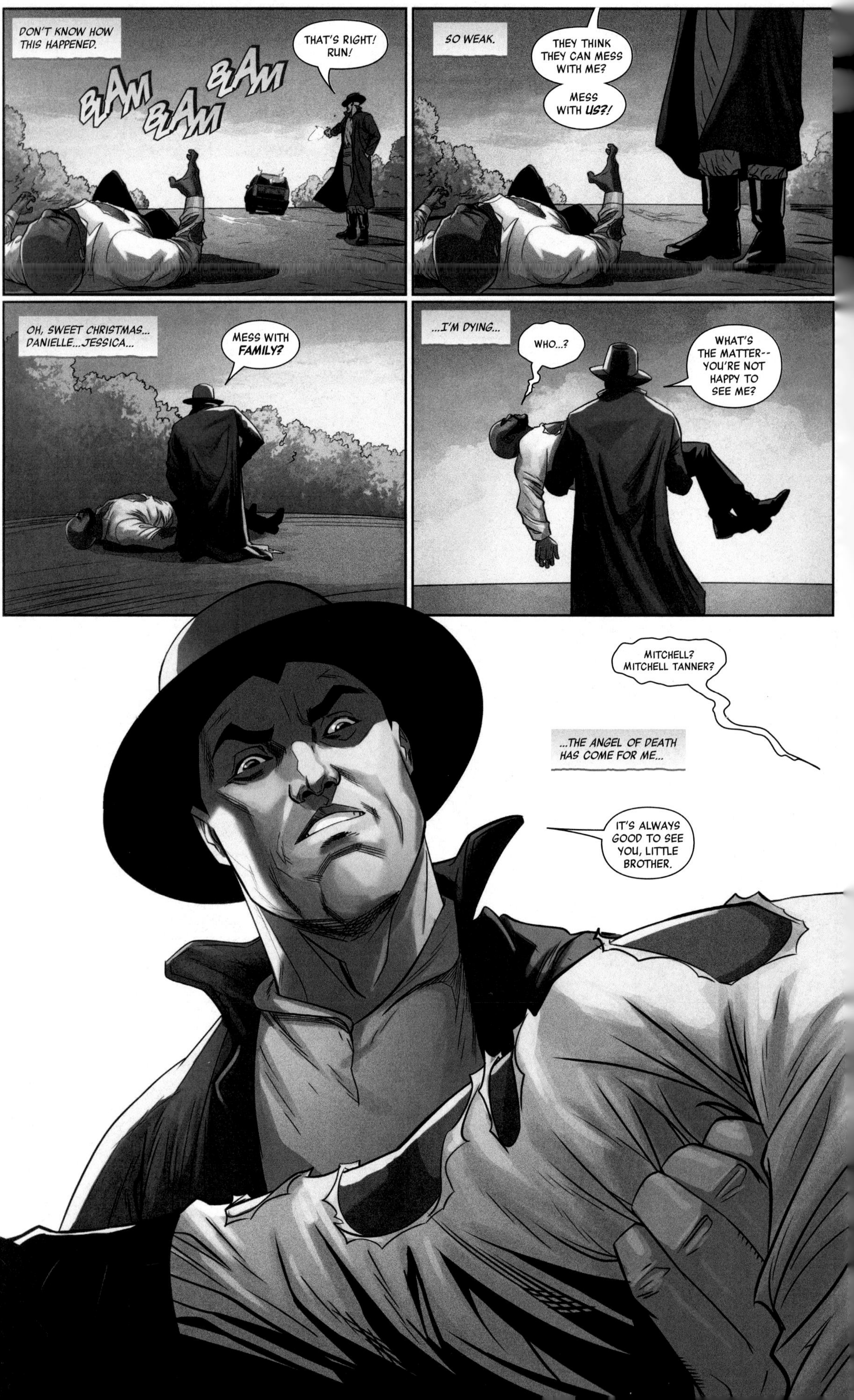
DON'T KNOW HOW THIS HAPPENED.
THAT'S RIGHT! RUN!
BLAM
BLAM
BLAM
SO WEAK.
THEY THINK THEY CAN MESS WITH ME?
MESS WITH US?!
OH, SWEET CHRISTMAS... DANIELLE...JESSICA...
MESS WITH FAMILY?
...I'M DYING...
WHO...?
WHAT'S THE MATTER--YOU'RE NOT HAPPY TO SEE ME?
MITCHELL? MITCHELL TANNER?
...THE ANGEL OF DEATH HAS COME FOR ME...
IT'S ALWAYS GOOD TO SEE YOU, LITTLE BROTHER.

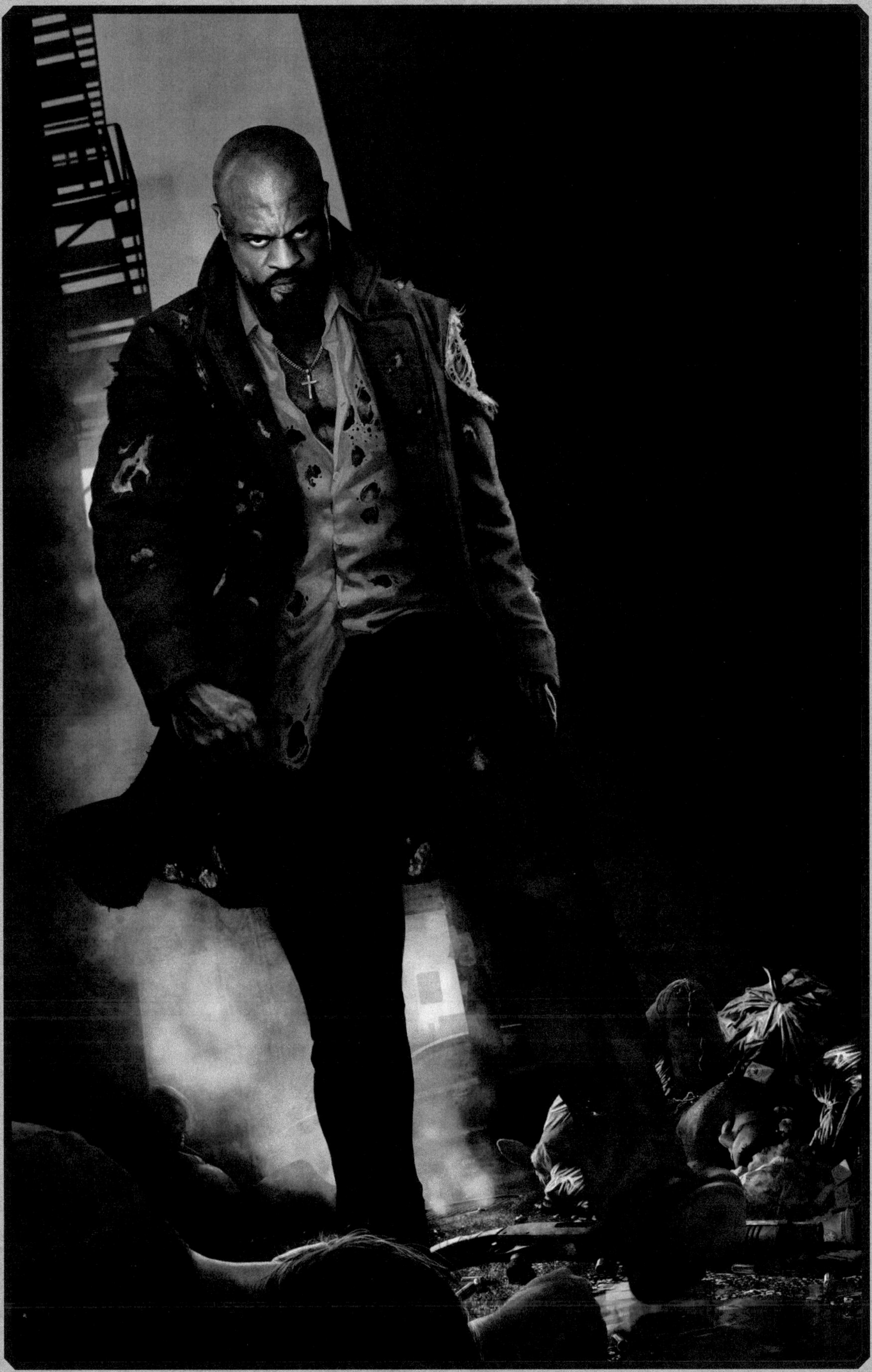

Z

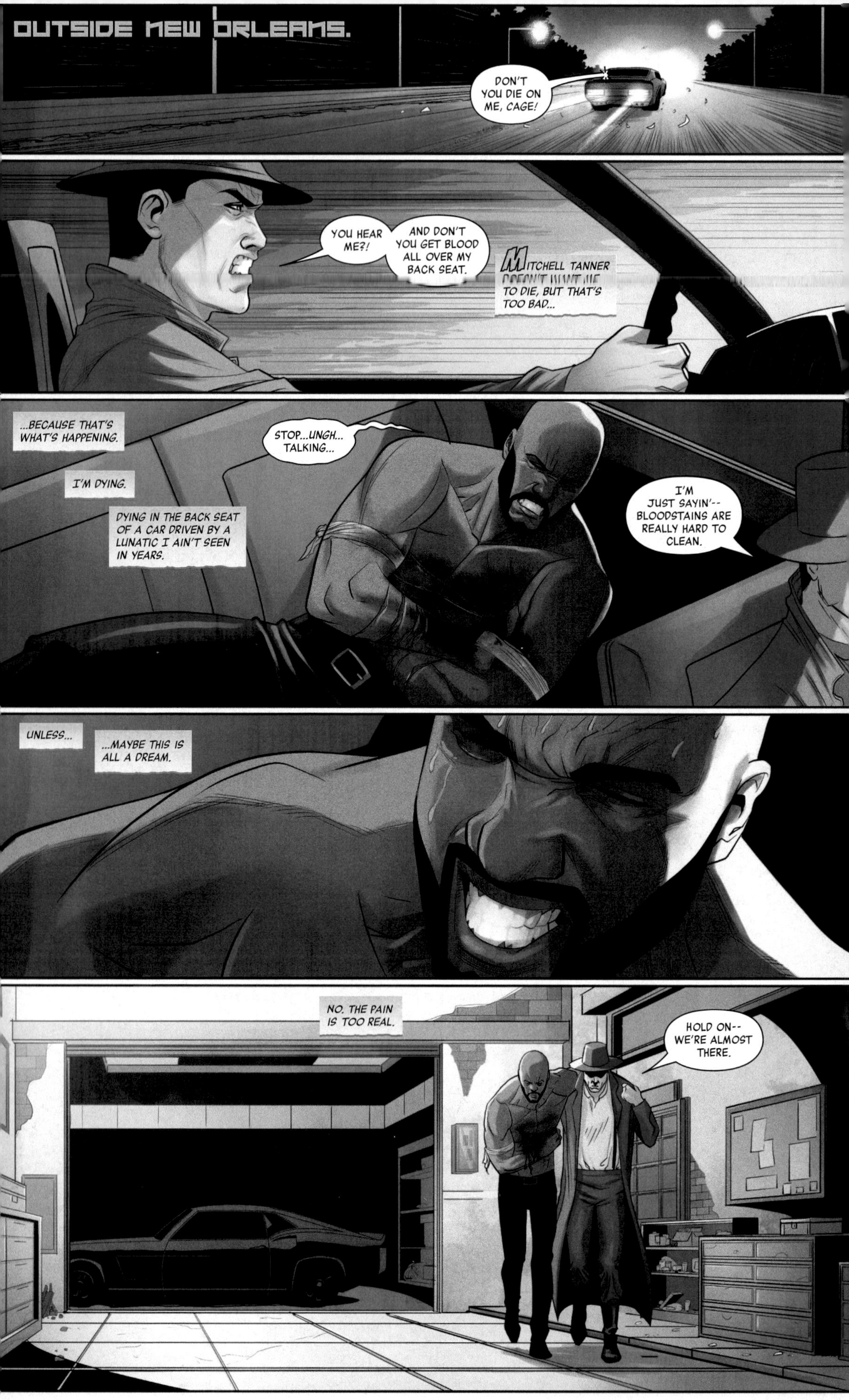
OUTSIDE NEW ORLEANS.
DON'T YOU DIE ON ME, CAGE!
YOU HEAR ME?!
AND DON'T YOU GET BLOOD ALL OVER MY BACK SEAT.
MITCHELL TANNER
TO DIE, BUT THAT'S TOO BAD...
...BECAUSE THAT'S WHAT'S HAPPENING.
STOP...UNGH... TALKING...
I'M DYING.
DYING IN THE BACK SEAT OF A CAR DRIVEN BY A LUNATIC I AIN'T SEEN IN YEARS.
I'M JUST SAYIN'-- BLOODSTAINS ARE REALLY HARD TO CLEAN.
UNLESS...
...MAYBE THIS IS ALL A DREAM.
NO. THE PAIN IS TOO REAL.
HOLD ON-- WE'RE ALMOST THERE.

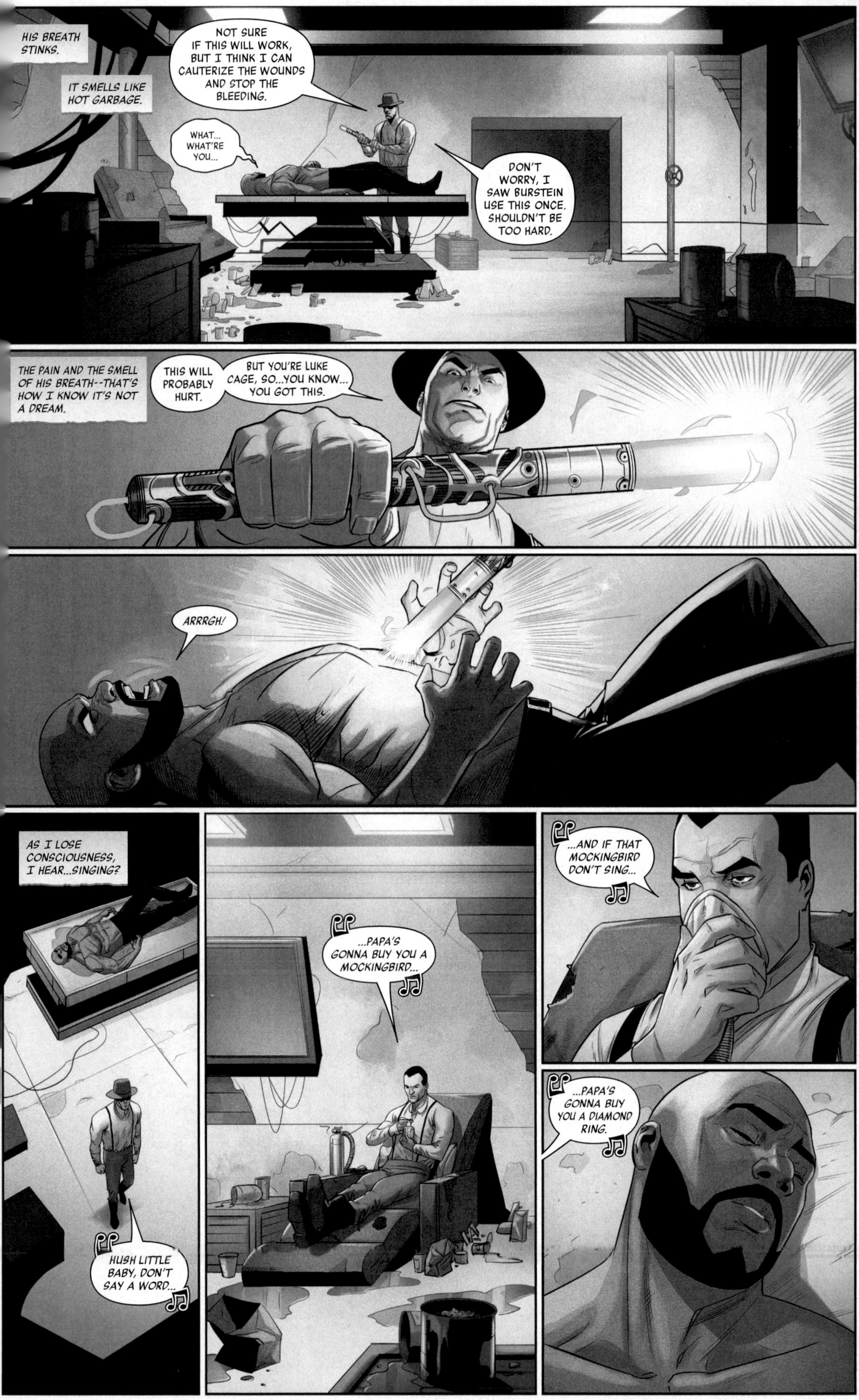
HIS BREATH STINKS.
IT SMELLS LIKE HOT GARBAGE.
NOT SURE IF THIS WILL WORK, BUT I THINK I CAN CAUTERIZE THE WOUNDS AND STOP THE BLEEDING.
WHAT... WHAT'RE YOU...
DON'T WORRY, I SAW BURSTEIN USE THIS ONCE. SHOULDN'T BE TOO HARD.
THE PAIN AND THE SMELL OF HIS BREATH--THAT'S HOW I KNOW IT'S NOT A DREAM.
THIS WILL PROBABLY HURT.
BUT YOU'RE LUKE CAGE, SO...YOU KNOW... YOU GOT THIS.
ARRRGH!
AS I LOSE CONSCIOUSNESS, I HEAR...SINGING?
HUSH LITTLE BABY, DON'T SAY A WORD...
...PAPA'S GONNA BUY YOU A MOCKINGBIRD...
...AND IF THAT MOCKINGBIRD DON'T SING...
...PAPA'S GONNA BUY YOU A DIAMOND RING.

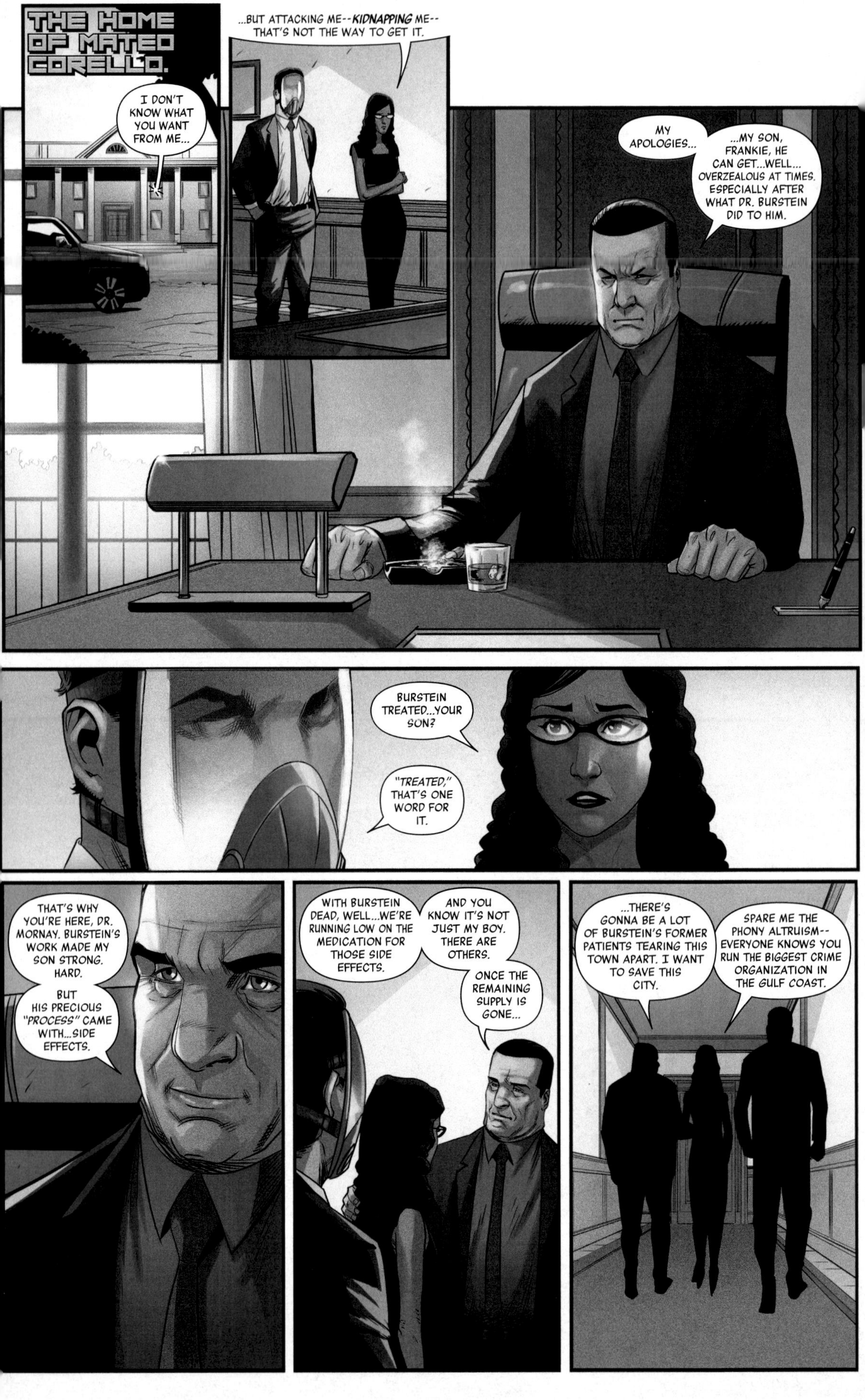
THE HOME OF MATEO CORELLO.
I DON'T KNOW WHAT YOU WANT FROM ME...
...BUT ATTACKING ME--KIDNAPPING ME--THAT'S NOT THE WAY TO GET IT.
MY APOLOGIES...
...MY SON, FRANKIE, HE CAN GET...WELL... OVERZEALOUS AT TIMES. ESPECIALLY AFTER WHAT DR. BURSTEIN DID TO HIM.
BURSTEIN TREATED...YOUR SON?
"TREATED," THAT'S ONE WORD FOR IT.
THAT'S WHY YOU'RE HERE, DR. MORNAY. BURSTEIN'S WORK MADE MY SON STRONG. HARD.
BUT HIS PRECIOUS "PROCESS" CAME WITH...SIDE EFFECTS.
WITH BURSTEIN DEAD, WELL...WE'RE RUNNING LOW ON THE MEDICATION FOR THOSE SIDE EFFECTS.
AND YOU KNOW IT'S NOT JUST MY BOY. THERE ARE OTHERS.
ONCE THE REMAINING SUPPLY IS GONE...
...THERE'S GONNA BE A LOT OF BURSTEIN'S FORMER PATIENTS TEARING THIS TOWN APART. I WANT TO SAVE THIS CITY.
SPARE ME THE PHONY ALTRUISM--EVERYONE KNOWS YOU RUN THE BIGGEST CRIME ORGANIZATION IN THE GULF COAST.

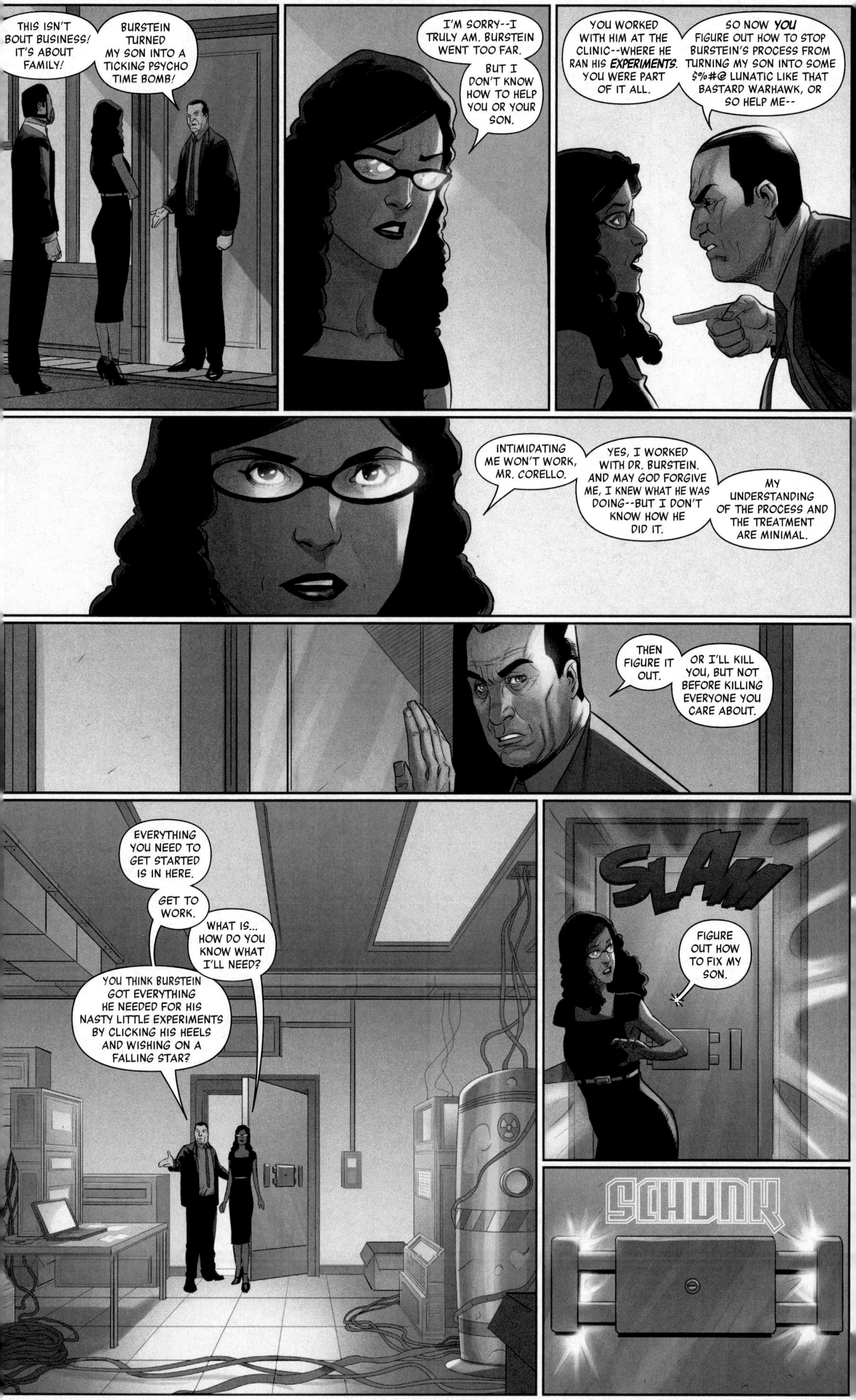
THIS ISN'T BOUT BUSINESS! IT'S ABOUT FAMILY!
BURSTEIN TURNED MY SON INTO A TICKING PSYCHO TIME BOMB!
I'M SORRY--I TRULY AM. BURSTEIN WENT TOO FAR.
BUT I DON'T KNOW HOW TO HELP YOU OR YOUR SON.
YOU WORKED WITH HIM AT THE CLINIC--WHERE HE RAN HIS EXPERIMENTS. YOU WERE PART OF IT ALL.
SO NOW YOU FIGURE OUT HOW TO STOP BURSTEIN'S PROCESS FROM TURNING MY SON INTO SOME $%#@ LUNATIC LIKE THAT BASTARD WARHAWK, OR SO HELP ME--
INTIMIDATING ME WON'T WORK, MR. CORELLO.
YES, I WORKED WITH DR. BURSTEIN. AND MAY GOD FORGIVE ME, I KNEW WHAT HE WAS DOING--BUT I DON'T KNOW HOW HE DID IT.
MY UNDERSTANDING OF THE PROCESS AND THE TREATMENT ARE MINIMAL.
THEN FIGURE IT OUT.
OR I'LL KILL YOU, BUT NOT BEFORE KILLING EVERYONE YOU CARE ABOUT.
EVERYTHING YOU NEED TO GET STARTED IS IN HERE.
GET TO WORK.
WHAT IS... HOW DO YOU KNOW WHAT I'LL NEED?
YOU THINK BURSTEIN GOT EVERYTHING HE NEEDED FOR HIS NASTY LITTLE EXPERIMENTS BY CLICKING HIS HEELS AND WISHING ON A FALLING STAR?
SLAM
FIGURE OUT HOW TO FIX MY SON.
SCHUNK

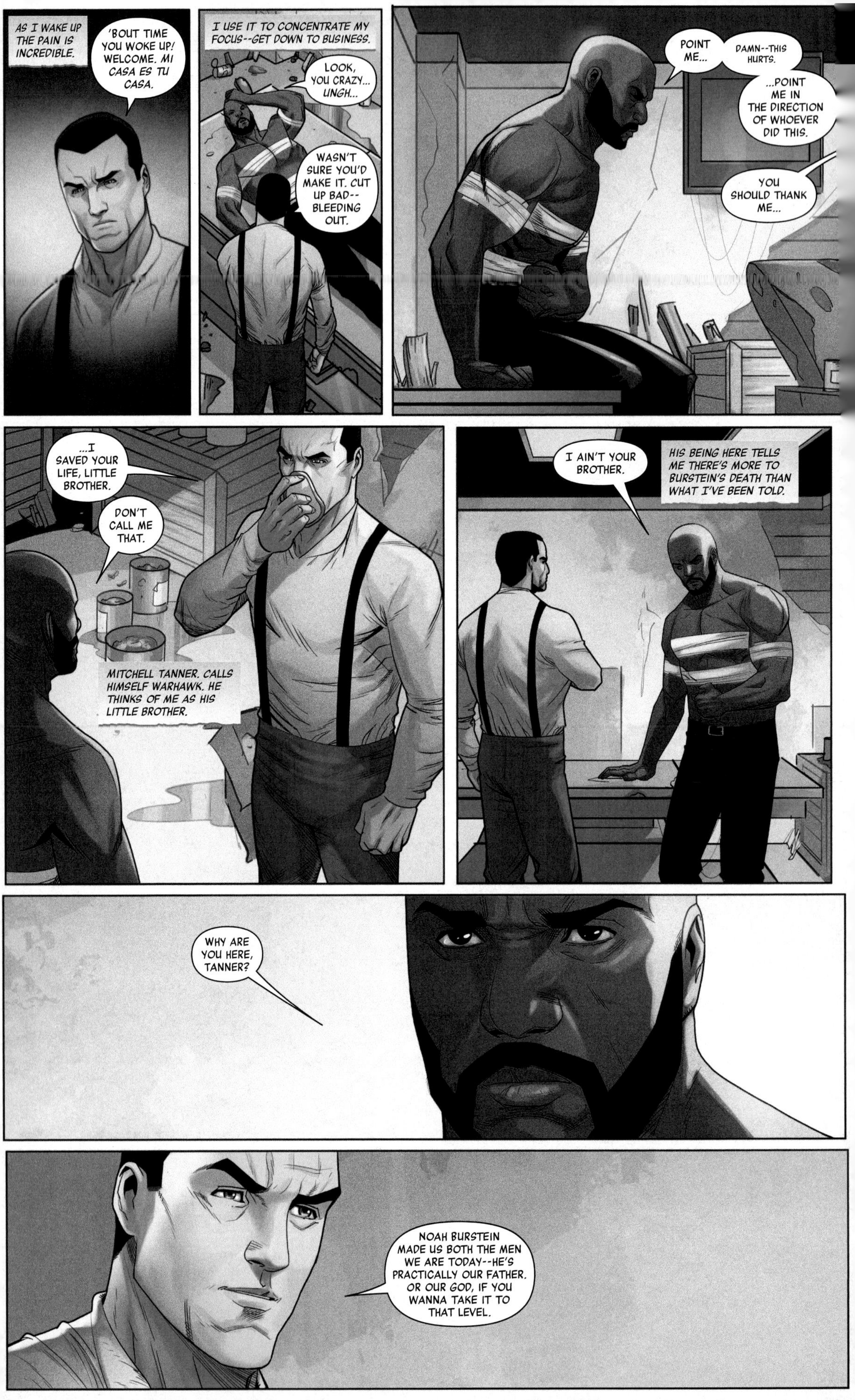
AS I WAKE UP THE PAIN IS INCREDIBLE.
'BOUT TIME YOU WOKE UP! WELCOME. MI CASA ES TU CASA.
I USE IT TO CONCENTRATE MY FOCUS--GET DOWN TO BUSINESS.
LOOK, YOU CRAZY... UNGH...
WASN'T SURE YOU'D MAKE IT. CUT UP BAD--BLEEDING OUT.
POINT ME...
DAMN--THIS HURTS.
...POINT ME IN THE DIRECTION OF WHOEVER DID THIS.
YOU SHOULD THANK ME...
...I SAVED YOUR LIFE, LITTLE BROTHER.
DON'T CALL ME THAT.
MITCHELL TANNER. CALLS HIMSELF WARHAWK. HE THINKS OF ME AS HIS LITTLE BROTHER.
I AIN'T YOUR BROTHER.
HIS BEING HERE TELLS ME THERE'S MORE TO BURSTEIN'S DEATH THAN WHAT I'VE BEEN TOLD.
WHY ARE YOU HERE, TANNER?
NOAH BURSTEIN MADE US BOTH THE MEN WE ARE TODAY--HE'S PRACTICALLY OUR FATHER. OR OUR GOD, IF YOU WANNA TAKE IT TO THAT LEVEL.

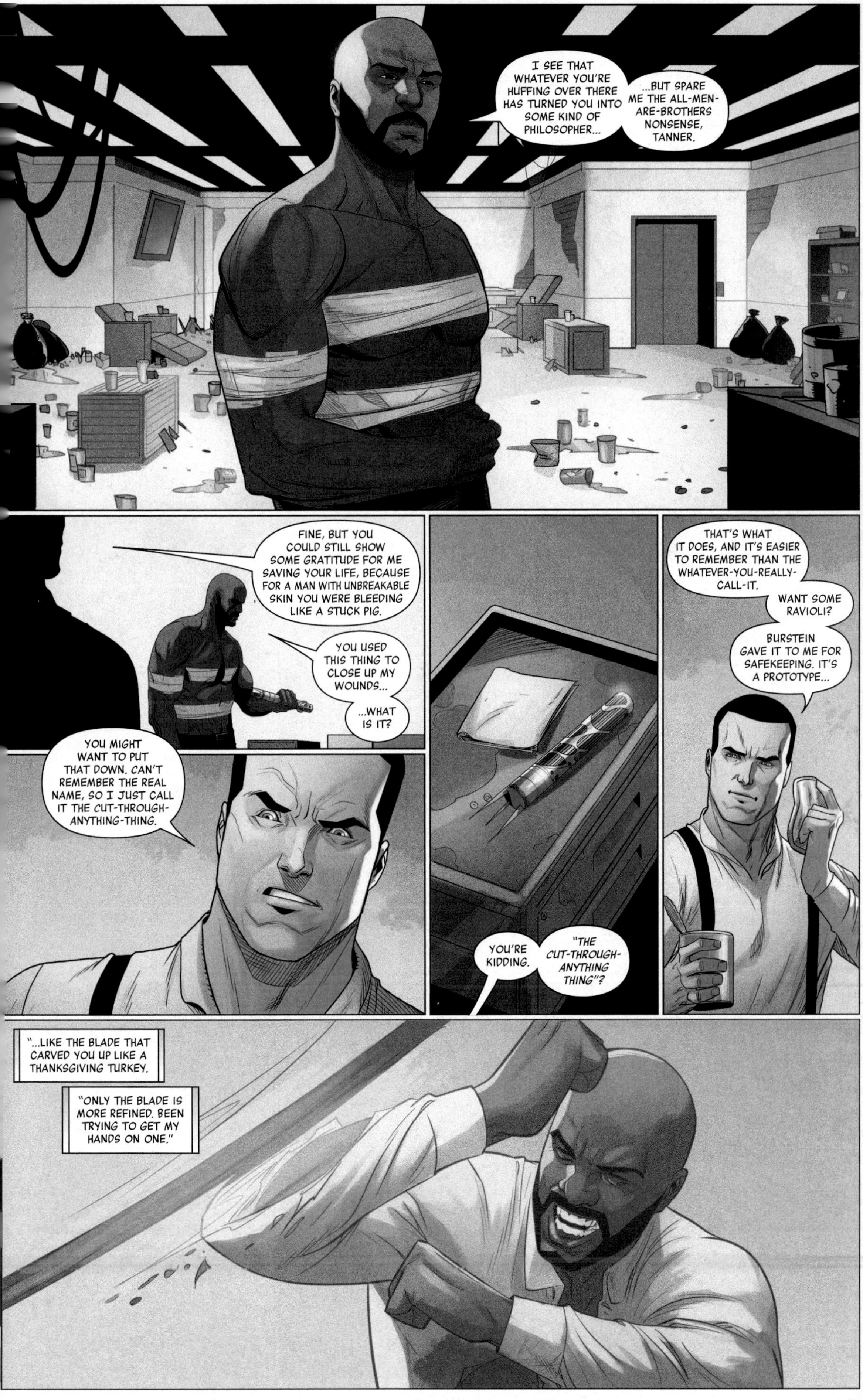
I SEE THAT WHATEVER YOU'RE HUFFING OVER THERE HAS TURNED YOU INTO SOME KIND OF PHILOSOPHER...
...BUT SPARE ME THE ALL-MEN-ARE-BROTHERS NONSENSE, TANNER.
FINE, BUT YOU COULD STILL SHOW SOME GRATITUDE FOR ME SAVING YOUR LIFE, BECAUSE FOR A MAN WITH UNBREAKABLE SKIN YOU WERE BLEEDING LIKE A STUCK PIG.
YOU USED THIS THING TO CLOSE UP MY WOUNDS...
...WHAT IS IT?
YOU MIGHT WANT TO PUT THAT DOWN. CAN'T REMEMBER THE REAL NAME, SO I JUST CALL IT THE CUT-THROUGH-ANYTHING-THING.
YOU'RE KIDDING.
"THE CUT-THROUGH-ANYTHING THING"?
THAT'S WHAT IT DOES, AND IT'S EASIER TO REMEMBER THAN THE WHATEVER-YOU-REALLY-CALL-IT.
WANT SOME RAVIOLI?
BURSTEIN GAVE IT TO ME FOR SAFEKEEPING. IT'S A PROTOTYPE...
"...LIKE THE BLADE THAT CARVED YOU UP LIKE A THANKSGIVING TURKEY.
"ONLY THE BLADE IS MORE REFINED. BEEN TRYING TO GET MY HANDS ON ONE."

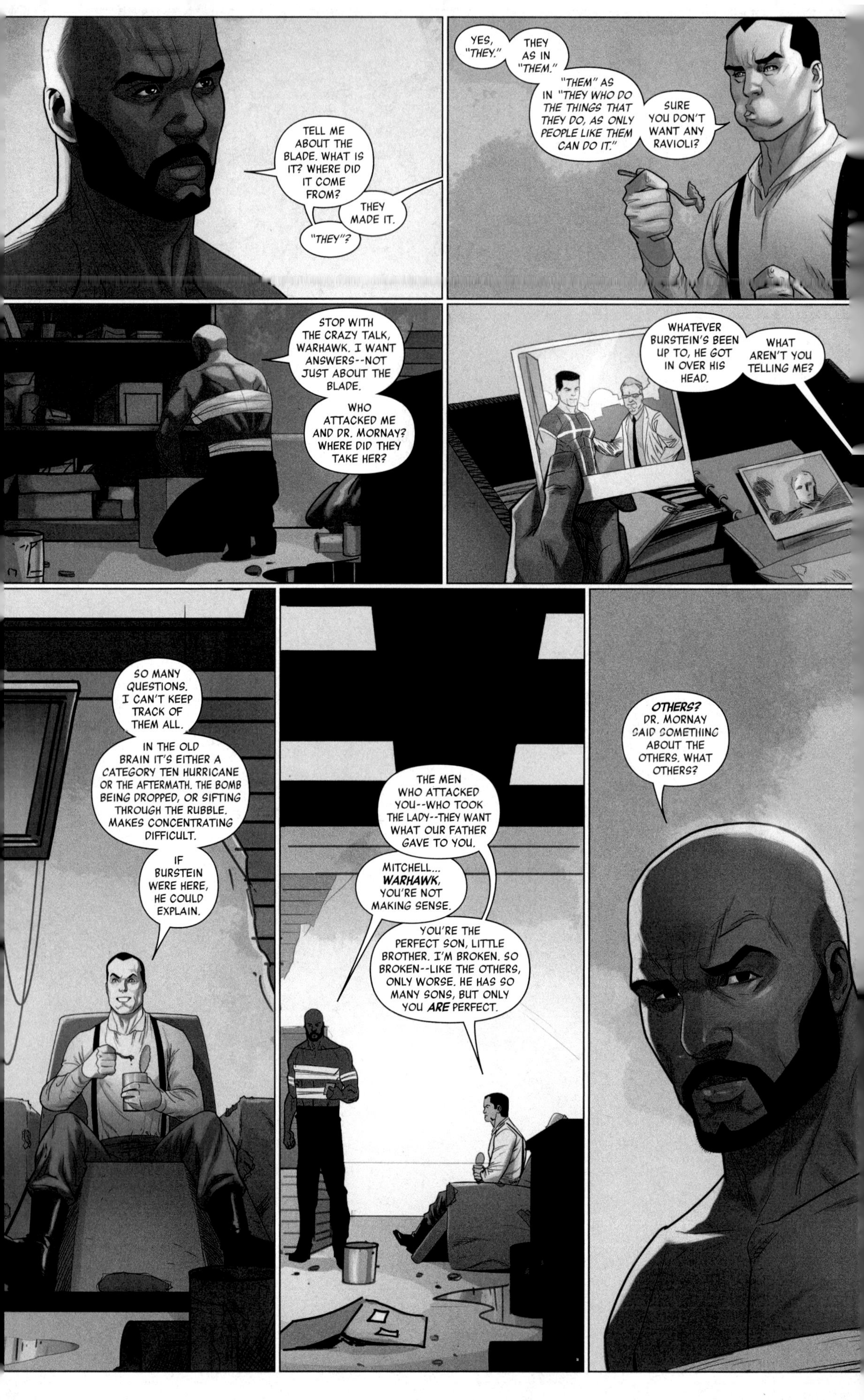
TELL ME ABOUT THE BLADE. WHAT IS IT? WHERE DID IT COME FROM?
THEY MADE IT.
"THEY"?
YES, "THEY."
THEY AS IN "THEM."
"THEM" AS IN "THEY WHO DO THE THINGS THAT THEY DO, AS ONLY PEOPLE LIKE THEM CAN DO IT."
SURE YOU DON'T WANT ANY RAVIOLI?
STOP WITH THE CRAZY TALK, WARHAWK. I WANT ANSWERS--NOT JUST ABOUT THE BLADE.
WHO ATTACKED ME AND DR. MORNAY? WHERE DID THEY TAKE HER?
WHATEVER BURSTEIN'S BEEN UP TO, HE GOT IN OVER HIS HEAD.
WHAT AREN'T YOU TELLING ME?
SO MANY QUESTIONS. I CAN'T KEEP TRACK OF THEM ALL.
IN THE OLD BRAIN IT'S EITHER A CATEGORY TEN HURRICANE OR THE AFTERMATH. THE BOMB BEING DROPPED, OR SIFTING THROUGH THE RUBBLE. MAKES CONCENTRATING DIFFICULT.
IF BURSTEIN WERE HERE, HE COULD EXPLAIN.
THE MEN WHO ATTACKED YOU--WHO TOOK THE LADY--THEY WANT WHAT OUR FATHER GAVE TO YOU.
MITCHELL... **WARHAWK,** YOU'RE NOT MAKING SENSE.
YOU'RE THE PERFECT SON, LITTLE BROTHER. I'M BROKEN. SO BROKEN--LIKE THE OTHERS, ONLY WORSE. HE HAS SO MANY SONS, BUT ONLY YOU **ARE** PERFECT.
OTHERS? DR. MORNAY SAID SOMETHING ABOUT THE OTHERS. WHAT OTHERS?

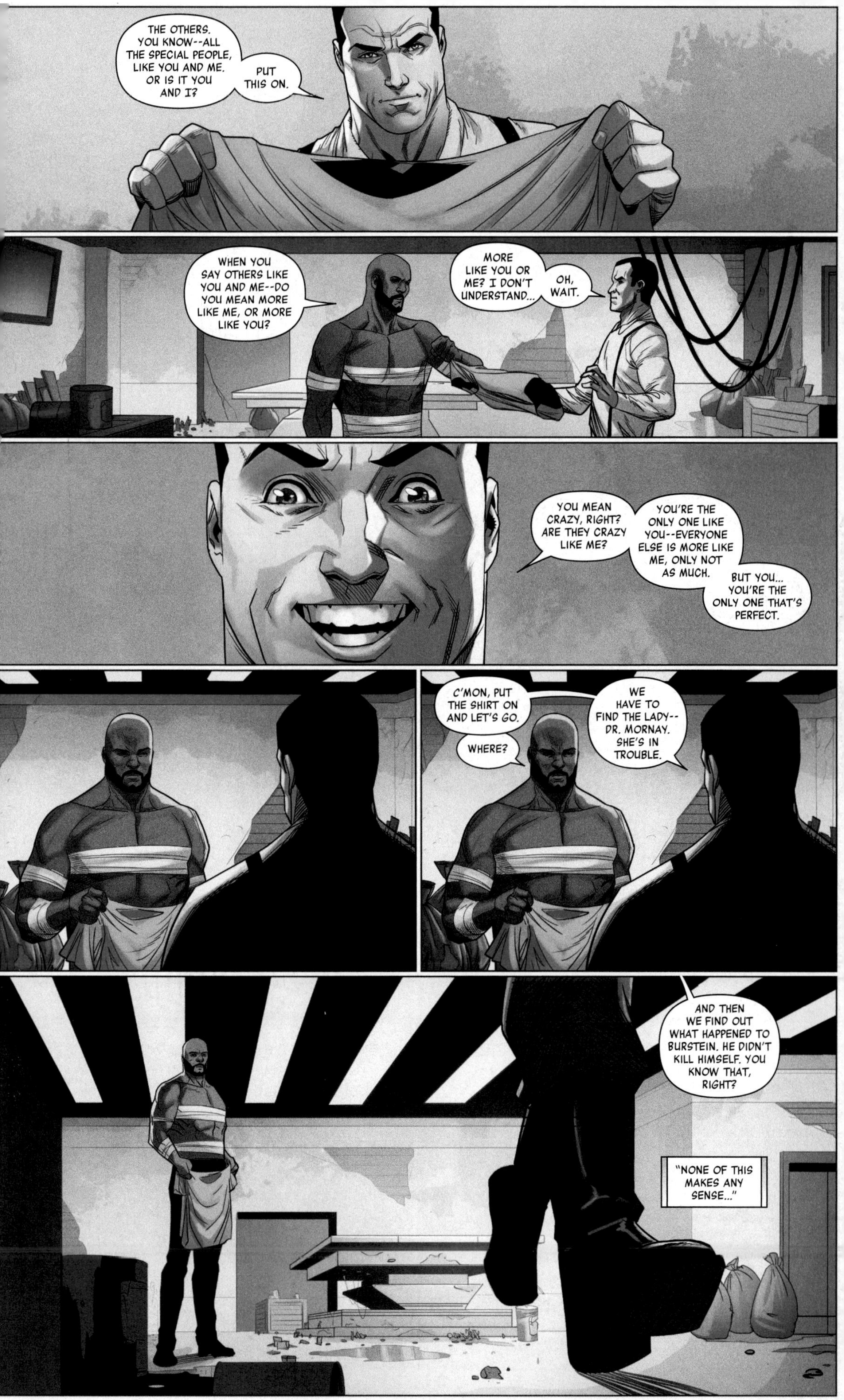
THE OTHERS. YOU KNOW--ALL THE SPECIAL PEOPLE, LIKE YOU AND ME. OR IS IT YOU AND I?
PUT THIS ON.
WHEN YOU SAY OTHERS LIKE YOU AND ME--DO YOU MEAN MORE LIKE ME, OR MORE LIKE YOU?
MORE LIKE YOU OR ME? I DON'T UNDERSTAND...
OH, WAIT.
YOU MEAN CRAZY, RIGHT? ARE THEY CRAZY LIKE ME?
YOU'RE THE ONLY ONE LIKE YOU--EVERYONE ELSE IS MORE LIKE ME, ONLY NOT AS MUCH.
BUT YOU... YOU'RE THE ONLY ONE THAT'S PERFECT.
C'MON, PUT THE SHIRT ON AND LET'S GO.
WHERE?
WE HAVE TO FIND THE LADY--DR. MORNAY. SHE'S IN TROUBLE.
AND THEN WE FIND OUT WHAT HAPPENED TO BURSTEIN. HE DIDN'T KILL HIMSELF. YOU KNOW THAT, RIGHT?
"NONE OF THIS MAKES ANY SENSE..."

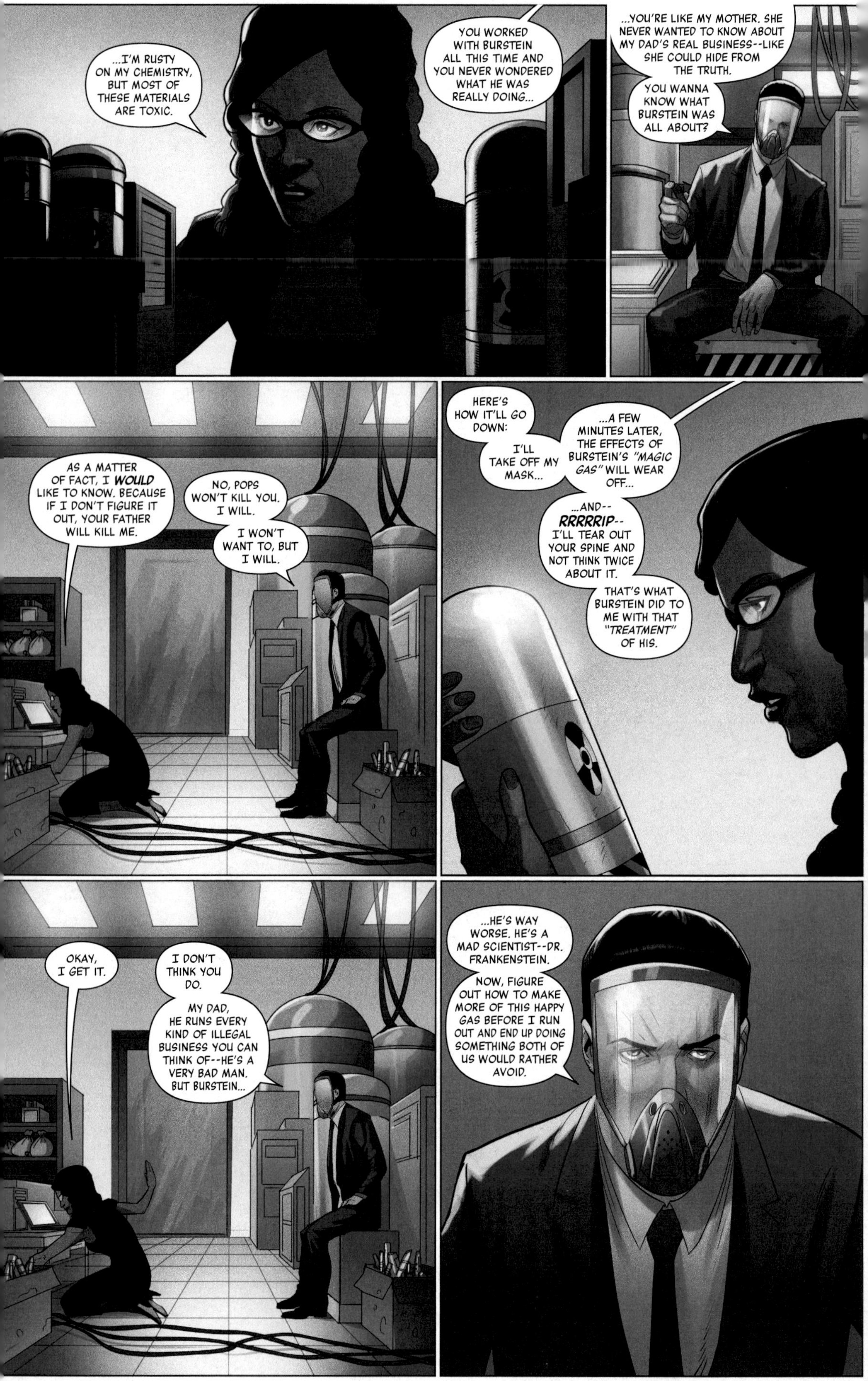
...I'M RUSTY ON MY CHEMISTRY, BUT MOST OF THESE MATERIALS ARE TOXIC.
YOU WORKED WITH BURSTEIN ALL THIS TIME AND YOU NEVER WONDERED WHAT HE WAS REALLY DOING...
...YOU'RE LIKE MY MOTHER. SHE NEVER WANTED TO KNOW ABOUT MY DAD'S REAL BUSINESS--LIKE SHE COULD HIDE FROM THE TRUTH.
YOU WANNA KNOW WHAT BURSTEIN WAS ALL ABOUT?
AS A MATTER OF FACT, I **WOULD** LIKE TO KNOW. BECAUSE IF I DON'T FIGURE IT OUT, YOUR FATHER WILL KILL ME.
NO, POPS WON'T KILL YOU. I WILL.
I WON'T WANT TO, BUT I WILL.
HERE'S HOW IT'LL GO DOWN:
I'LL TAKE OFF MY MASK...
...A FEW MINUTES LATER, THE EFFECTS OF BURSTEIN'S *"MAGIC GAS"* WILL WEAR OFF...
...AND-- ***RRRRRIP***-- I'LL TEAR OUT YOUR SPINE AND NOT THINK TWICE ABOUT IT.
THAT'S WHAT BURSTEIN DID TO ME WITH THAT *"TREATMENT"* OF HIS.
OKAY, I GET IT.
I DON'T THINK YOU DO.
MY DAD, HE RUNS EVERY KIND OF ILLEGAL BUSINESS YOU CAN THINK OF--HE'S A VERY BAD MAN. BUT BURSTEIN...
...HE'S WAY WORSE. HE'S A MAD SCIENTIST--DR. FRANKENSTEIN.
NOW, FIGURE OUT HOW TO MAKE MORE OF THIS HAPPY GAS BEFORE I RUN OUT AND END UP DOING SOMETHING BOTH OF US WOULD RATHER AVOID.

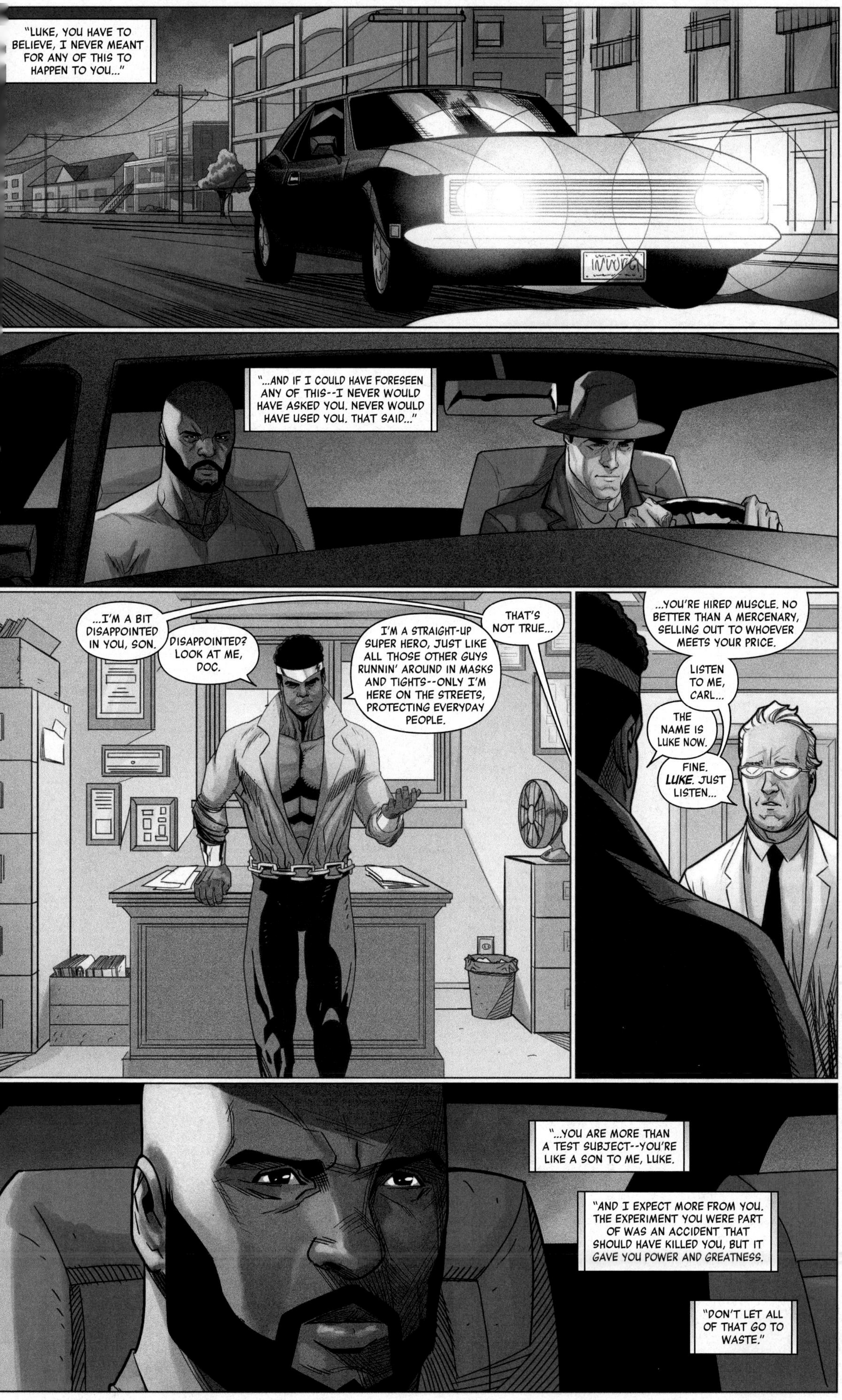
"LUKE, YOU HAVE TO BELIEVE, I NEVER MEANT FOR ANY OF THIS TO HAPPEN TO YOU..."
"...AND IF I COULD HAVE FORESEEN ANY OF THIS--I NEVER WOULD HAVE ASKED YOU. NEVER WOULD HAVE USED YOU. THAT SAID..."
...I'M A BIT DISAPPOINTED IN YOU, SON.
DISAPPOINTED? LOOK AT ME, DOC.
I'M A STRAIGHT-UP SUPER HERO, JUST LIKE ALL THOSE OTHER GUYS RUNNIN' AROUND IN MASKS AND TIGHTS--ONLY I'M HERE ON THE STREETS, PROTECTING EVERYDAY PEOPLE.
THAT'S NOT TRUE...
...YOU'RE HIRED MUSCLE. NO BETTER THAN A MERCENARY, SELLING OUT TO WHOEVER MEETS YOUR PRICE.
LISTEN TO ME, CARL...
THE NAME IS LUKE NOW.
FINE. *LUKE*. JUST LISTEN...
"...YOU ARE MORE THAN A TEST SUBJECT--YOU'RE LIKE A SON TO ME, LUKE.
"AND I EXPECT MORE FROM YOU. THE EXPERIMENT YOU WERE PART OF WAS AN ACCIDENT THAT SHOULD HAVE KILLED YOU, BUT IT GAVE YOU POWER AND GREATNESS.
"DON'T LET ALL OF THAT GO TO WASTE."

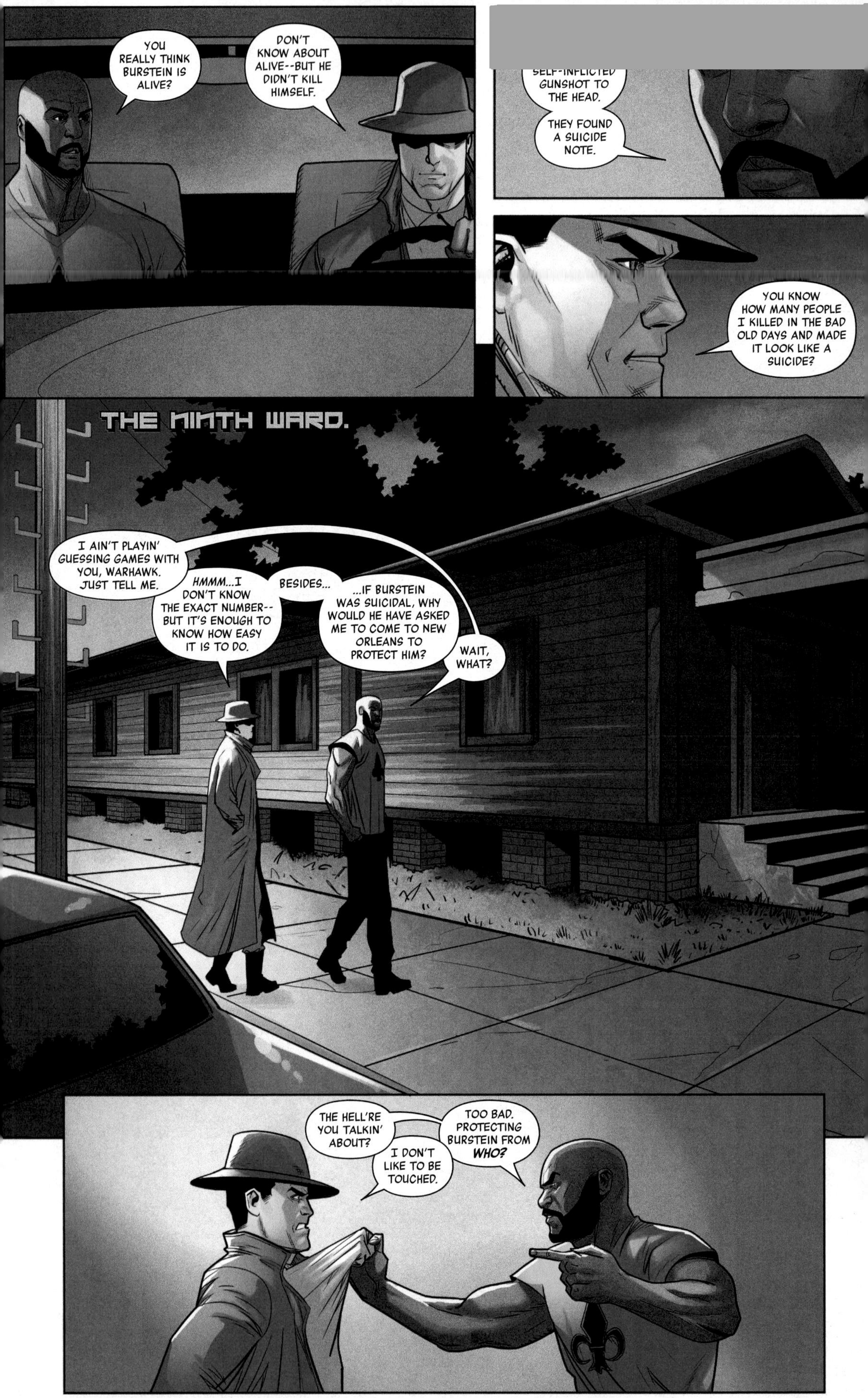
YOU REALLY THINK BURSTEIN IS ALIVE?
DON'T KNOW ABOUT ALIVE--BUT HE DIDN'T KILL HIMSELF.
SELF-INFLICTED GUNSHOT TO THE HEAD.
THEY FOUND A SUICIDE NOTE.
YOU KNOW HOW MANY PEOPLE I KILLED IN THE BAD OLD DAYS AND MADE IT LOOK LIKE A SUICIDE?
THE NINTH WARD.
I AIN'T PLAYIN' GUESSING GAMES WITH YOU, WARHAWK. JUST TELL ME.
HMMM...I DON'T KNOW THE EXACT NUMBER--BUT IT'S ENOUGH TO KNOW HOW EASY IT IS TO DO.
BESIDES...
...IF BURSTEIN WAS SUICIDAL, WHY WOULD HE HAVE ASKED ME TO COME TO NEW ORLEANS TO PROTECT HIM?
WAIT, WHAT?
THE HELL'RE YOU TALKIN' ABOUT?
TOO BAD. PROTECTING BURSTEIN FROM WHO?
I DON'T LIKE TO BE TOUCHED.

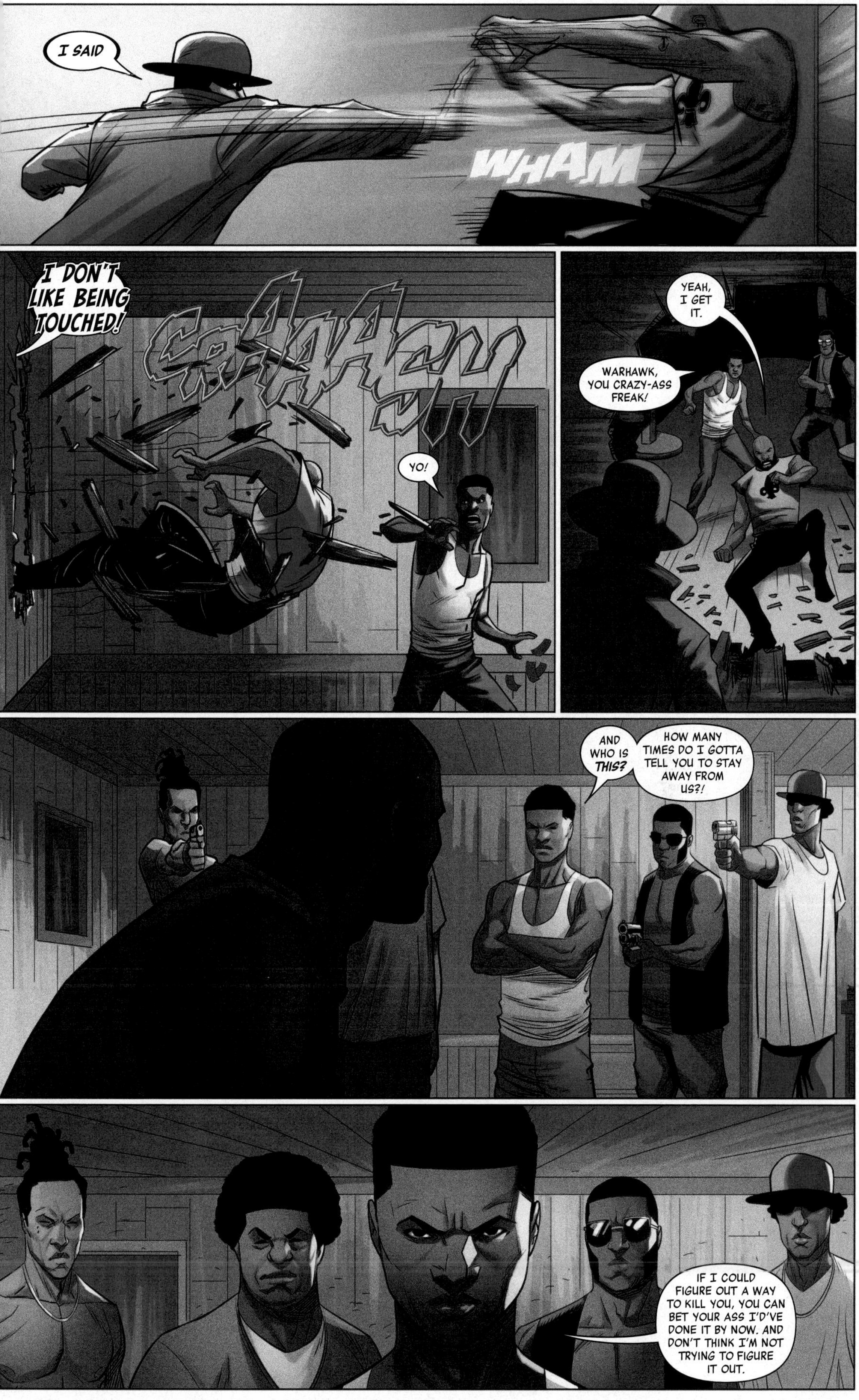
I SAID
WHAM
I DON'T LIKE BEING TOUCHED!
CRAAASH
YO!
YEAH, I GET IT.
WARHAWK, YOU CRAZY-ASS FREAK!
AND WHO IS THIS?
HOW MANY TIMES DO I GOTTA TELL YOU TO STAY AWAY FROM US?!
IF I COULD FIGURE OUT A WAY TO KILL YOU, YOU CAN BET YOUR ASS I'D'VE DONE IT BY NOW. AND DON'T THINK I'M NOT TRYING TO FIGURE IT OUT.

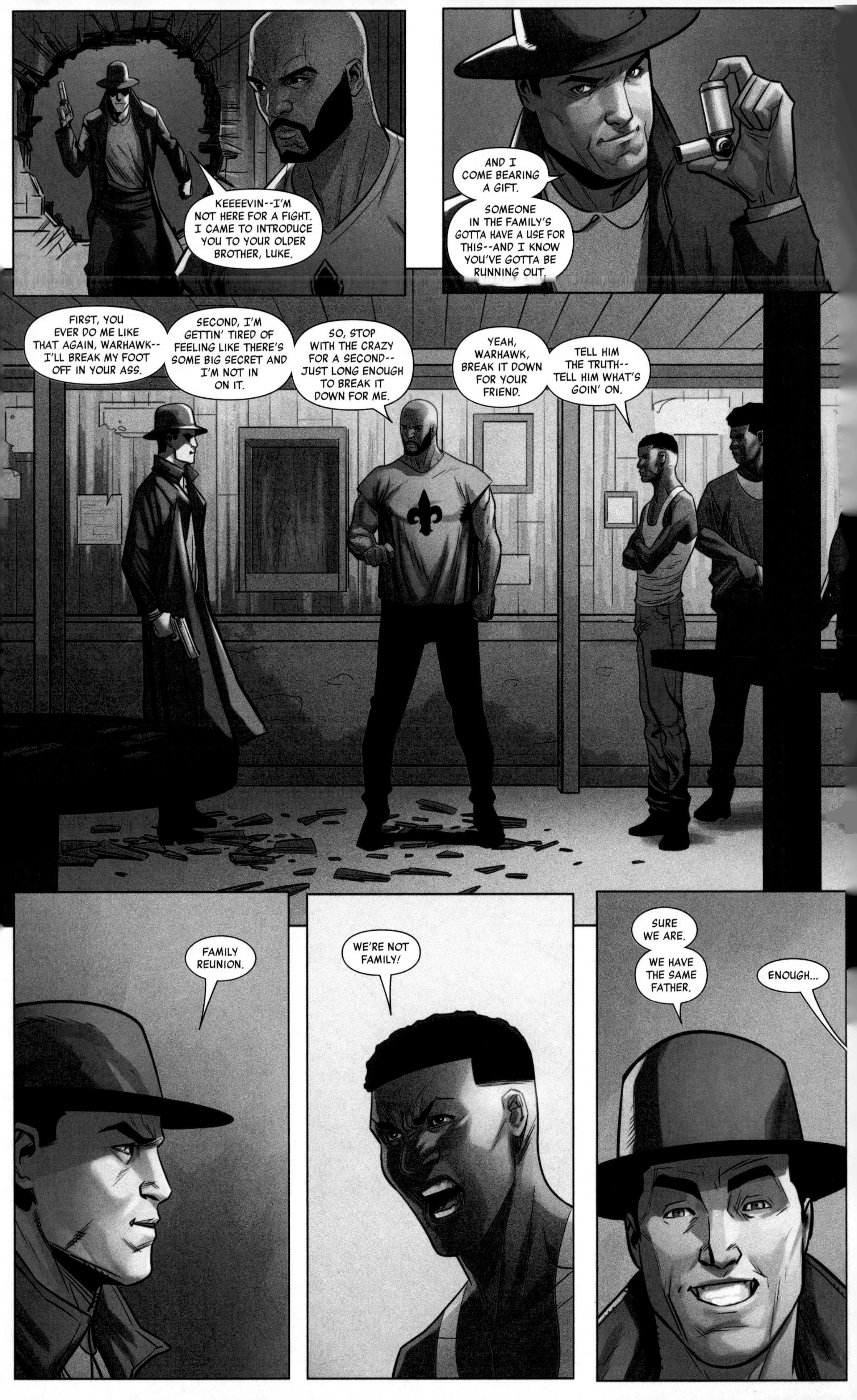
KEEEEVIN--I'M NOT HERE FOR A FIGHT. I CAME TO INTRODUCE YOU TO YOUR OLDER BROTHER, LUKE.
AND I COME BEARING A GIFT.
SOMEONE IN THE FAMILY'S GOTTA HAVE A USE FOR THIS--AND I KNOW YOU'VE GOTTA BE RUNNING OUT.
FIRST, YOU EVER DO ME LIKE THAT AGAIN, WARHAWK--I'LL BREAK MY FOOT OFF IN YOUR ASS.
SECOND, I'M GETTIN' TIRED OF FEELING LIKE THERE'S SOME BIG SECRET AND I'M NOT IN ON IT.
SO, STOP WITH THE CRAZY FOR A SECOND--JUST LONG ENOUGH TO BREAK IT DOWN FOR ME.
YEAH, WARHAWK, BREAK IT DOWN FOR YOUR FRIEND.
TELL HIM THE TRUTH--TELL HIM WHAT'S GOIN' ON.
FAMILY REUNION.
WE'RE NOT FAMILY!
SURE WE ARE.
WE HAVE THE SAME FATHER.
ENOUGH...

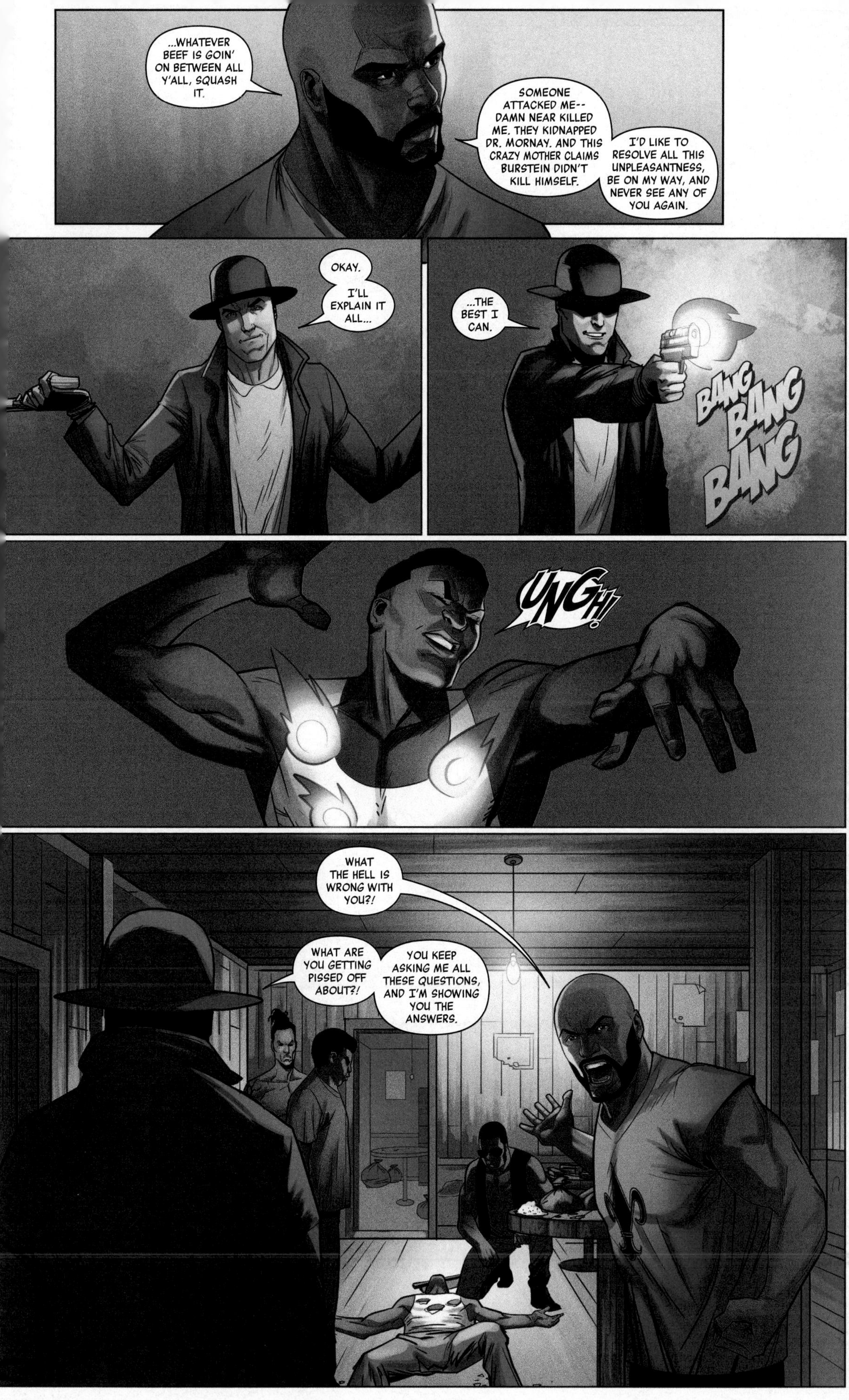
...WHATEVER BEEF IS GOIN' ON BETWEEN ALL Y'ALL, SQUASH IT.
SOMEONE ATTACKED ME--DAMN NEAR KILLED ME. THEY KIDNAPPED DR. MORNAY. AND THIS CRAZY MOTHER CLAIMS BURSTEIN DIDN'T KILL HIMSELF.
I'D LIKE TO RESOLVE ALL THIS UNPLEASANTNESS, BE ON MY WAY, AND NEVER SEE ANY OF YOU AGAIN.
OKAY.
I'LL EXPLAIN IT ALL...
...THE BEST I CAN.
BANG BANG BANG
UNGH!
WHAT THE HELL IS WRONG WITH YOU?!
WHAT ARE YOU GETTING PISSED OFF ABOUT?!
YOU KEEP ASKING ME ALL THESE QUESTIONS, AND I'M SHOWING YOU THE ANSWERS.

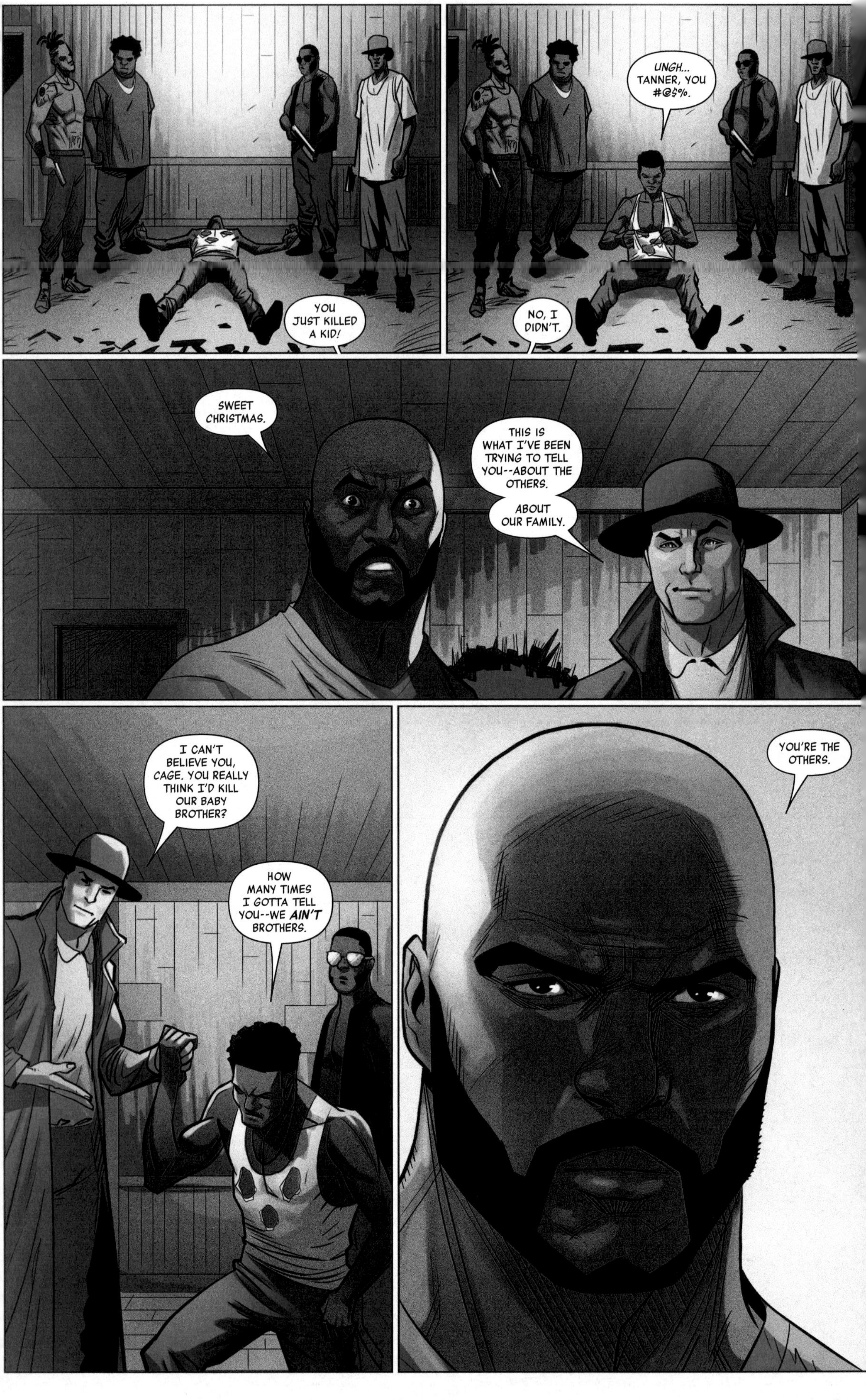
YOU JUST KILLED A KID!
UNGH... TANNER, YOU #@$%.
NO, I DIDN'T.
SWEET CHRISTMAS.
THIS IS WHAT I'VE BEEN TRYING TO TELL YOU--ABOUT THE OTHERS.
ABOUT OUR FAMILY.
I CAN'T BELIEVE YOU, CAGE. YOU REALLY THINK I'D KILL OUR BABY BROTHER?
HOW MANY TIMES I GOTTA TELL YOU--WE *AIN'T* BROTHERS.
YOU'RE THE OTHERS.

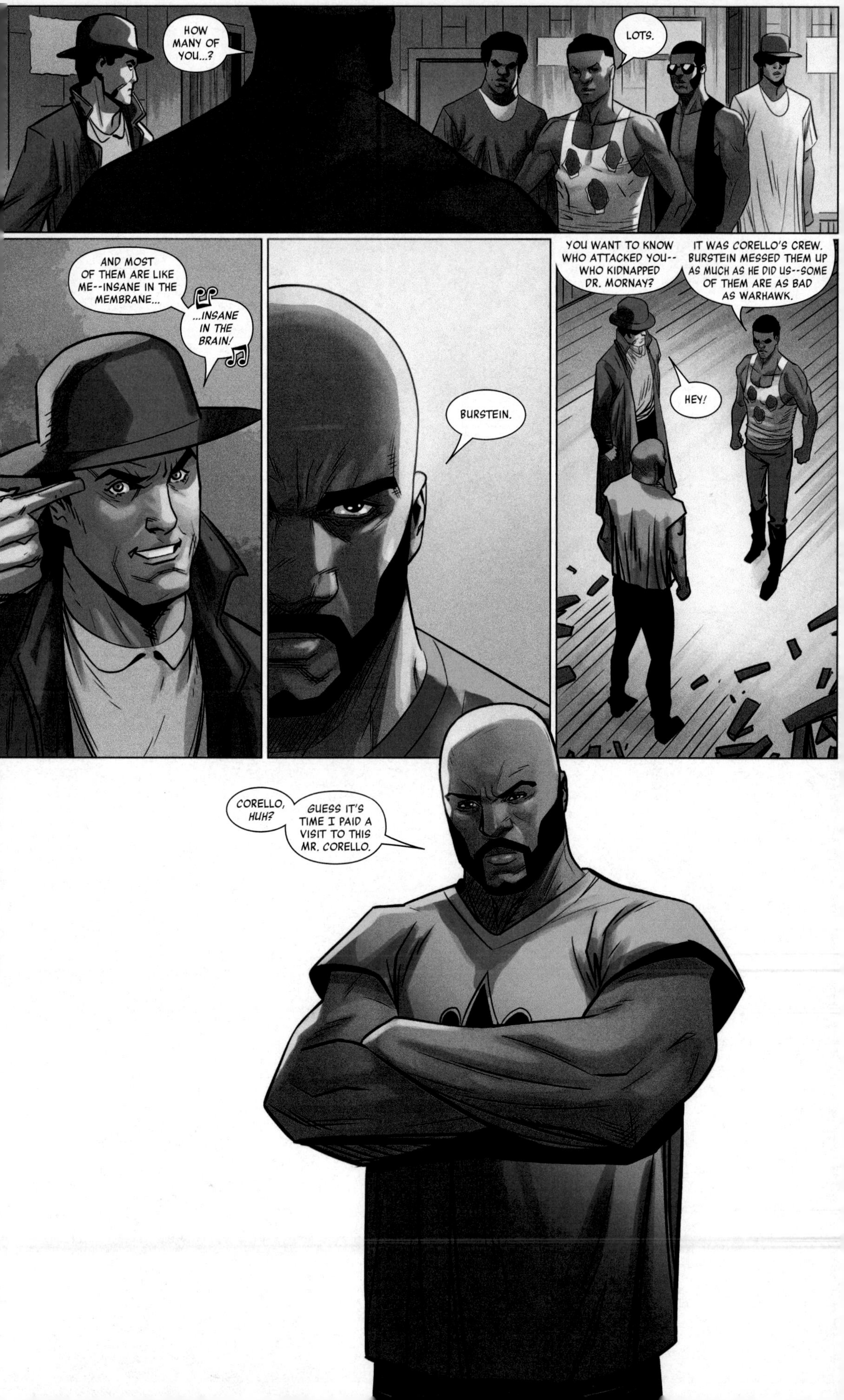
HOW MANY OF YOU...?
LOTS.
AND MOST OF THEM ARE LIKE ME--INSANE IN THE MEMBRANE...
...INSANE IN THE BRAIN!
BURSTEIN.
YOU WANT TO KNOW WHO ATTACKED YOU--WHO KIDNAPPED DR. MORNAY?
IT WAS CORELLO'S CREW. BURSTEIN MESSED THEM UP AS MUCH AS HE DID US--SOME OF THEM ARE AS BAD AS WARHAWK.
HEY!
CORELLO, HUH?
GUESS IT'S TIME I PAID A VISIT TO THIS MR. CORELLO.

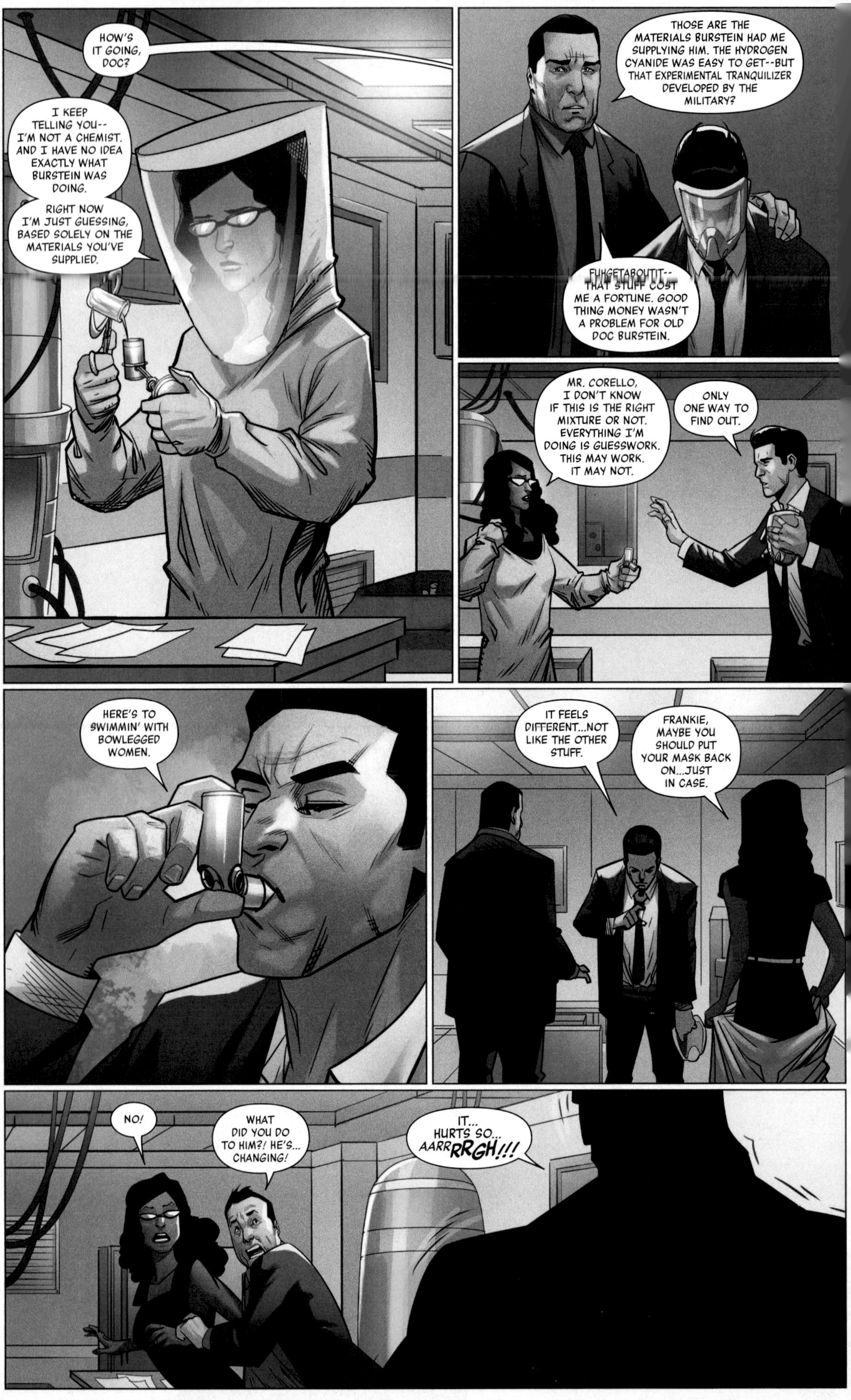
HOW'S IT GOING, DOC?
I KEEP TELLING YOU-- I'M NOT A CHEMIST. AND I HAVE NO IDEA EXACTLY WHAT BURSTEIN WAS DOING.
RIGHT NOW I'M JUST GUESSING, BASED SOLELY ON THE MATERIALS YOU'VE SUPPLIED.
THOSE ARE THE MATERIALS BURSTEIN HAD ME SUPPLYING HIM. THE HYDROGEN CYANIDE WAS EASY TO GET--BUT THAT EXPERIMENTAL TRANQUILIZER DEVELOPED BY THE MILITARY?
FUHGETABOUTIT-- THAT STUFF COST ME A FORTUNE. GOOD THING MONEY WASN'T A PROBLEM FOR OLD DOC BURSTEIN.
MR. CORELLO, I DON'T KNOW IF THIS IS THE RIGHT MIXTURE OR NOT. EVERYTHING I'M DOING IS GUESSWORK. THIS MAY WORK. IT MAY NOT.
ONLY ONE WAY TO FIND OUT.
HERE'S TO SWIMMIN' WITH BOWLEGGED WOMEN.
IT FEELS DIFFERENT...NOT LIKE THE OTHER STUFF.
FRANKIE, MAYBE YOU SHOULD PUT YOUR MASK BACK ON...JUST IN CASE.
NO!
WHAT DID YOU DO TO HIM?! HE'S... CHANGING!
IT... HURTS SO... AARRRRGH!!!

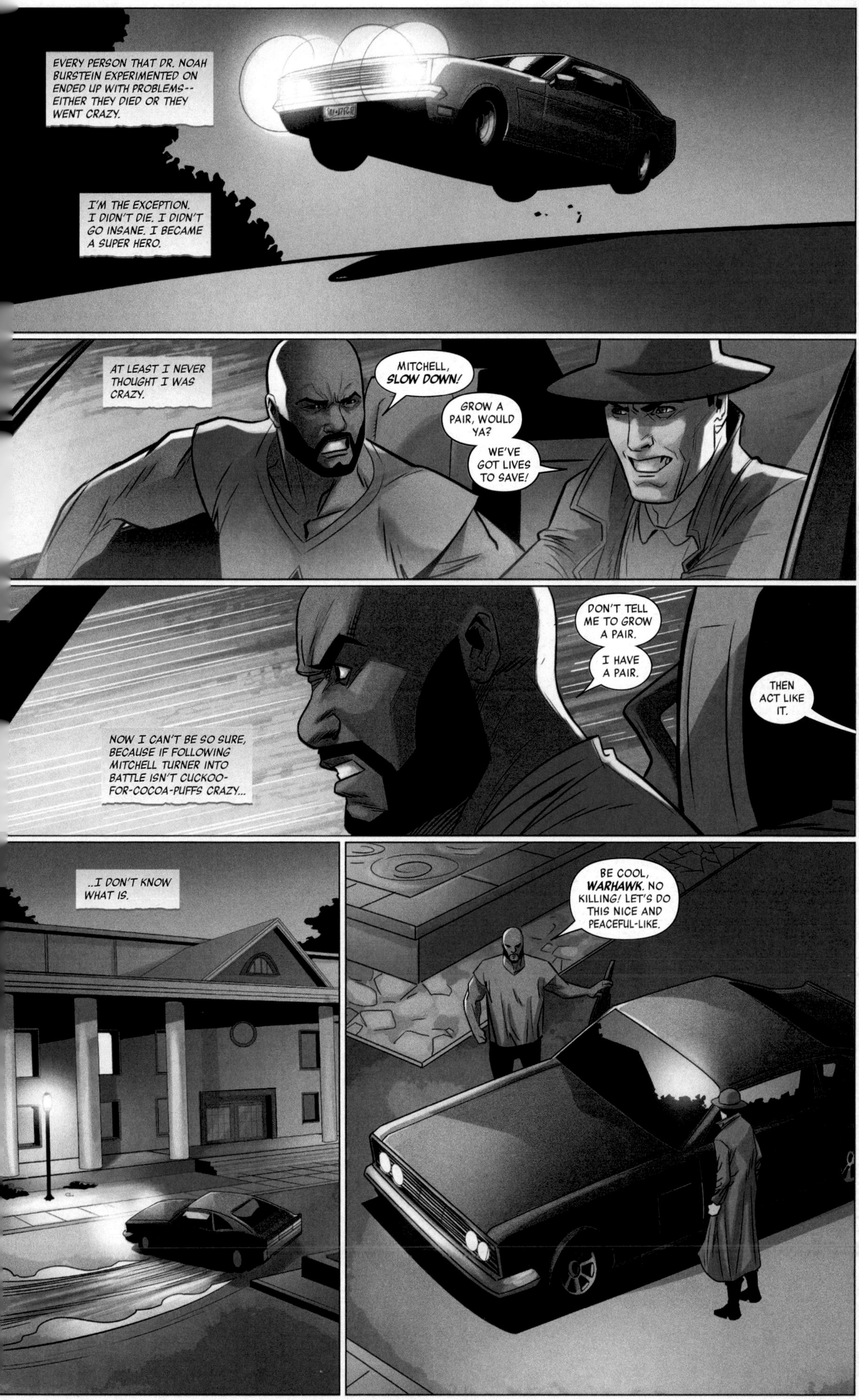
EVERY PERSON THAT DR. NOAH BURSTEIN EXPERIMENTED ON ENDED UP WITH PROBLEMS--EITHER THEY DIED OR THEY WENT CRAZY.
I'M THE EXCEPTION. I DIDN'T DIE. I DIDN'T GO INSANE. I BECAME A SUPER HERO.
AT LEAST I NEVER THOUGHT I WAS CRAZY.
MITCHELL, SLOW DOWN!
GROW A PAIR, WOULD YA?
WE'VE GOT LIVES TO SAVE!
NOW I CAN'T BE SO SURE, BECAUSE IF FOLLOWING MITCHELL TURNER INTO BATTLE ISN'T CUCKOO-FOR-COCOA-PUFFS CRAZY...
DON'T TELL ME TO GROW A PAIR.
I HAVE A PAIR.
THEN ACT LIKE IT.
...I DON'T KNOW WHAT IS.
BE COOL, WARHAWK. NO KILLING! LET'S DO THIS NICE AND PEACEFUL-LIKE.

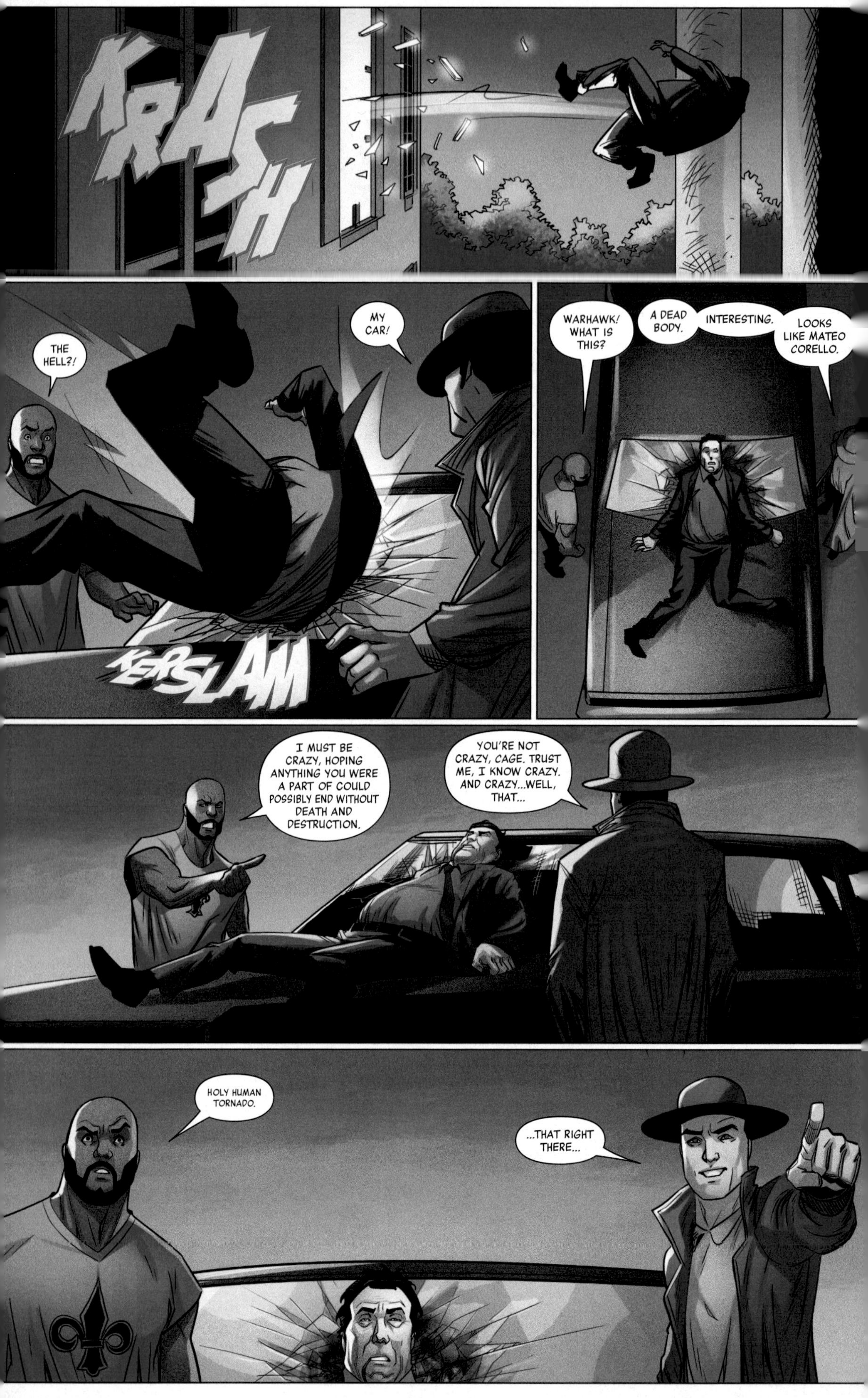
KRASH
THE HELL?!
MY CAR!
KERSLAM
WARHAWK! WHAT IS THIS?
A DEAD BODY.
INTERESTING.
LOOKS LIKE MATEO CORELLO.
I MUST BE CRAZY, HOPING ANYTHING YOU WERE A PART OF COULD POSSIBLY END WITHOUT DEATH AND DESTRUCTION.
YOU'RE NOT CRAZY, CAGE. TRUST ME, I KNOW CRAZY. AND CRAZY...WELL, THAT...
HOLY HUMAN TORNADO.
...THAT RIGHT THERE...

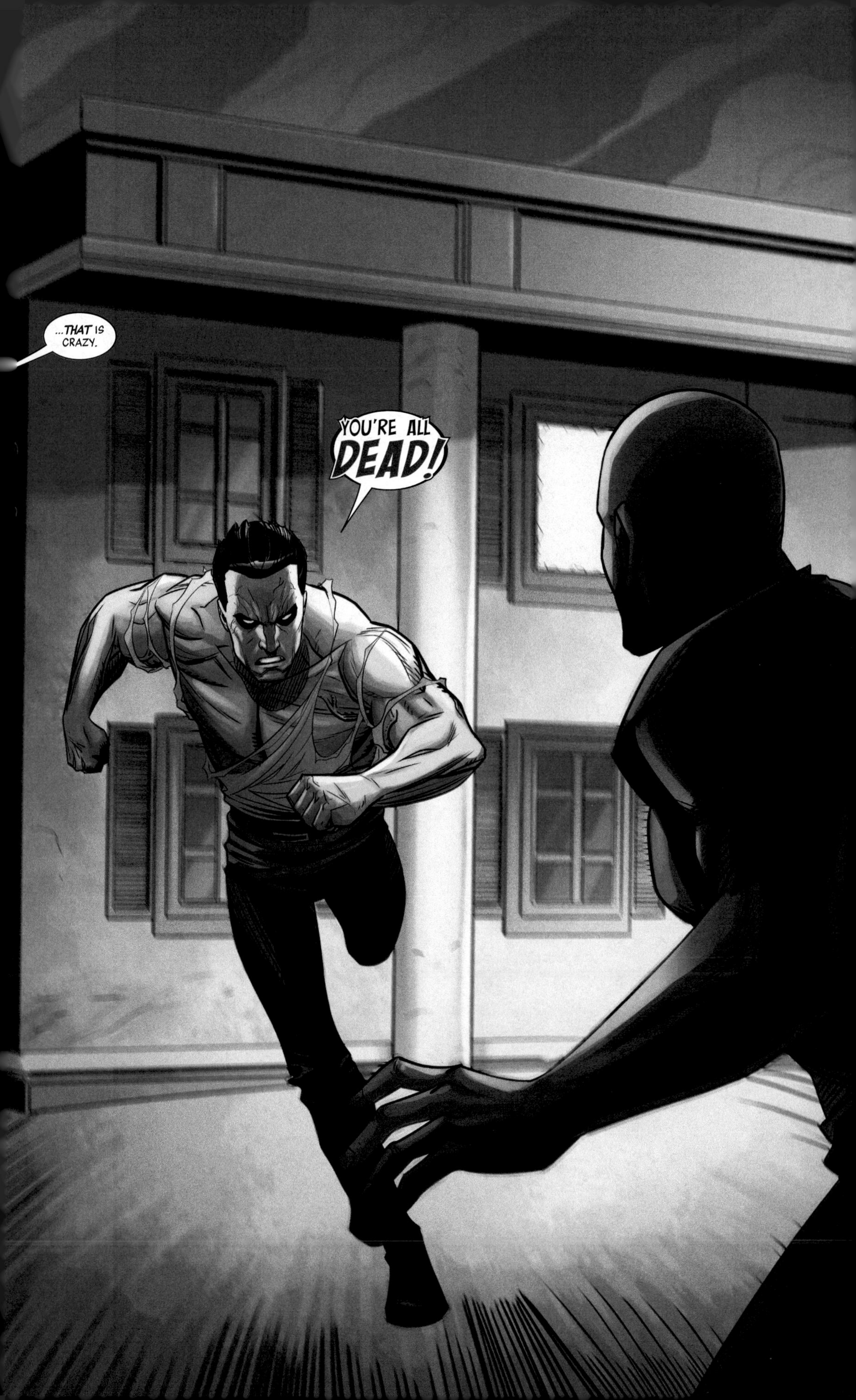
...THAT IS CRAZY.
YOU'RE ALL DEAD!

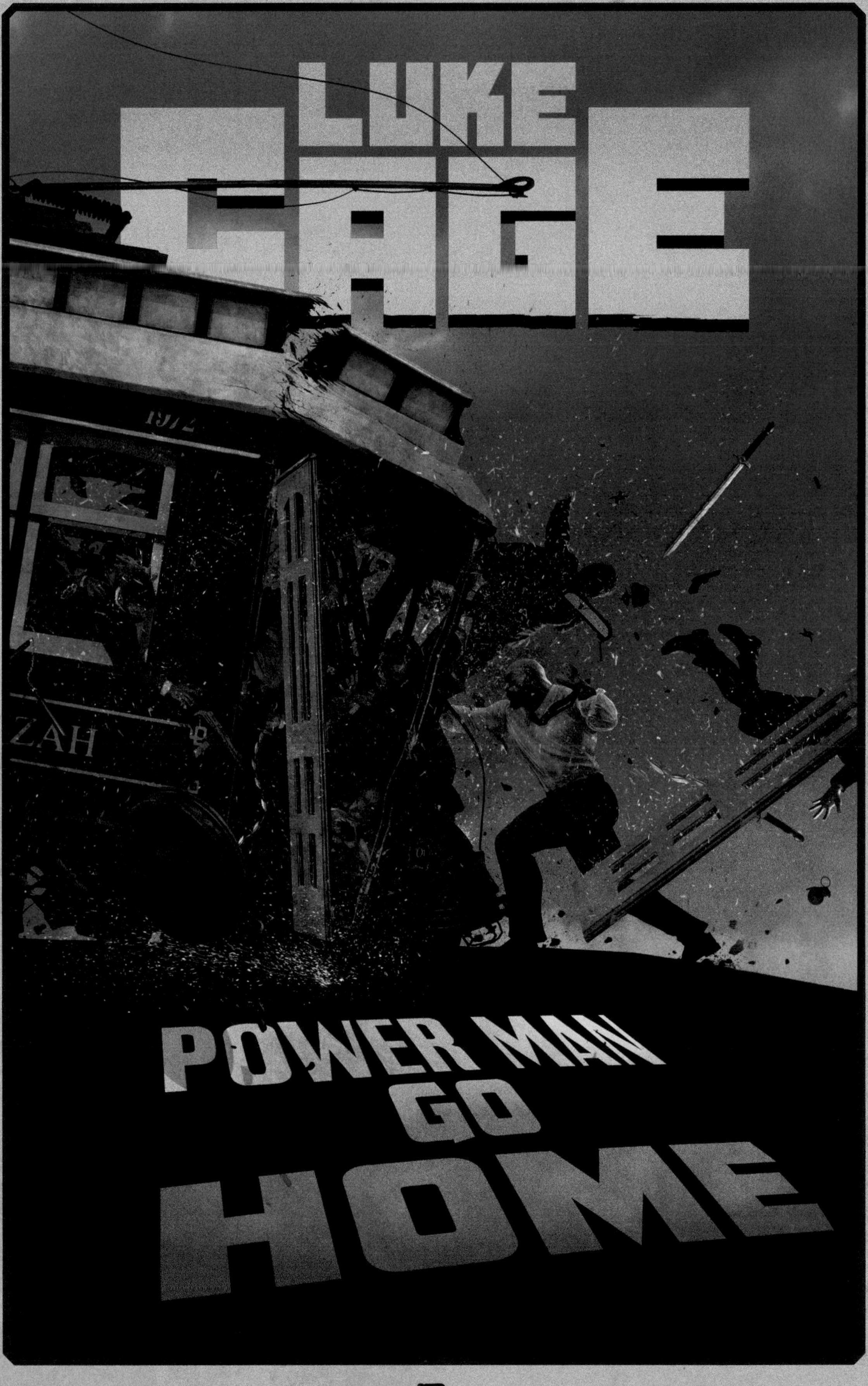
LUKE
CAGE
1972
ZAH
POWER MAN
GO
HOME

3

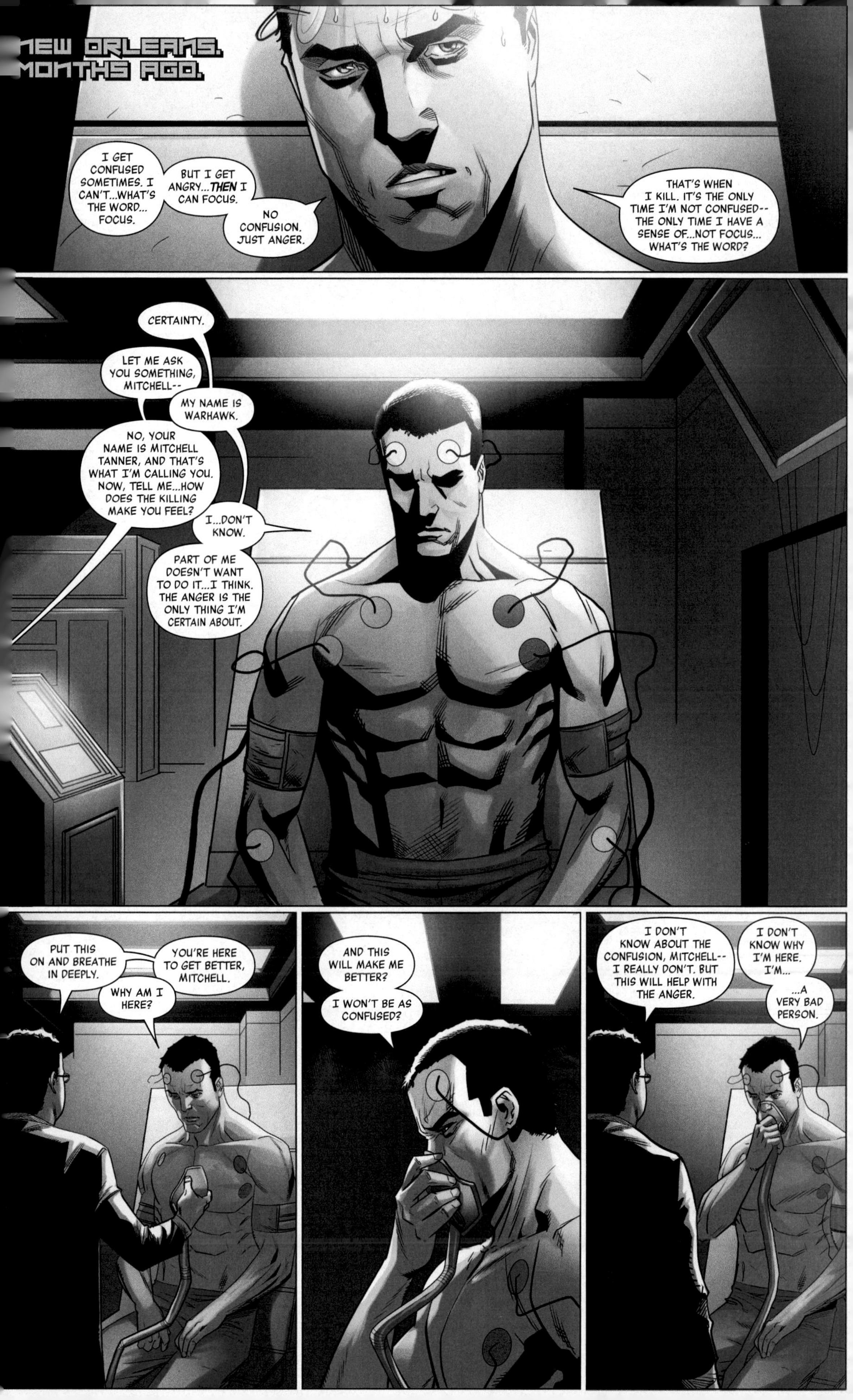
NEW ORLEANS. MONTHS AGO.
I GET CONFUSED SOMETIMES. I CAN'T...WHAT'S THE WORD... FOCUS.
BUT I GET ANGRY...THEN I CAN FOCUS.
NO CONFUSION. JUST ANGER.
THAT'S WHEN I KILL. IT'S THE ONLY TIME I'M NOT CONFUSED-- THE ONLY TIME I HAVE A SENSE OF...NOT FOCUS... WHAT'S THE WORD?
CERTAINTY.
LET ME ASK YOU SOMETHING, MITCHELL--
MY NAME IS WARHAWK.
NO, YOUR NAME IS MITCHELL TANNER, AND THAT'S WHAT I'M CALLING YOU. NOW, TELL ME...HOW DOES THE KILLING MAKE YOU FEEL?
I...DON'T KNOW.
PART OF ME DOESN'T WANT TO DO IT...I THINK. THE ANGER IS THE ONLY THING I'M CERTAIN ABOUT.
PUT THIS ON AND BREATHE IN DEEPLY.
YOU'RE HERE TO GET BETTER, MITCHELL.
WHY AM I HERE?
AND THIS WILL MAKE ME BETTER?
I WON'T BE AS CONFUSED?
I DON'T KNOW ABOUT THE CONFUSION, MITCHELL-- I REALLY DON'T. BUT THIS WILL HELP WITH THE ANGER.
I DON'T KNOW WHY I'M HERE. I'M...
...A VERY BAD PERSON.

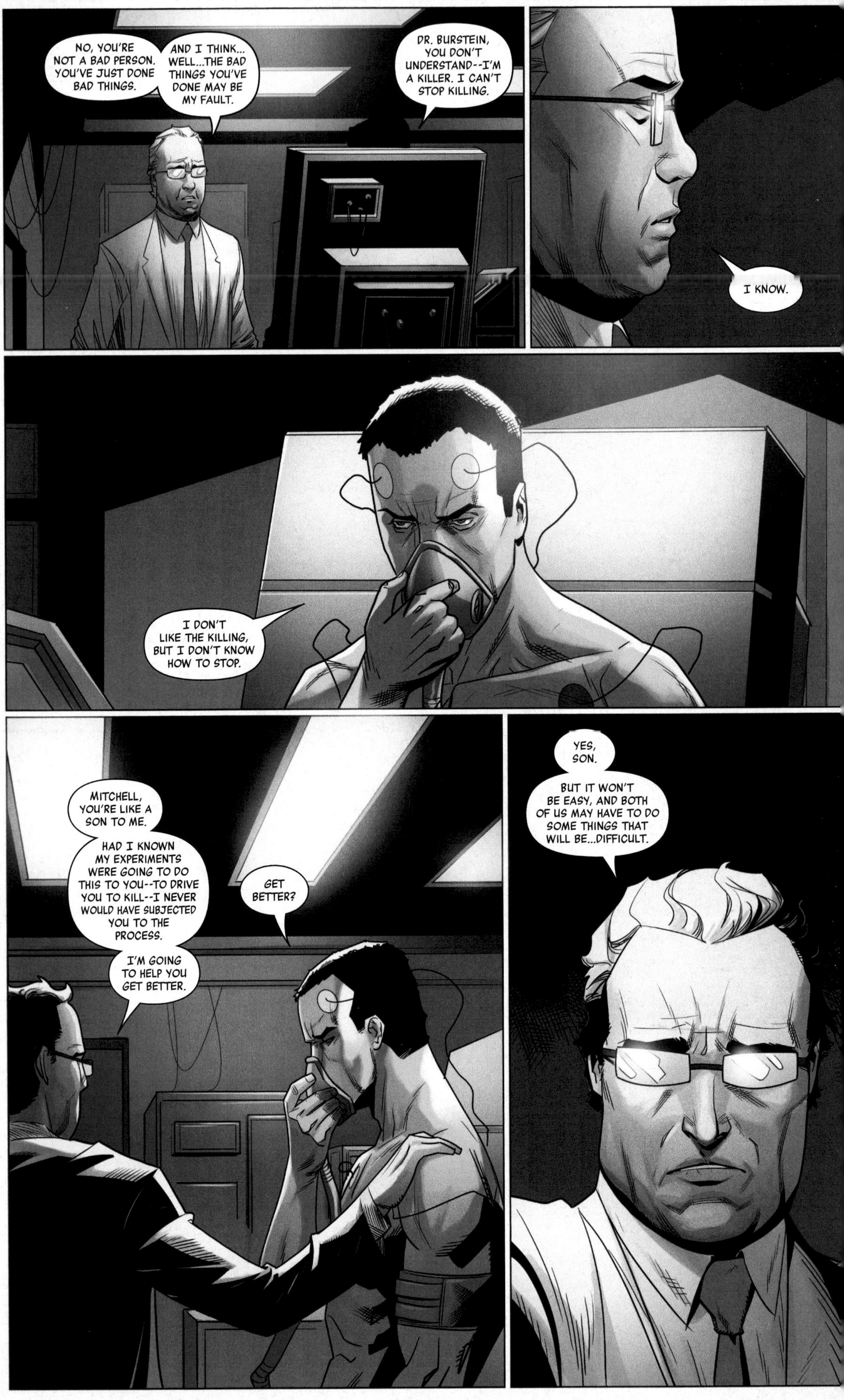

NO, YOU'RE NOT A BAD PERSON. YOU'VE JUST DONE BAD THINGS.
AND I THINK... WELL...THE BAD THINGS YOU'VE DONE MAY BE MY FAULT.
DR. BURSTEIN, YOU DON'T UNDERSTAND--I'M A KILLER. I CAN'T STOP KILLING.
I KNOW.
I DON'T LIKE THE KILLING, BUT I DON'T KNOW HOW TO STOP.
MITCHELL, YOU'RE LIKE A SON TO ME.
HAD I KNOWN MY EXPERIMENTS WERE GOING TO DO THIS TO YOU--TO DRIVE YOU TO KILL--I NEVER WOULD HAVE SUBJECTED YOU TO THE PROCESS.
I'M GOING TO HELP YOU GET BETTER.
GET BETTER?
YES, SON.
BUT IT WON'T BE EASY, AND BOTH OF US MAY HAVE TO DO SOME THINGS THAT WILL BE...DIFFICULT.

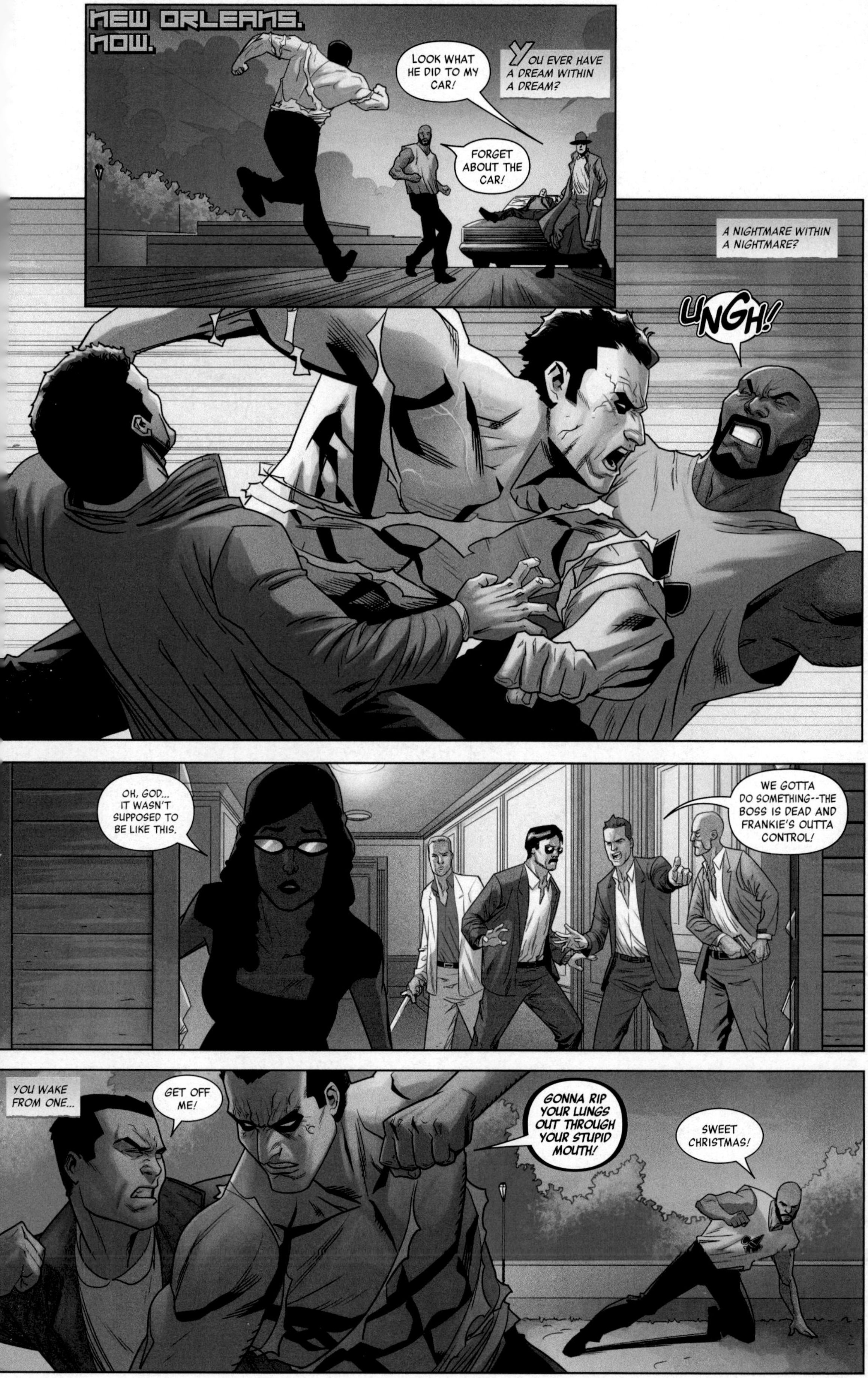

NEW ORLEANS. NOW.
LOOK WHAT HE DID TO MY CAR!
YOU EVER HAVE A DREAM WITHIN A DREAM?
FORGET ABOUT THE CAR!
A NIGHTMARE WITHIN A NIGHTMARE?
UNGH!
OH, GOD... IT WASN'T SUPPOSED TO BE LIKE THIS.
WE GOTTA DO SOMETHING--THE BOSS IS DEAD AND FRANKIE'S OUTTA CONTROL!
YOU WAKE FROM ONE...
GET OFF ME!
GONNA RIP YOUR LUNGS OUT THROUGH YOUR STUPID MOUTH!
SWEET CHRISTMAS!

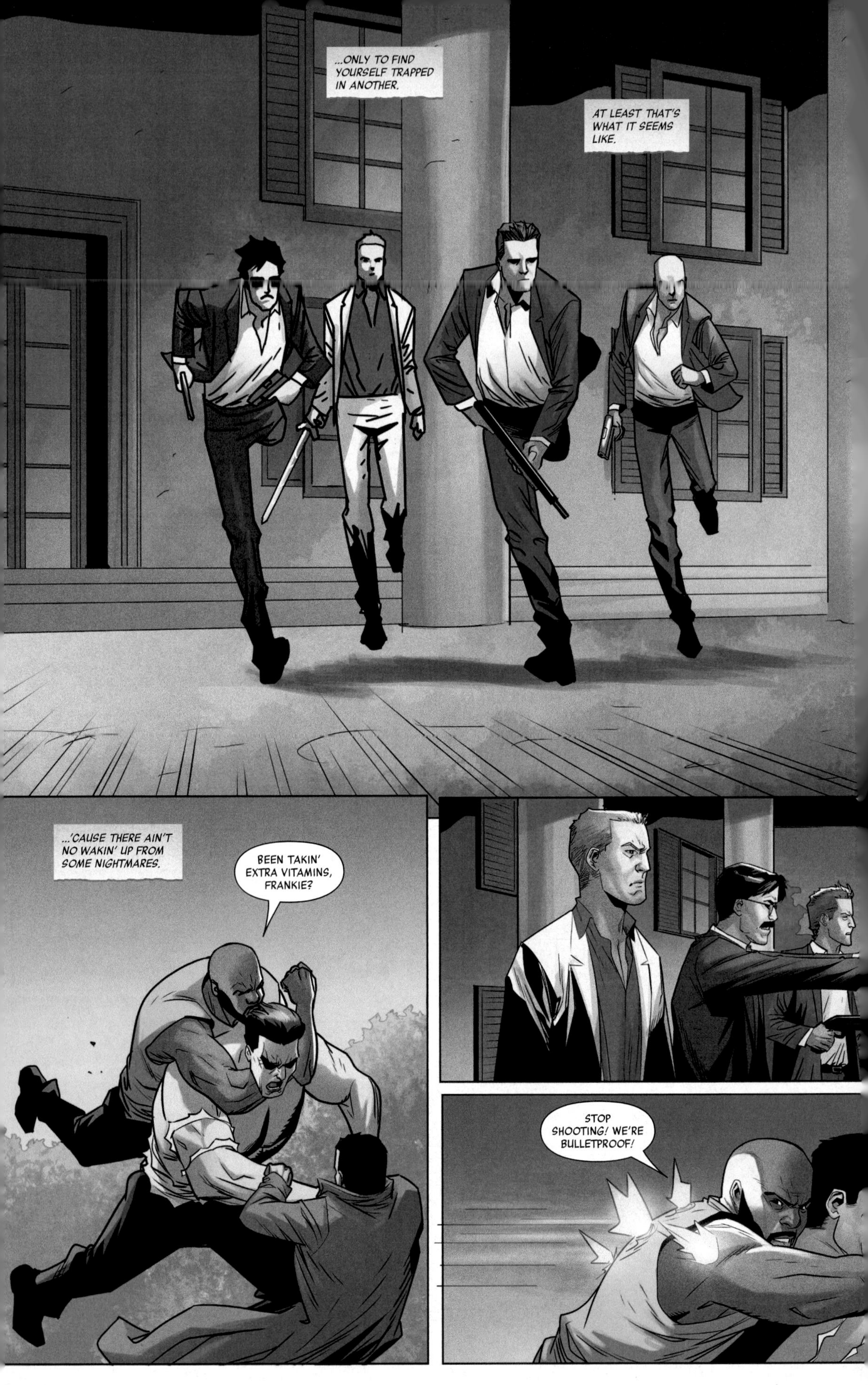
...ONLY TO FIND YOURSELF TRAPPED IN ANOTHER.
AT LEAST THAT'S WHAT IT SEEMS LIKE.
...'CAUSE THERE AIN'T NO WAKIN' UP FROM SOME NIGHTMARES.
BEEN TAKIN' EXTRA VITAMINS, FRANKIE?
STOP SHOOTING! WE'RE BULLETPROOF!

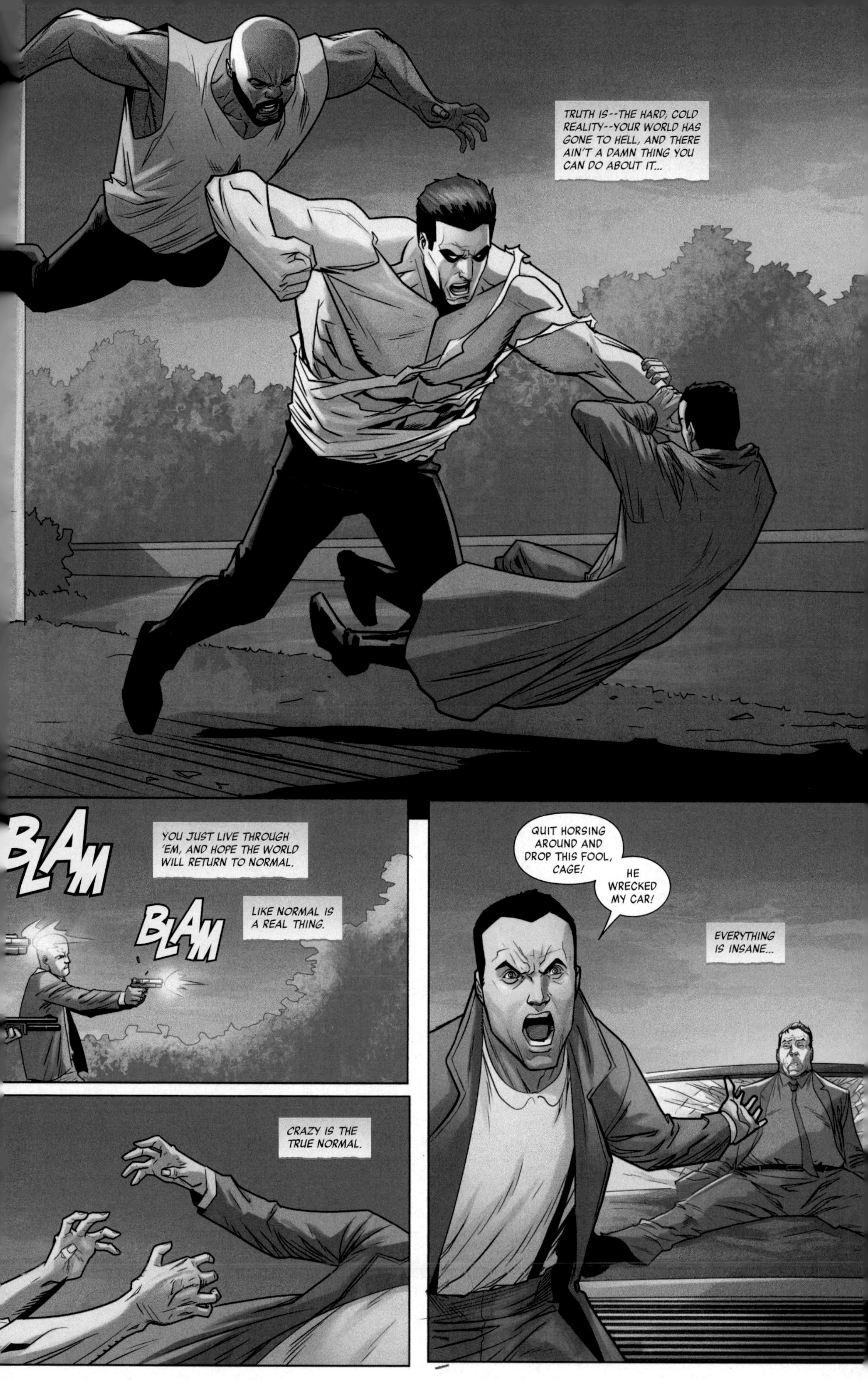
TRUTH IS--THE HARD, COLD REALITY--YOUR WORLD HAS GONE TO HELL, AND THERE AIN'T A DAMN THING YOU CAN DO ABOUT IT...
BLAM
YOU JUST LIVE THROUGH 'EM, AND HOPE THE WORLD WILL RETURN TO NORMAL.
BLAM
LIKE NORMAL IS A REAL THING.
CRAZY IS THE TRUE NORMAL.
QUIT HORSING AROUND AND DROP THIS FOOL, CAGE!
HE WRECKED MY CAR!
EVERYTHING IS INSANE...

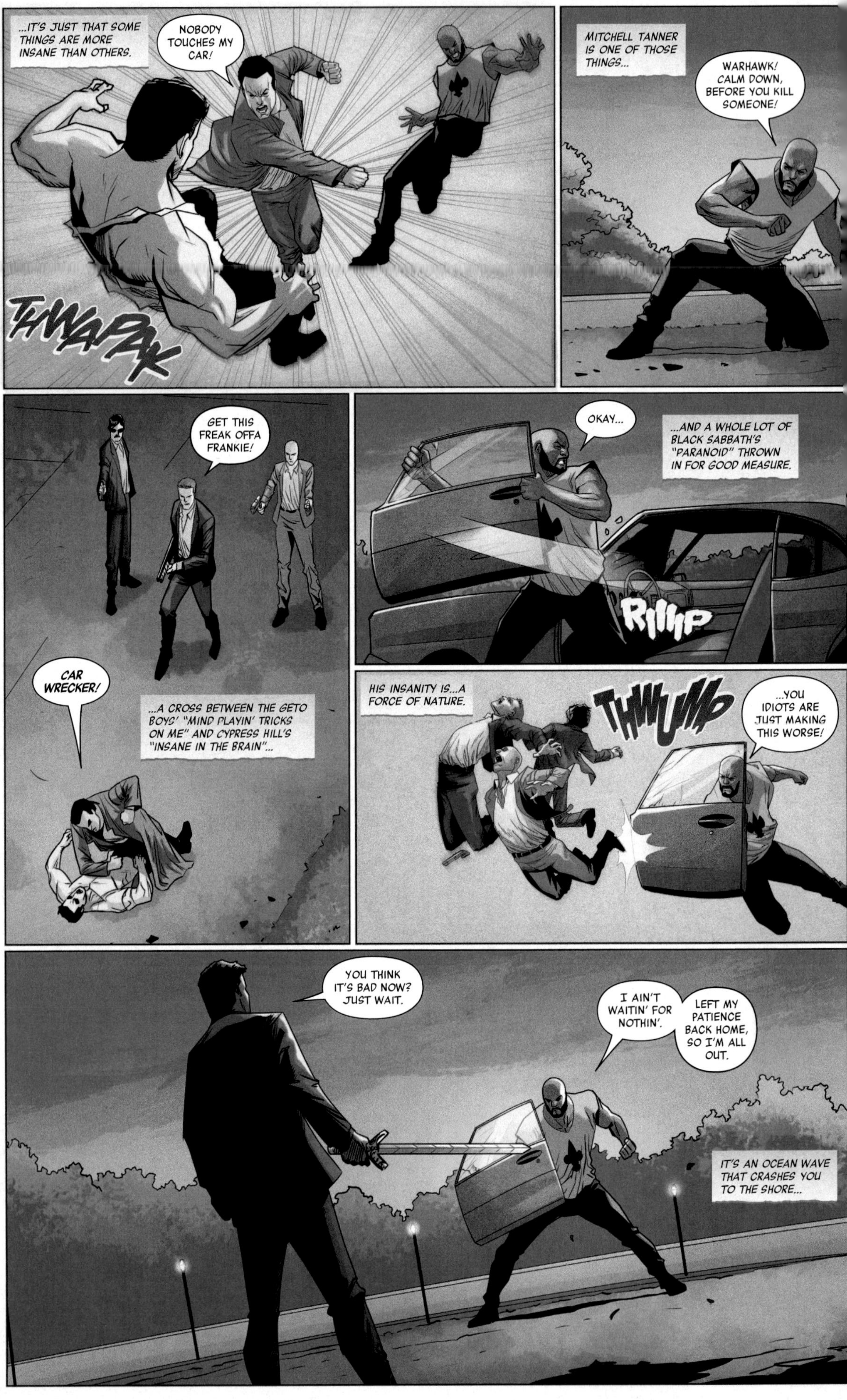

...IT'S JUST THAT SOME THINGS ARE MORE INSANE THAN OTHERS.
NOBODY TOUCHES MY CAR!
THWAPAK
MITCHELL TANNER IS ONE OF THOSE THINGS...
WARHAWK! CALM DOWN, BEFORE YOU KILL SOMEONE!
GET THIS FREAK OFFA FRANKIE!
CAR WRECKER!
...A CROSS BETWEEN THE GETO BOYS' "MIND PLAYIN' TRICKS ON ME" AND CYPRESS HILL'S "INSANE IN THE BRAIN"...
OKAY...
...AND A WHOLE LOT OF BLACK SABBATH'S "PARANOID" THROWN IN FOR GOOD MEASURE.
RIIIP
HIS INSANITY IS...A FORCE OF NATURE.
THWUMP
...YOU IDIOTS ARE JUST MAKING THIS WORSE!
YOU THINK IT'S BAD NOW? JUST WAIT.
I AIN'T WAITIN' FOR NOTHIN'.
LEFT MY PATIENCE BACK HOME, SO I'M ALL OUT.
IT'S AN OCEAN WAVE THAT CRASHES YOU TO THE SHORE...

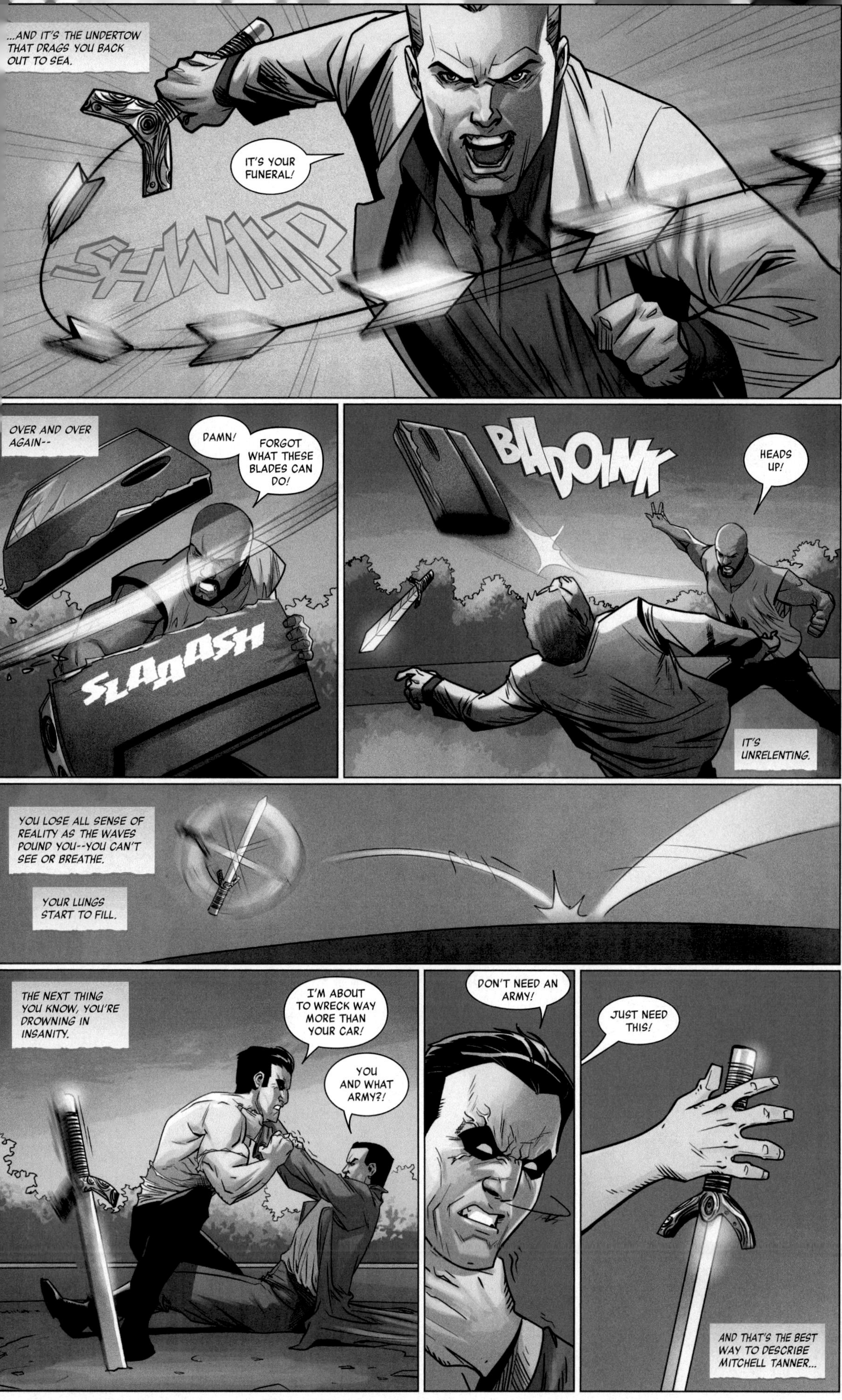
...AND IT'S THE UNDERTOW THAT DRAGS YOU BACK OUT TO SEA.
IT'S YOUR FUNERAL!
SHWIIIP
OVER AND OVER AGAIN--
DAMN!
FORGOT WHAT THESE BLADES CAN DO!
SLAAASH
BADOINK
HEADS UP!
IT'S UNRELENTING.
YOU LOSE ALL SENSE OF REALITY AS THE WAVES POUND YOU--YOU CAN'T SEE OR BREATHE.
YOUR LUNGS START TO FILL.
THE NEXT THING YOU KNOW, YOU'RE DROWNING IN INSANITY.
I'M ABOUT TO WRECK WAY MORE THAN YOUR CAR!
YOU AND WHAT ARMY?!
DON'T NEED AN ARMY!
JUST NEED THIS!
AND THAT'S THE BEST WAY TO DESCRIBE MITCHELL TANNER...

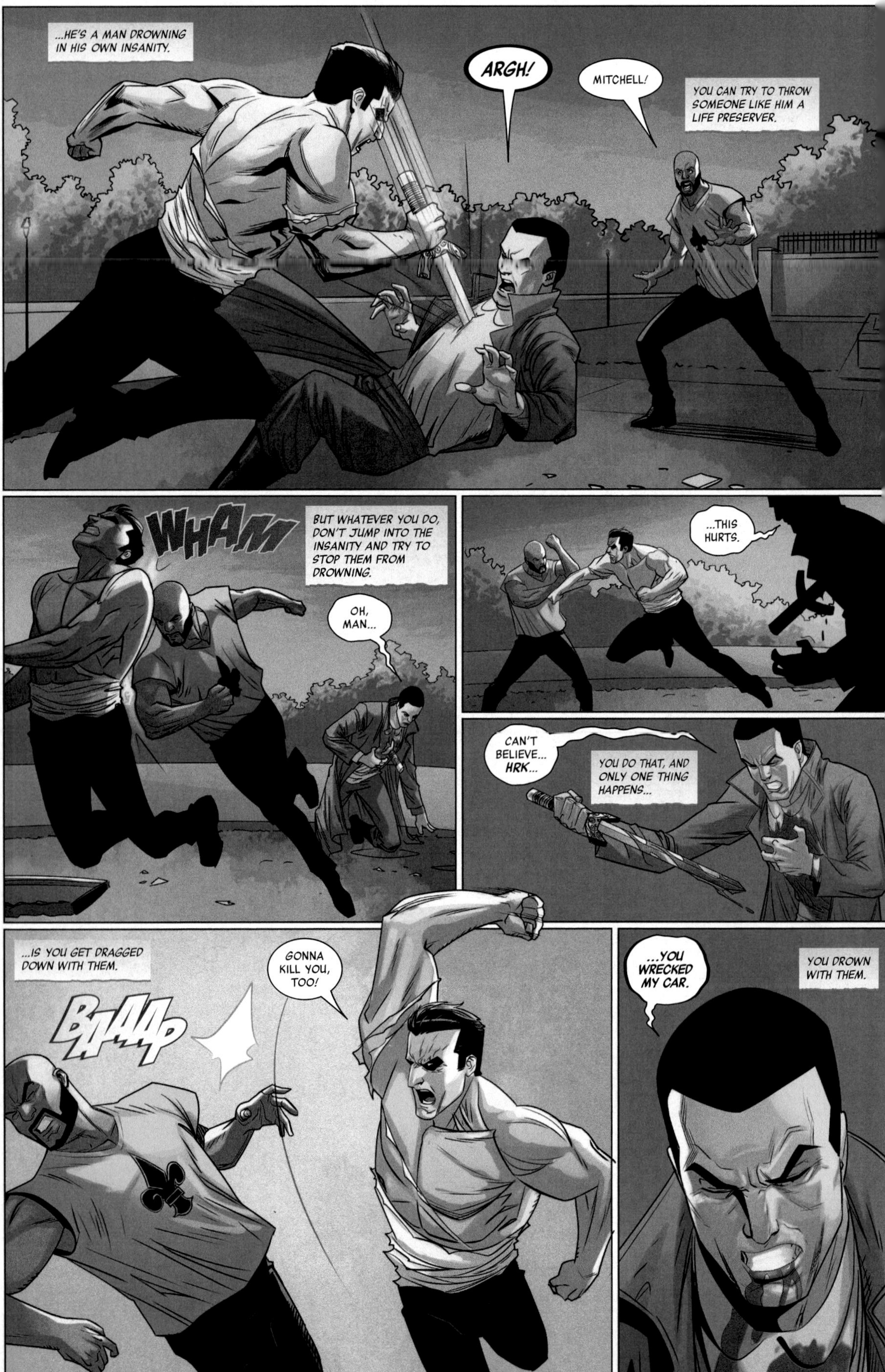
...HE'S A MAN DROWNING IN HIS OWN INSANITY.
ARGH!
MITCHELL!
YOU CAN TRY TO THROW SOMEONE LIKE HIM A LIFE PRESERVER.
WHAM
BUT WHATEVER YOU DO, DON'T JUMP INTO THE INSANITY AND TRY TO STOP THEM FROM DROWNING.
OH, MAN...
...THIS HURTS.
CAN'T BELIEVE... HRK...
YOU DO THAT, AND ONLY ONE THING HAPPENS...
...IS YOU GET DRAGGED DOWN WITH THEM.
GONNA KILL YOU, TOO!
BAAAP
...YOU WRECKED MY CAR.
YOU DROWN WITH THEM.

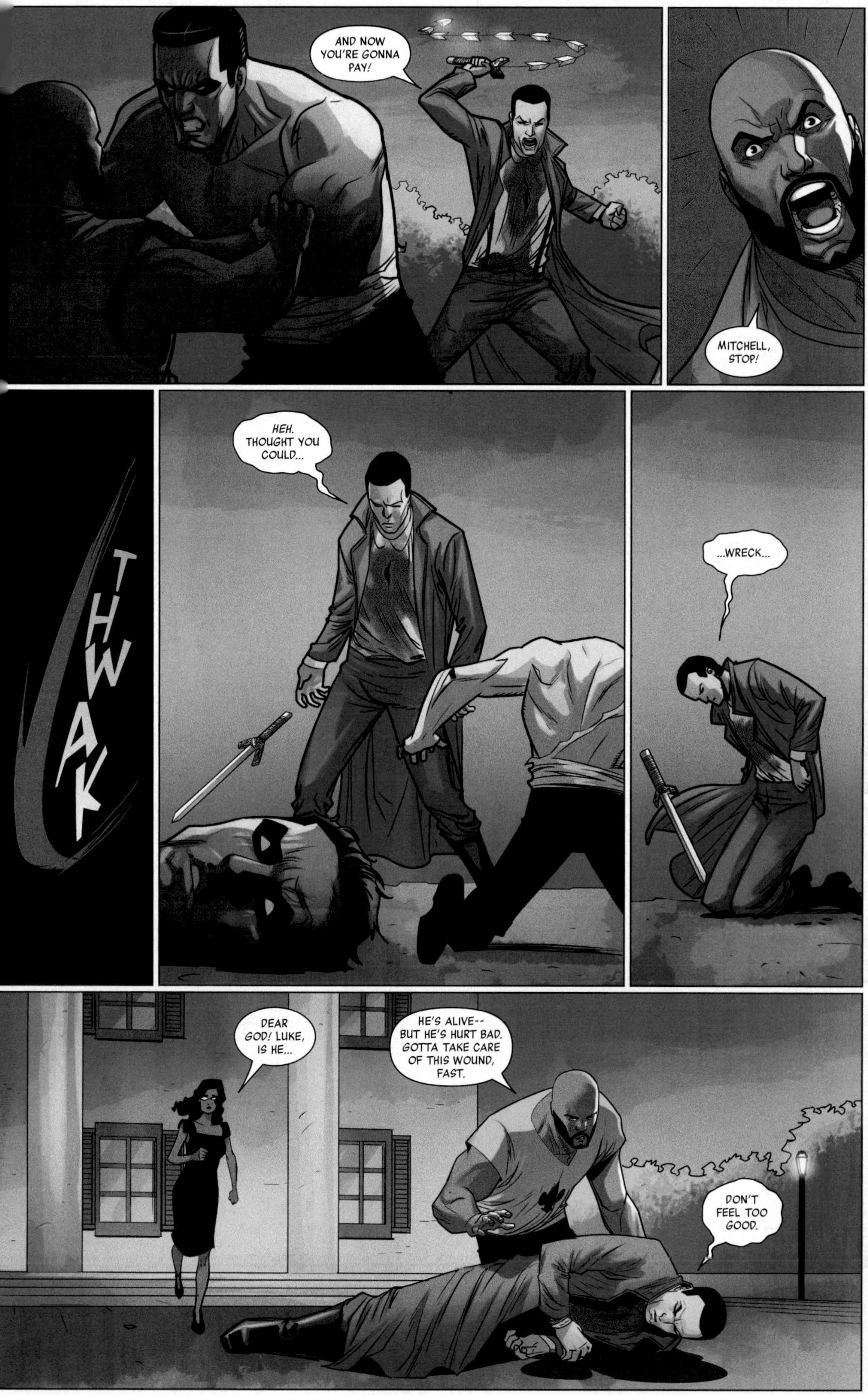
AND NOW YOU'RE GONNA PAY!
MITCHELL, STOP!
THWAK
HEH. THOUGHT YOU COULD...
...WRECK...
DEAR GOD! LUKE, IS HE...
HE'S ALIVE-- BUT HE'S HURT BAD. GOTTA TAKE CARE OF THIS WOUND, FAST.
DON'T FEEL TOO GOOD.

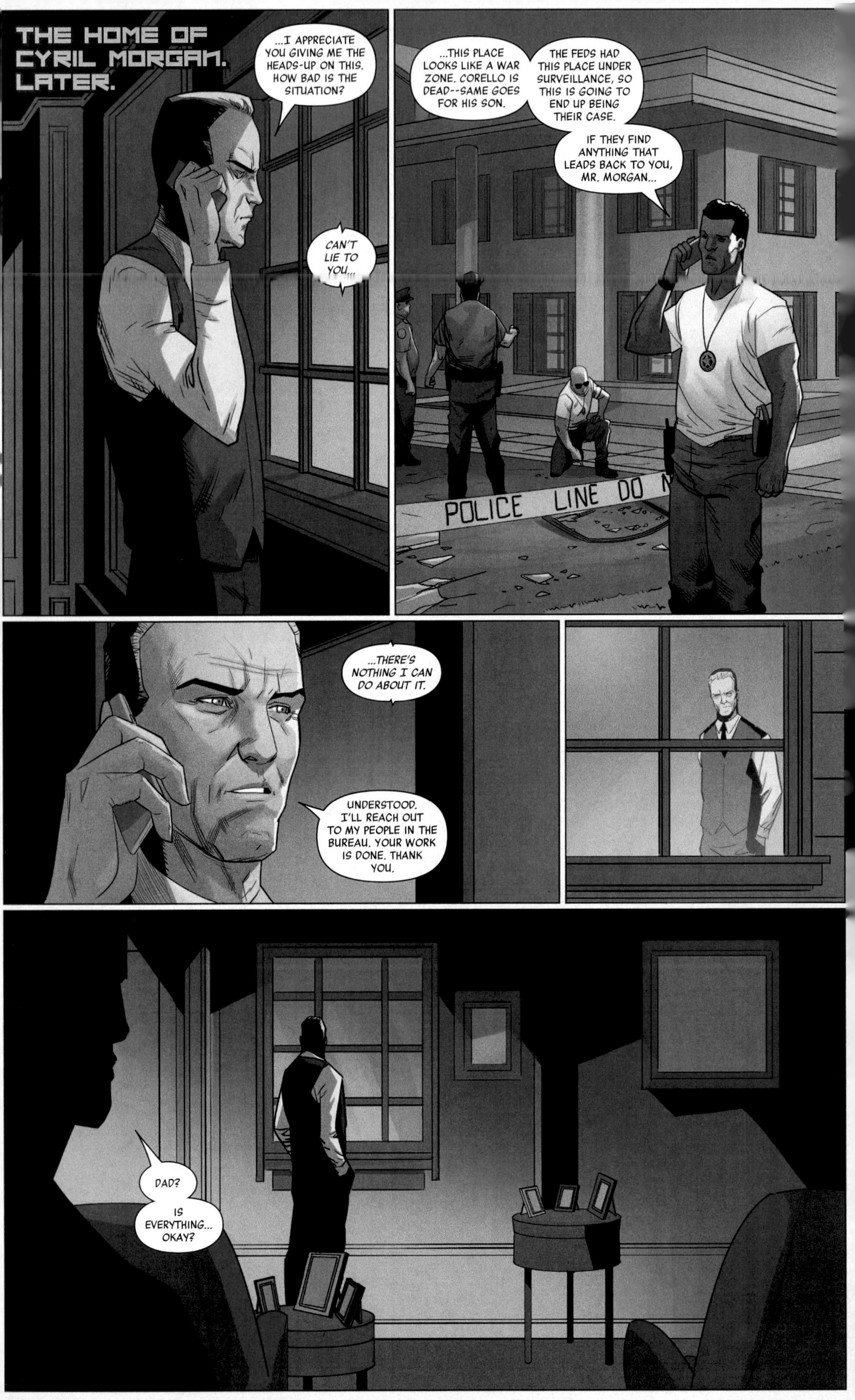
THE HOME OF CYRIL MORGAN. LATER.
...I APPRECIATE YOU GIVING ME THE HEADS-UP ON THIS. HOW BAD IS THE SITUATION?
CAN'T LIE TO YOU...
...THIS PLACE LOOKS LIKE A WAR ZONE. CORELLO IS DEAD--SAME GOES FOR HIS SON.
THE FEDS HAD THIS PLACE UNDER SURVEILLANCE, SO THIS IS GOING TO END UP BEING THEIR CASE.
IF THEY FIND ANYTHING THAT LEADS BACK TO YOU, MR. MORGAN...
POLICE LINE DO
...THERE'S NOTHING I CAN DO ABOUT IT.
UNDERSTOOD. I'LL REACH OUT TO MY PEOPLE IN THE BUREAU. YOUR WORK IS DONE. THANK YOU.
DAD?
IS EVERYTHING... OKAY?

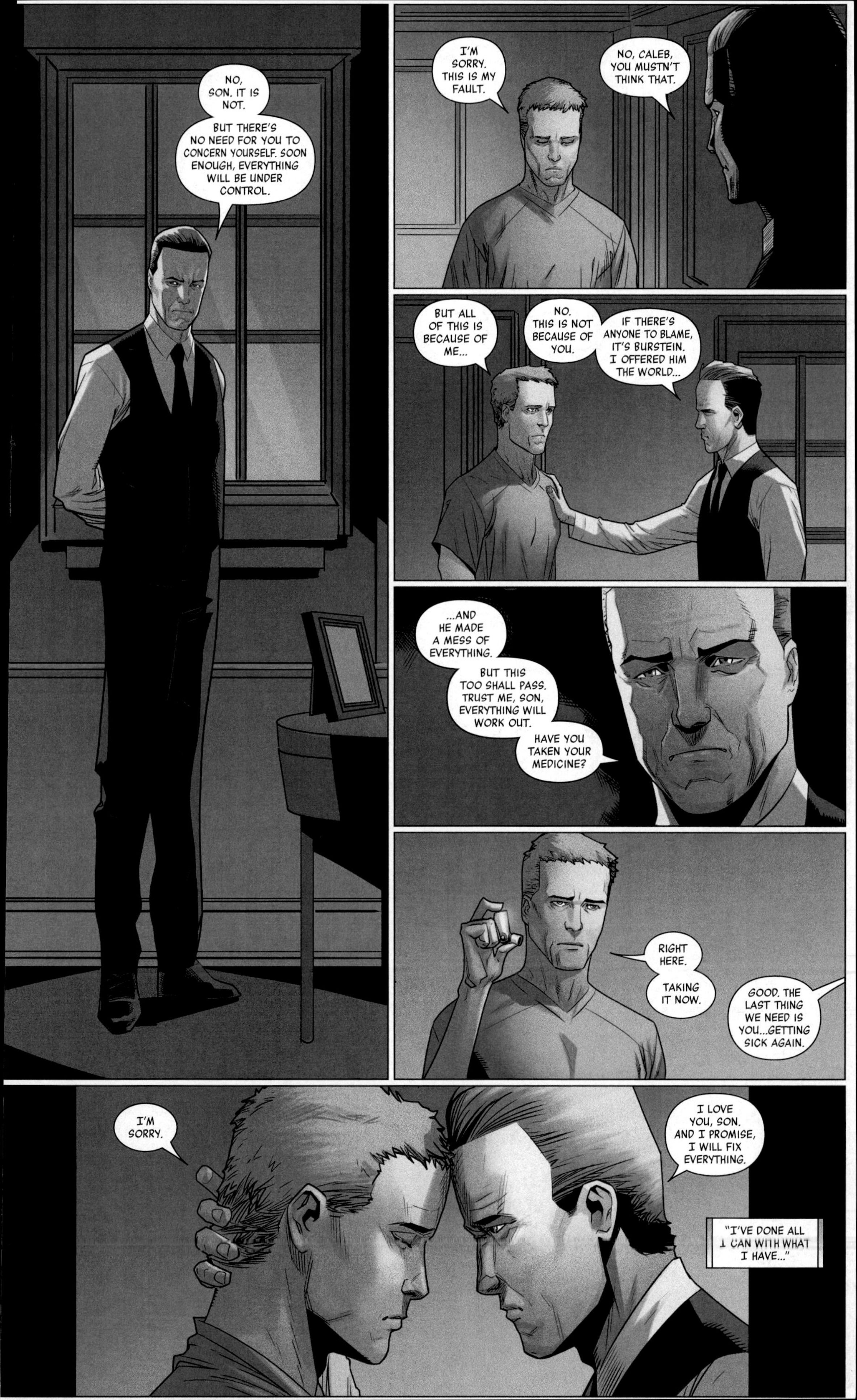

NO, SON. IT IS NOT.
BUT THERE'S NO NEED FOR YOU TO CONCERN YOURSELF. SOON ENOUGH, EVERYTHING WILL BE UNDER CONTROL.
I'M SORRY. THIS IS MY FAULT.
NO, CALEB, YOU MUSTN'T THINK THAT.
BUT ALL OF THIS IS BECAUSE OF ME...
NO. THIS IS NOT BECAUSE OF YOU.
IF THERE'S ANYONE TO BLAME, IT'S BURSTEIN. I OFFERED HIM THE WORLD...
...AND HE MADE A MESS OF EVERYTHING.
BUT THIS TOO SHALL PASS. TRUST ME, SON, EVERYTHING WILL WORK OUT.
HAVE YOU TAKEN YOUR MEDICINE?
RIGHT HERE.
TAKING IT NOW.
GOOD. THE LAST THING WE NEED IS YOU...GETTING SICK AGAIN.
I'M SORRY.
I LOVE YOU, SON. AND I PROMISE, I WILL FIX EVERYTHING.
"I'VE DONE ALL I CAN WITH WHAT I HAVE..."

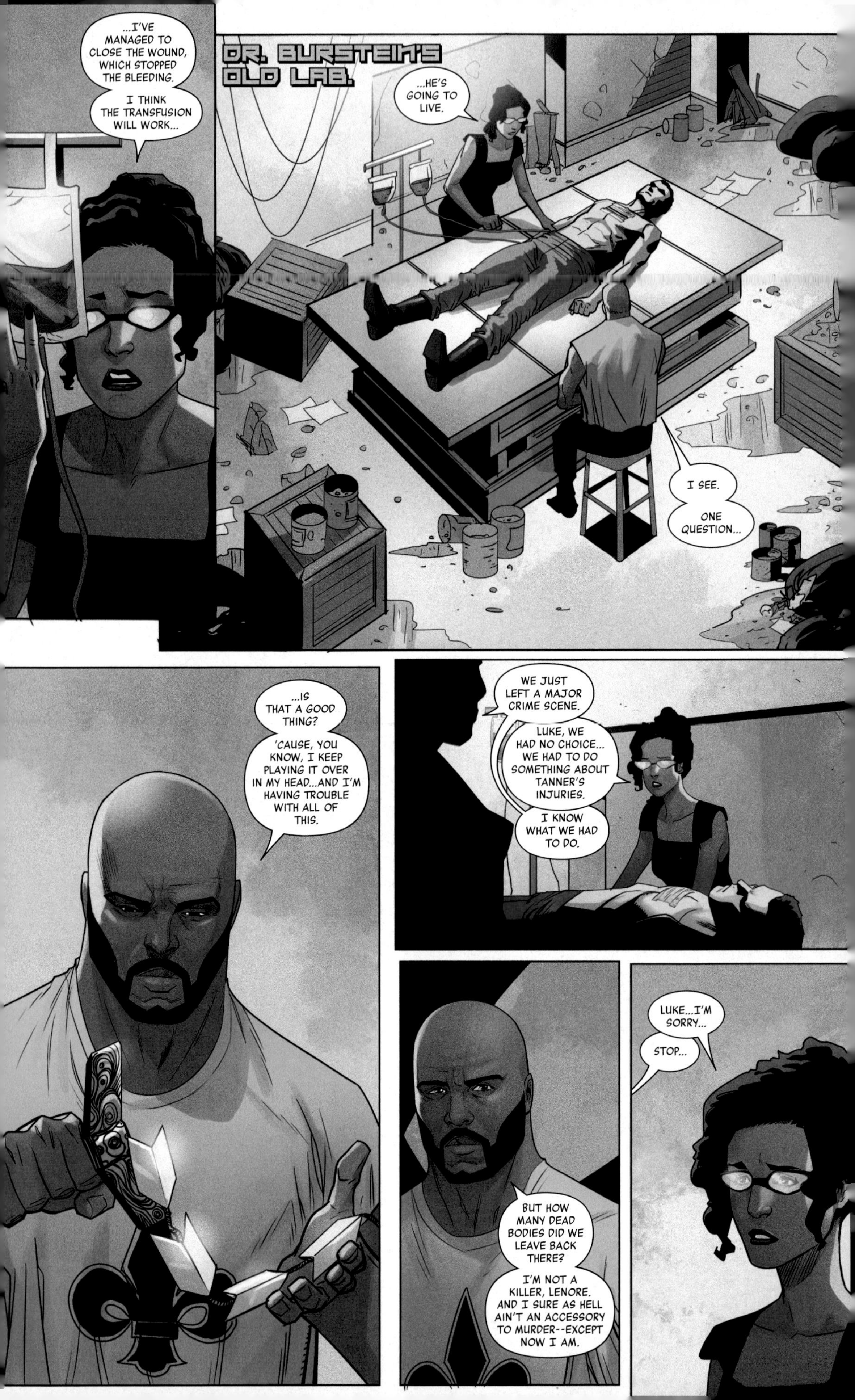
...I'VE MANAGED TO CLOSE THE WOUND, WHICH STOPPED THE BLEEDING.
I THINK THE TRANSFUSION WILL WORK...
DR. BURSTEIN'S OLD LAB.
...HE'S GOING TO LIVE.
I SEE.
ONE QUESTION...
...IS THAT A GOOD THING?
'CAUSE, YOU KNOW, I KEEP PLAYING IT OVER IN MY HEAD...AND I'M HAVING TROUBLE WITH ALL OF THIS.
WE JUST LEFT A MAJOR CRIME SCENE.
LUKE, WE HAD NO CHOICE... WE HAD TO DO SOMETHING ABOUT TANNER'S INJURIES.
I KNOW WHAT WE HAD TO DO.
BUT HOW MANY DEAD BODIES DID WE LEAVE BACK THERE?
I'M NOT A KILLER, LENORE. AND I SURE AS HELL AIN'T AN ACCESSORY TO MURDER--EXCEPT NOW I AM.
LUKE...I'M SORRY...
STOP...

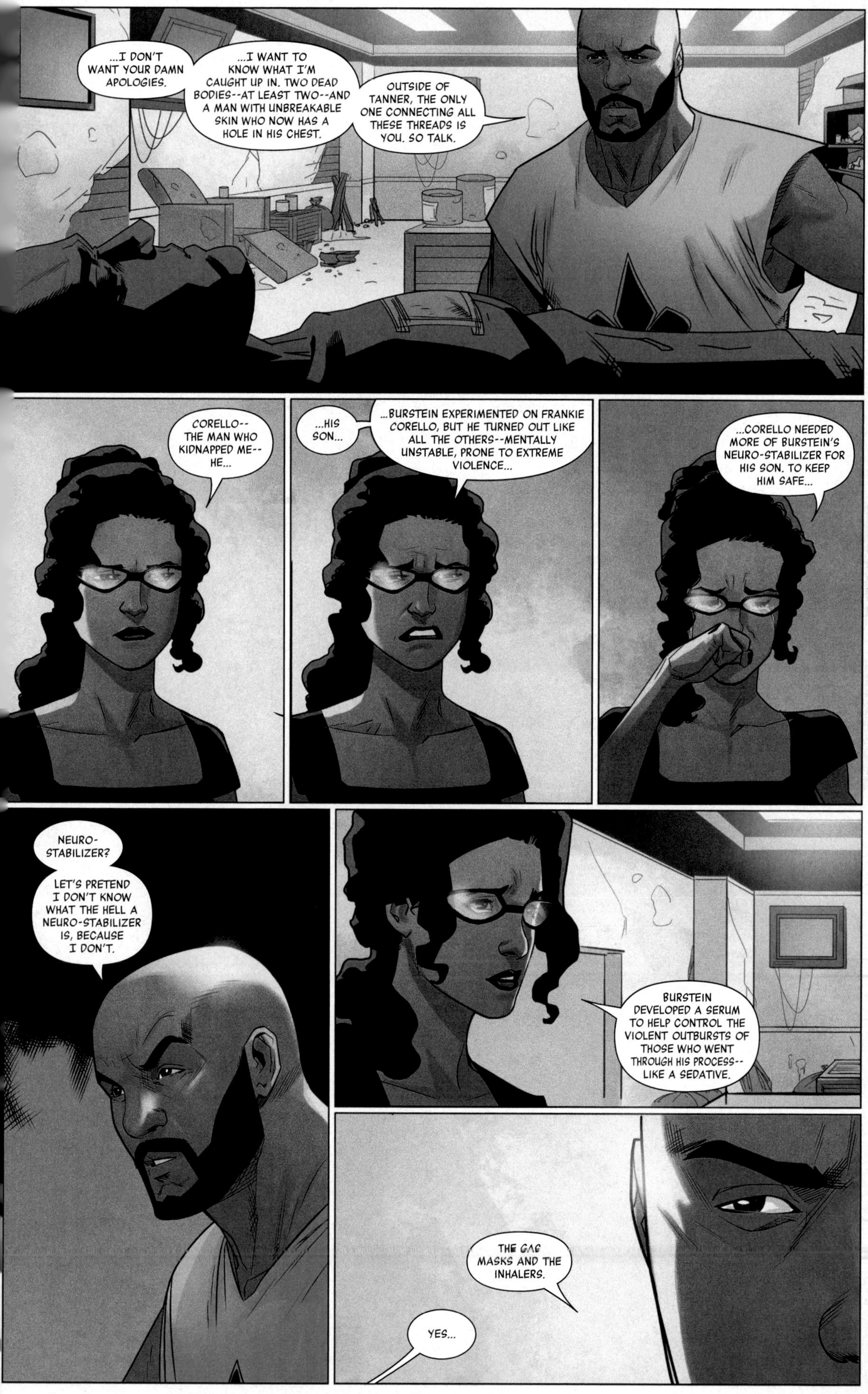
...I DON'T WANT YOUR DAMN APOLOGIES.
...I WANT TO KNOW WHAT I'M CAUGHT UP IN. TWO DEAD BODIES--AT LEAST TWO--AND A MAN WITH UNBREAKABLE SKIN WHO NOW HAS A HOLE IN HIS CHEST.
OUTSIDE OF TANNER, THE ONLY ONE CONNECTING ALL THESE THREADS IS YOU. SO TALK.
CORELLO--THE MAN WHO KIDNAPPED ME--HE...
...HIS SON...
...BURSTEIN EXPERIMENTED ON FRANKIE CORELLO, BUT HE TURNED OUT LIKE ALL THE OTHERS--MENTALLY UNSTABLE, PRONE TO EXTREME VIOLENCE...
...CORELLO NEEDED MORE OF BURSTEIN'S NEURO-STABILIZER FOR HIS SON. TO KEEP HIM SAFE...
NEURO-STABILIZER?
LET'S PRETEND I DON'T KNOW WHAT THE HELL A NEURO-STABILIZER IS, BECAUSE I DON'T.
BURSTEIN DEVELOPED A SERUM TO HELP CONTROL THE VIOLENT OUTBURSTS OF THOSE WHO WENT THROUGH HIS PROCESS--LIKE A SEDATIVE.
THE GAS MASKS AND THE INHALERS.
YES...

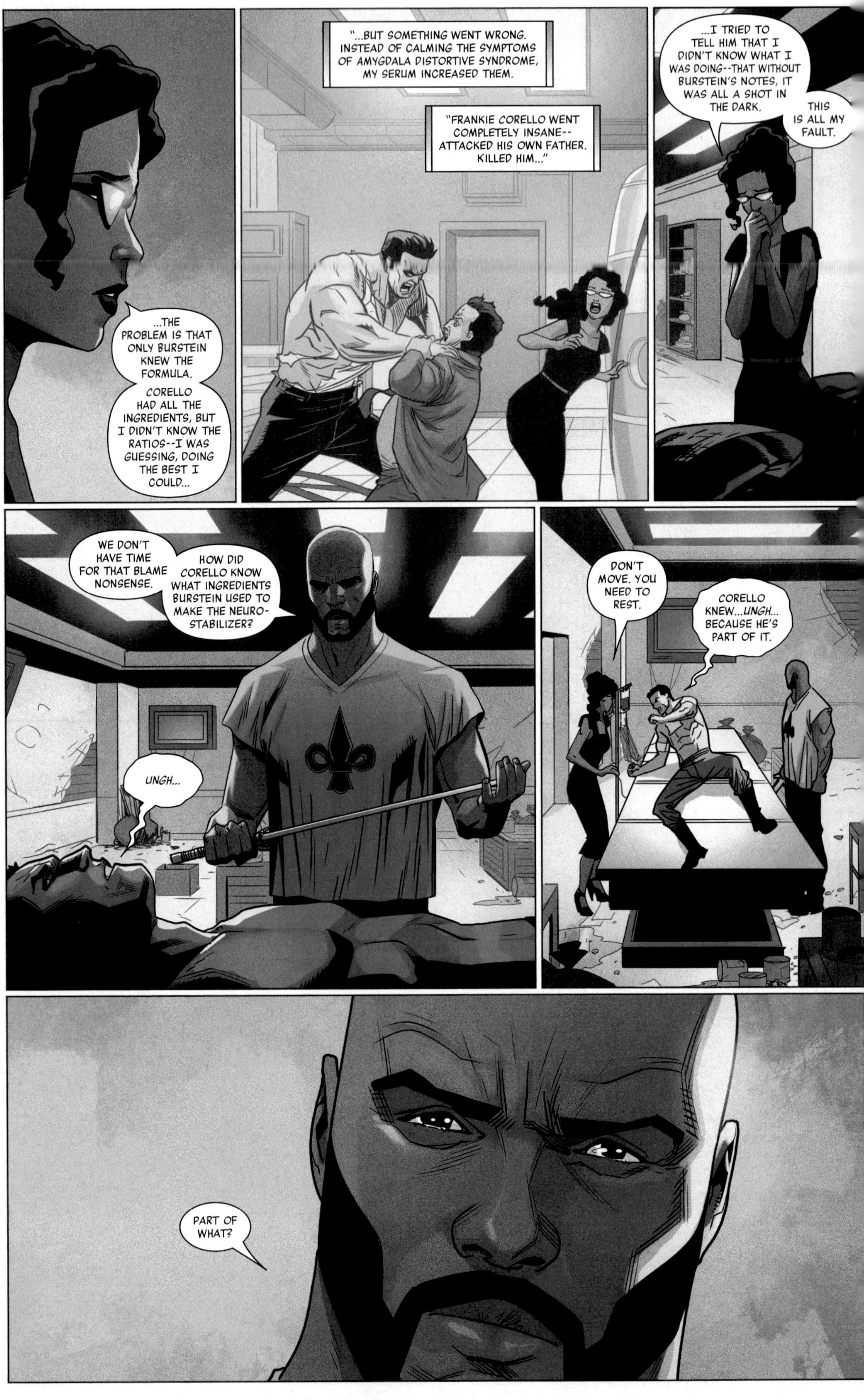
...THE PROBLEM IS THAT ONLY BURSTEIN KNEW THE FORMULA.
CORELLO HAD ALL THE INGREDIENTS, BUT I DIDN'T KNOW THE RATIOS--I WAS GUESSING, DOING THE BEST I COULD...
"...BUT SOMETHING WENT WRONG. INSTEAD OF CALMING THE SYMPTOMS OF AMYGDALA DISTORTIVE SYNDROME, MY SERUM INCREASED THEM.
"FRANKIE CORELLO WENT COMPLETELY INSANE--ATTACKED HIS OWN FATHER. KILLED HIM..."
...I TRIED TO TELL HIM THAT I DIDN'T KNOW WHAT I WAS DOING--THAT WITHOUT BURSTEIN'S NOTES, IT WAS ALL A SHOT IN THE DARK.
THIS IS ALL MY FAULT.
WE DON'T HAVE TIME FOR THAT BLAME NONSENSE.
HOW DID CORELLO KNOW WHAT INGREDIENTS BURSTEIN USED TO MAKE THE NEURO-STABILIZER?
UNGH...
DON'T MOVE. YOU NEED TO REST.
CORELLO KNEW...UNGH... BECAUSE HE'S PART OF IT.
PART OF WHAT?

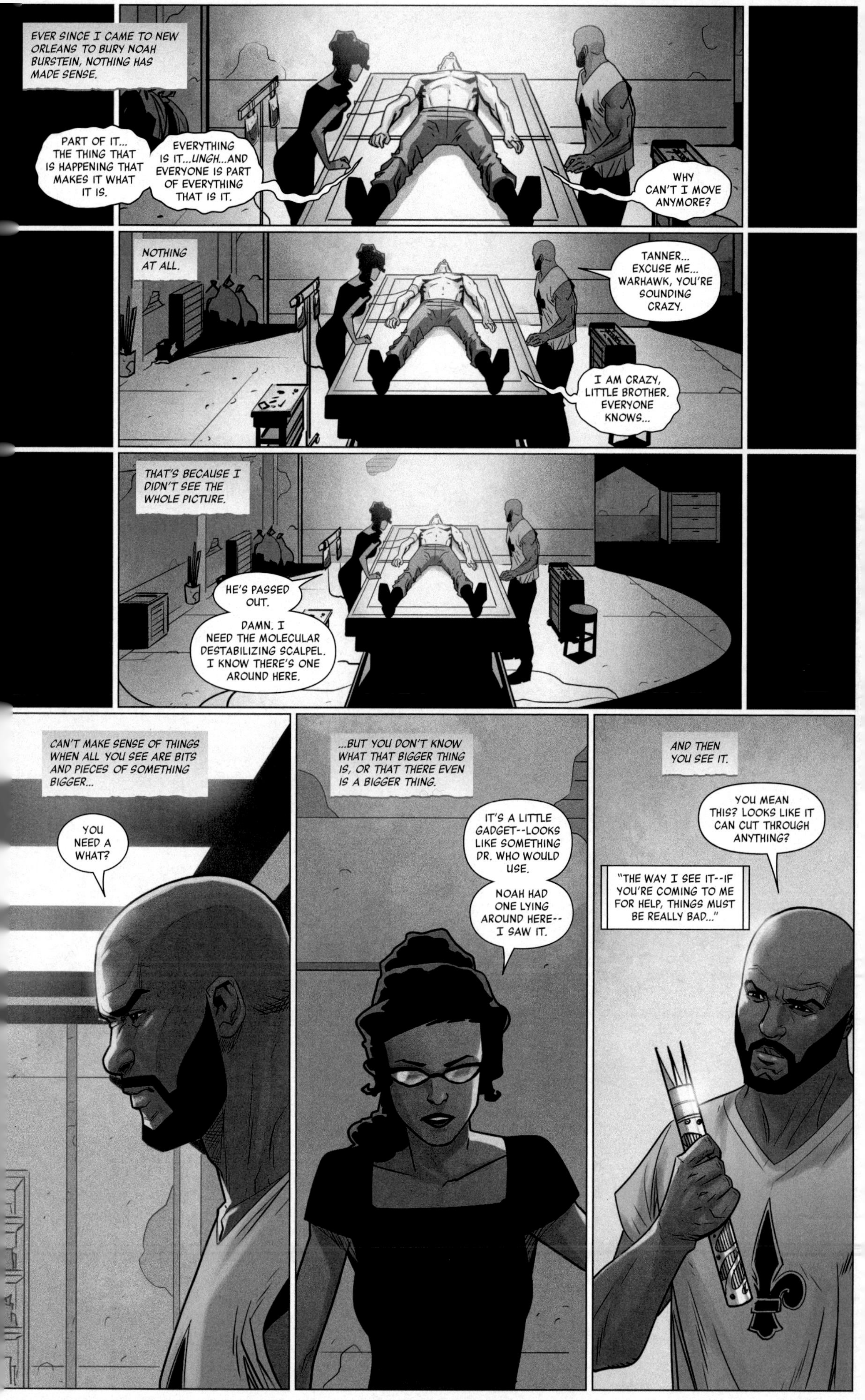
EVER SINCE I CAME TO NEW ORLEANS TO BURY NOAH BURSTEIN, NOTHING HAS MADE SENSE.
PART OF IT... THE THING THAT IS HAPPENING THAT MAKES IT WHAT IT IS.
EVERYTHING IS IT...UNGH...AND EVERYONE IS PART OF EVERYTHING THAT IS IT.
WHY CAN'T I MOVE ANYMORE?
NOTHING AT ALL.
TANNER... EXCUSE ME... WARHAWK, YOU'RE SOUNDING CRAZY.
I AM CRAZY, LITTLE BROTHER. EVERYONE KNOWS...
THAT'S BECAUSE I DIDN'T SEE THE WHOLE PICTURE.
HE'S PASSED OUT.
DAMN. I NEED THE MOLECULAR DESTABILIZING SCALPEL. I KNOW THERE'S ONE AROUND HERE.
CAN'T MAKE SENSE OF THINGS WHEN ALL YOU SEE ARE BITS AND PIECES OF SOMETHING BIGGER...
YOU NEED A WHAT?
...BUT YOU DON'T KNOW WHAT THAT BIGGER THING IS, OR THAT THERE EVEN IS A BIGGER THING.
IT'S A LITTLE GADGET--LOOKS LIKE SOMETHING DR. WHO WOULD USE.
NOAH HAD ONE LYING AROUND HERE-- I SAW IT.
AND THEN YOU SEE IT.
YOU MEAN THIS? LOOKS LIKE IT CAN CUT THROUGH ANYTHING?
"THE WAY I SEE IT--IF YOU'RE COMING TO ME FOR HELP, THINGS MUST BE REALLY BAD..."

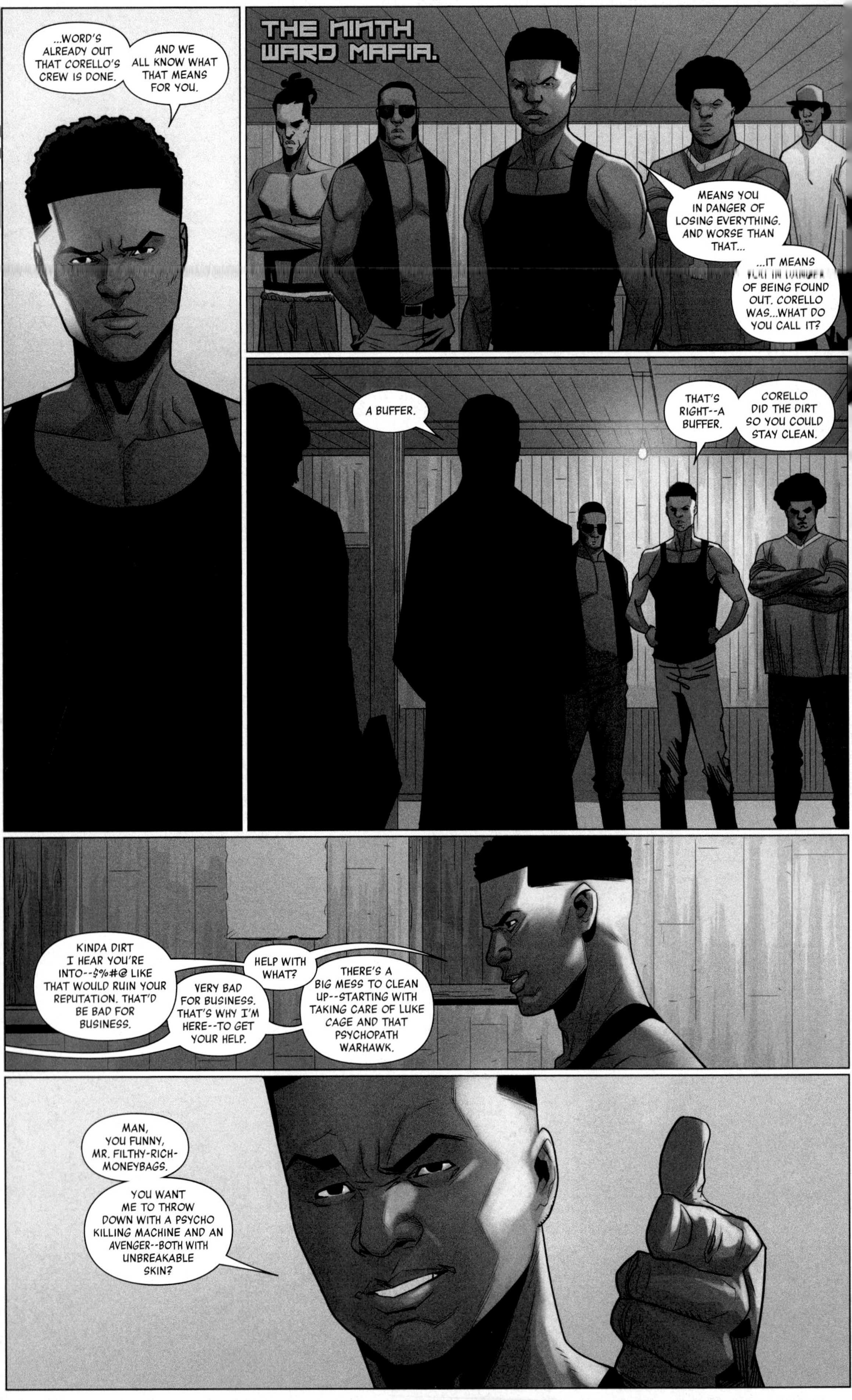
...WORD'S ALREADY OUT THAT CORELLO'S CREW IS DONE.
AND WE ALL KNOW WHAT THAT MEANS FOR YOU.
THE NINTH WARD MAFIA.
MEANS YOU IN DANGER OF LOSING EVERYTHING. AND WORSE THAN THAT...
...IT MEANS
OF BEING FOUND OUT. CORELLO WAS...WHAT DO YOU CALL IT?
A BUFFER.
THAT'S RIGHT--A BUFFER.
CORELLO DID THE DIRT SO YOU COULD STAY CLEAN.
KINDA DIRT I HEAR YOU'RE INTO--$%#@ LIKE THAT WOULD RUIN YOUR REPUTATION. THAT'D BE BAD FOR BUSINESS.
VERY BAD FOR BUSINESS. THAT'S WHY I'M HERE--TO GET YOUR HELP.
HELP WITH WHAT?
THERE'S A BIG MESS TO CLEAN UP--STARTING WITH TAKING CARE OF LUKE CAGE AND THAT PSYCHOPATH WARHAWK.
MAN, YOU FUNNY, MR. FILTHY-RICH-MONEYBAGS.
YOU WANT ME TO THROW DOWN WITH A PSYCHO KILLING MACHINE AND AN AVENGER--BOTH WITH UNBREAKABLE SKIN?

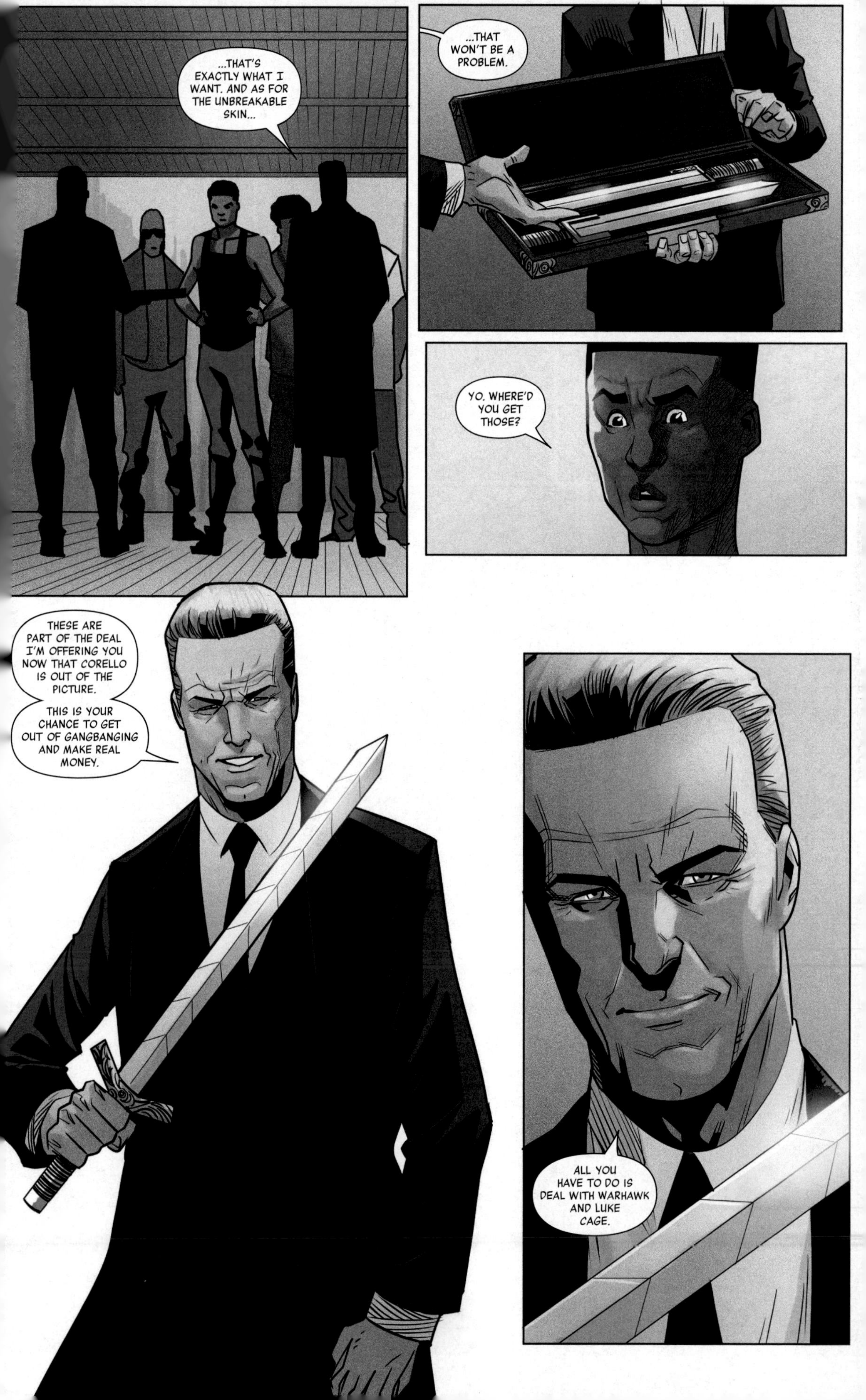
...THAT'S EXACTLY WHAT I WANT. AND AS FOR THE UNBREAKABLE SKIN...
...THAT WON'T BE A PROBLEM.
YO. WHERE'D YOU GET THOSE?
THESE ARE PART OF THE DEAL I'M OFFERING YOU NOW THAT CORELLO IS OUT OF THE PICTURE.
THIS IS YOUR CHANCE TO GET OUT OF GANGBANGING AND MAKE REAL MONEY.
ALL YOU HAVE TO DO IS DEAL WITH WARHAWK AND LUKE CAGE.

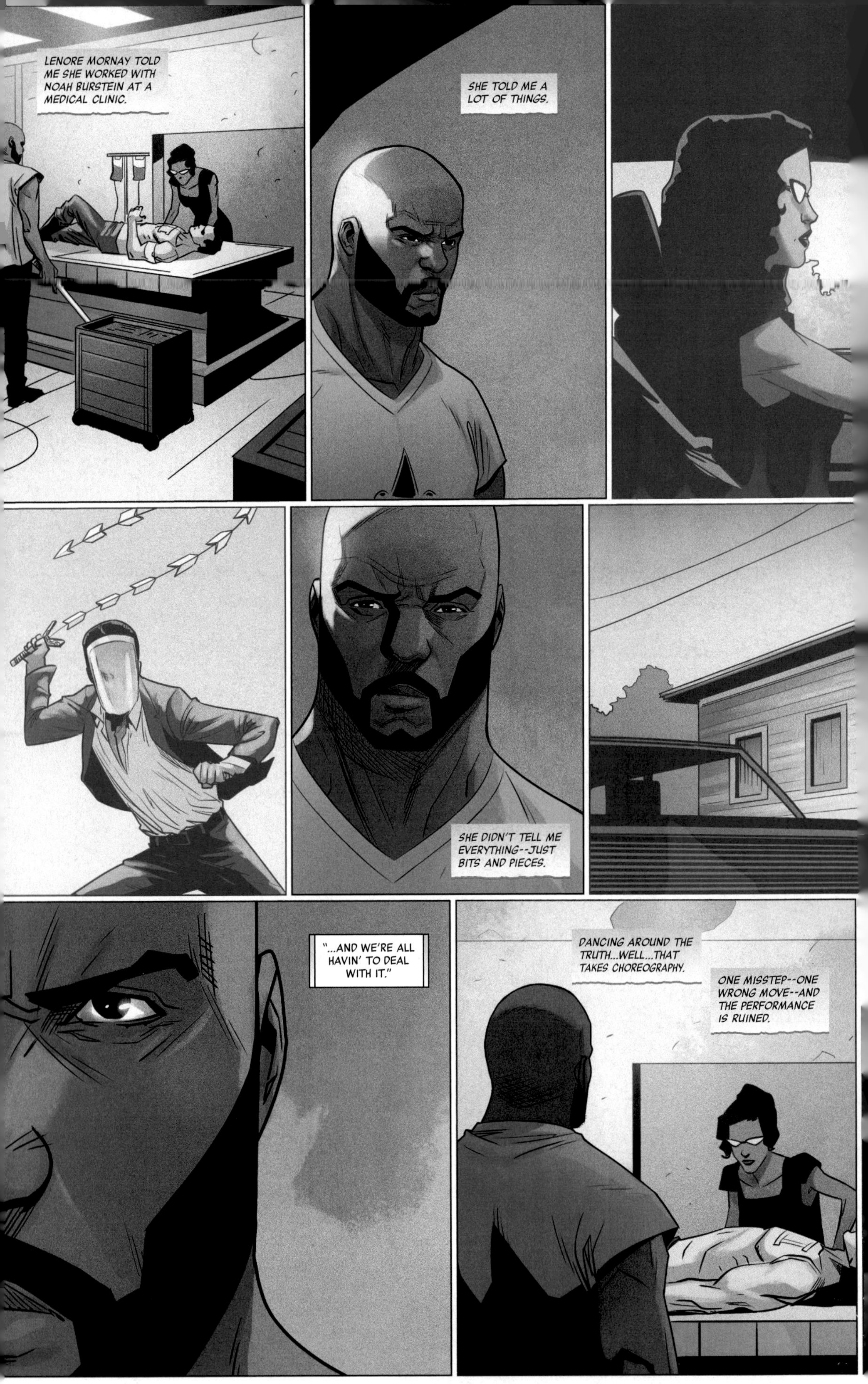
LENORE MORNAY TOLD ME SHE WORKED WITH NOAH BURSTEIN AT A MEDICAL CLINIC.
SHE TOLD ME A LOT OF THINGS.
SHE DIDN'T TELL ME EVERYTHING--JUST BITS AND PIECES.
"...AND WE'RE ALL HAVIN' TO DEAL WITH IT."
DANCING AROUND THE TRUTH...WELL...THAT TAKES CHOREOGRAPHY.
ONE MISSTEP--ONE WRONG MOVE--AND THE PERFORMANCE IS RUINED.

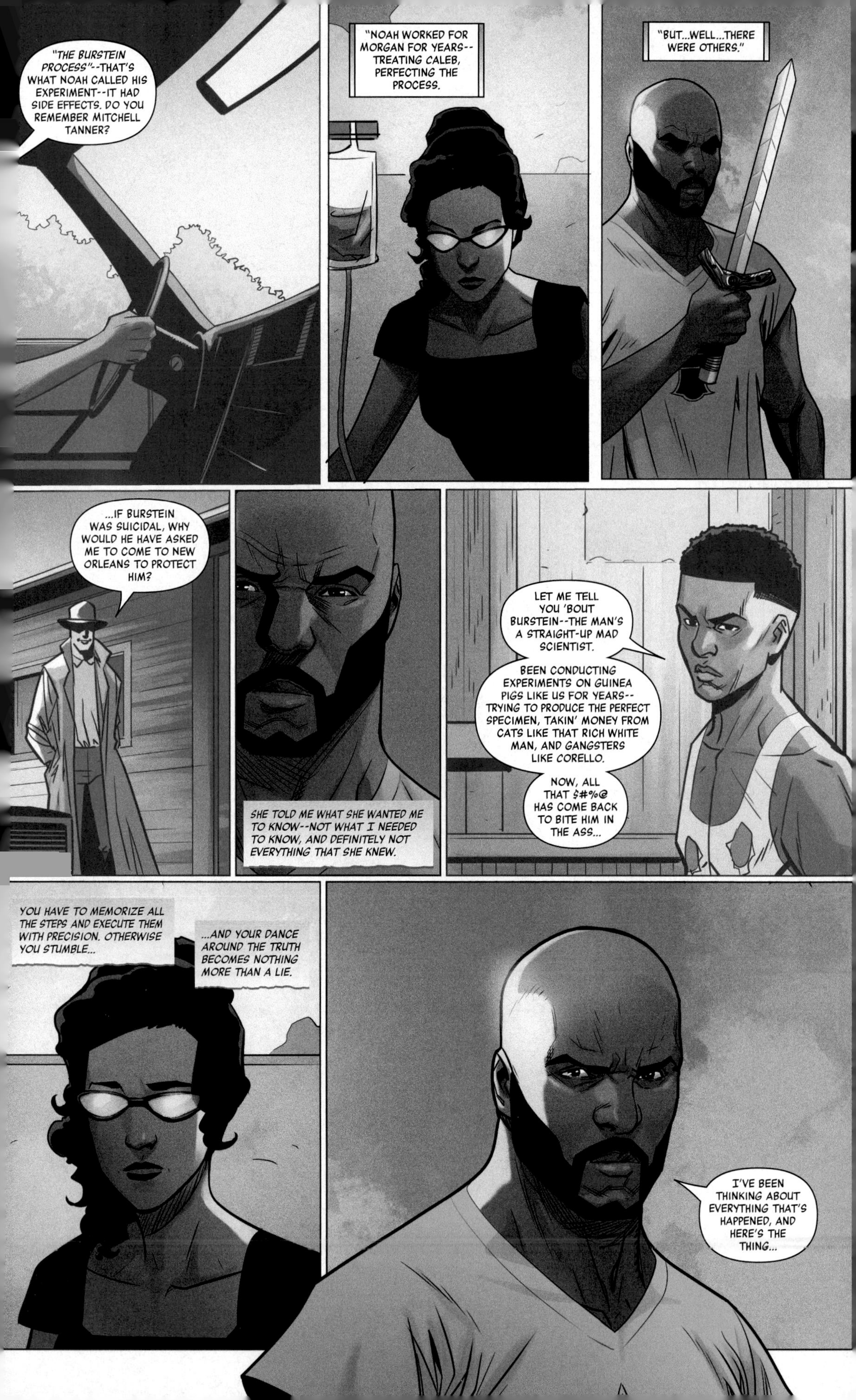
"THE BURSTEIN PROCESS"--THAT'S WHAT NOAH CALLED HIS EXPERIMENT--IT HAD SIDE EFFECTS. DO YOU REMEMBER MITCHELL TANNER?
"NOAH WORKED FOR MORGAN FOR YEARS--TREATING CALEB, PERFECTING THE PROCESS.
"BUT...WELL...THERE WERE OTHERS."
...IF BURSTEIN WAS SUICIDAL, WHY WOULD HE HAVE ASKED ME TO COME TO NEW ORLEANS TO PROTECT HIM?
SHE TOLD ME WHAT SHE WANTED ME TO KNOW--NOT WHAT I NEEDED TO KNOW, AND DEFINITELY NOT EVERYTHING THAT SHE KNEW.
LET ME TELL YOU 'BOUT BURSTEIN--THE MAN'S A STRAIGHT-UP MAD SCIENTIST.
BEEN CONDUCTING EXPERIMENTS ON GUINEA PIGS LIKE US FOR YEARS--TRYING TO PRODUCE THE PERFECT SPECIMEN, TAKIN' MONEY FROM CATS LIKE THAT RICH WHITE MAN, AND GANGSTERS LIKE CORELLO.
NOW, ALL THAT $#%@ HAS COME BACK TO BITE HIM IN THE ASS...
YOU HAVE TO MEMORIZE ALL THE STEPS AND EXECUTE THEM WITH PRECISION. OTHERWISE YOU STUMBLE...
...AND YOUR DANCE AROUND THE TRUTH BECOMES NOTHING MORE THAN A LIE.
I'VE BEEN THINKING ABOUT EVERYTHING THAT'S HAPPENED, AND HERE'S THE THING...

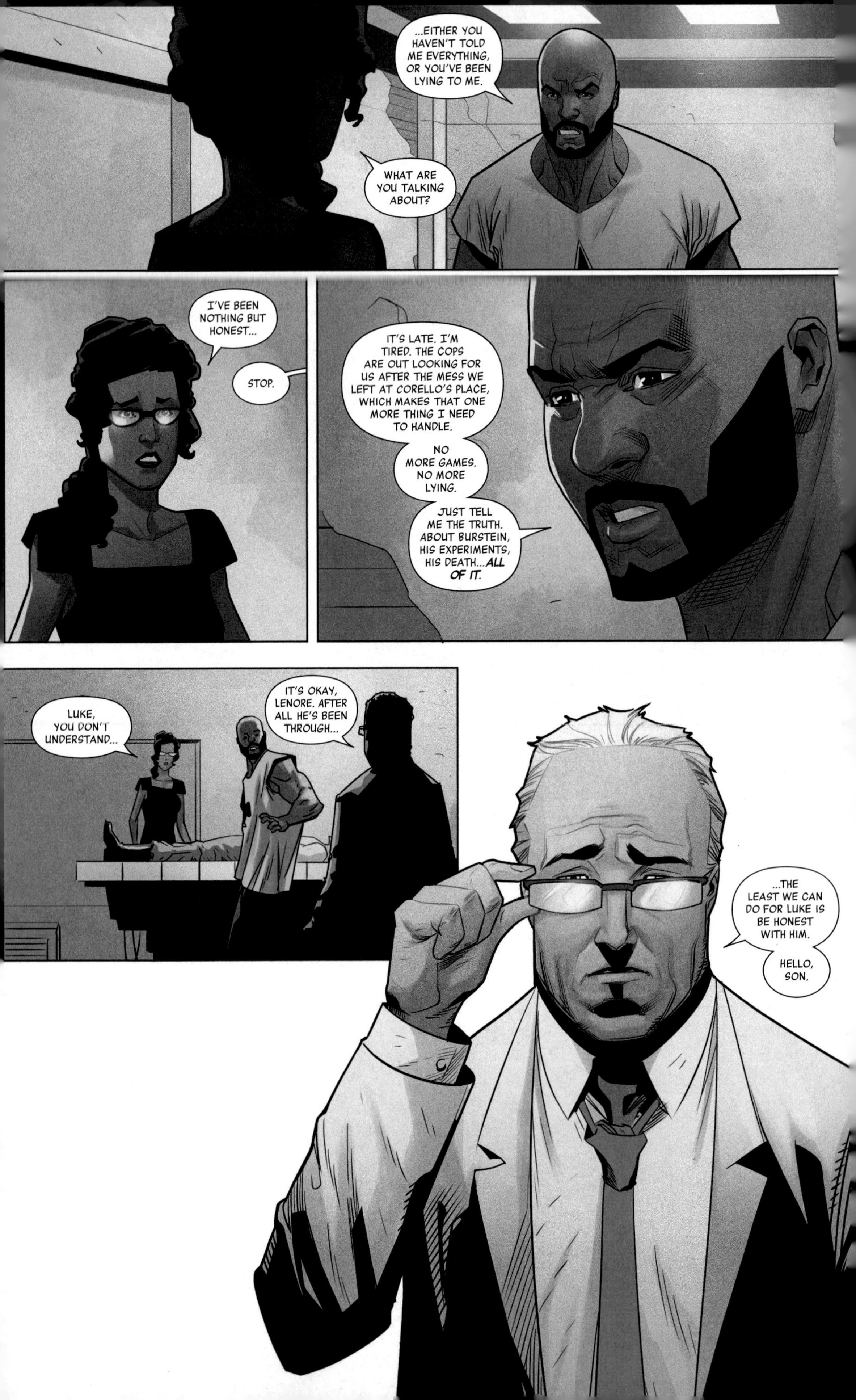

...EITHER YOU HAVEN'T TOLD ME EVERYTHING, OR YOU'VE BEEN LYING TO ME.
WHAT ARE YOU TALKING ABOUT?
I'VE BEEN NOTHING BUT HONEST...
STOP.
IT'S LATE. I'M TIRED. THE COPS ARE OUT LOOKING FOR US AFTER THE MESS WE LEFT AT CORELLO'S PLACE, WHICH MAKES THAT ONE MORE THING I NEED TO HANDLE.
NO MORE GAMES. NO MORE LYING.
JUST TELL ME THE TRUTH. ABOUT BURSTEIN, HIS EXPERIMENTS, HIS DEATH...ALL OF IT.
LUKE, YOU DON'T UNDERSTAND...
IT'S OKAY, LENORE. AFTER ALL HE'S BEEN THROUGH...
...THE LEAST WE CAN DO FOR LUKE IS BE HONEST WITH HIM.
HELLO, SON.

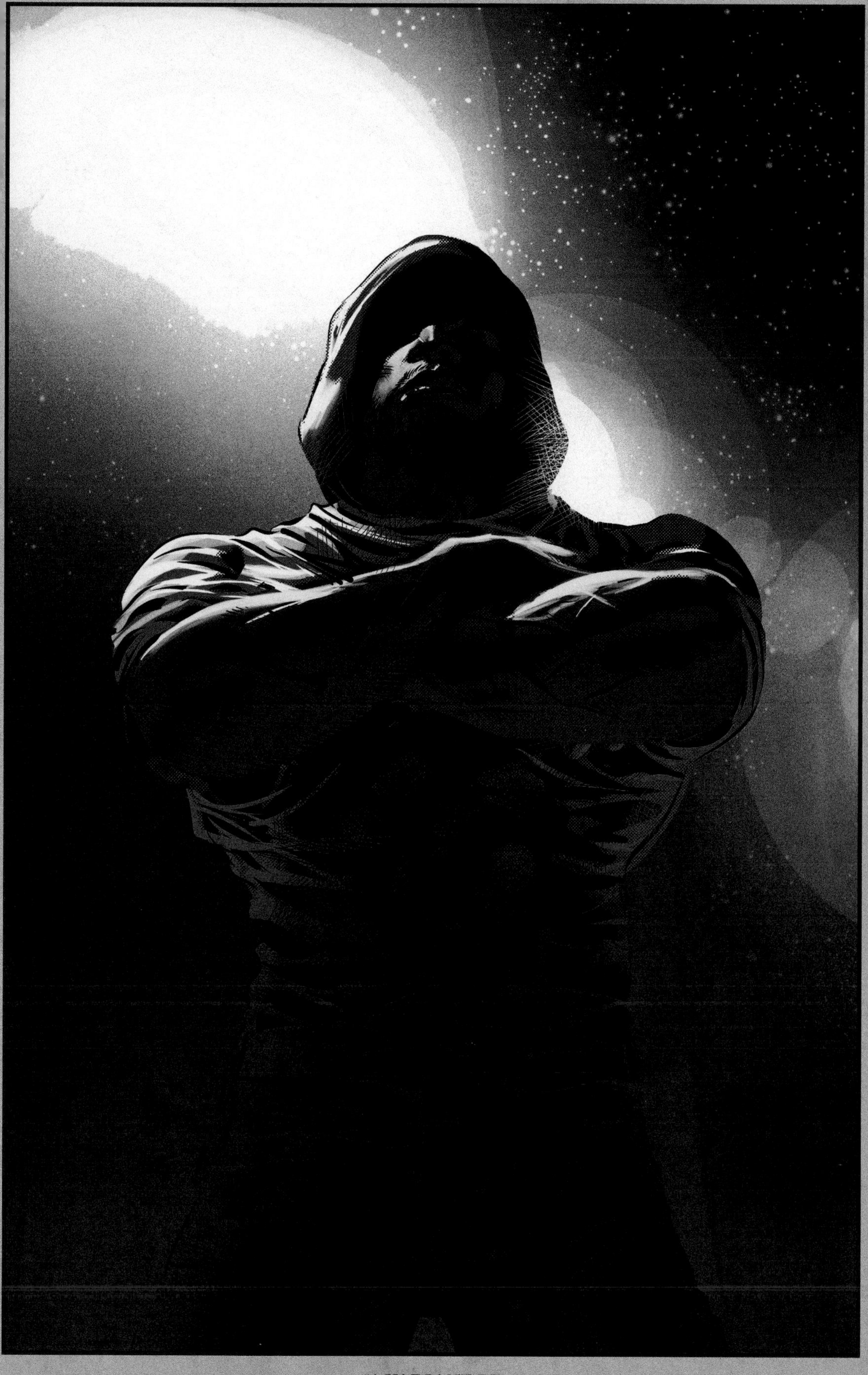

#1 VARIANT BY
MIKE DEODATO JR. & FRANK MARTIN

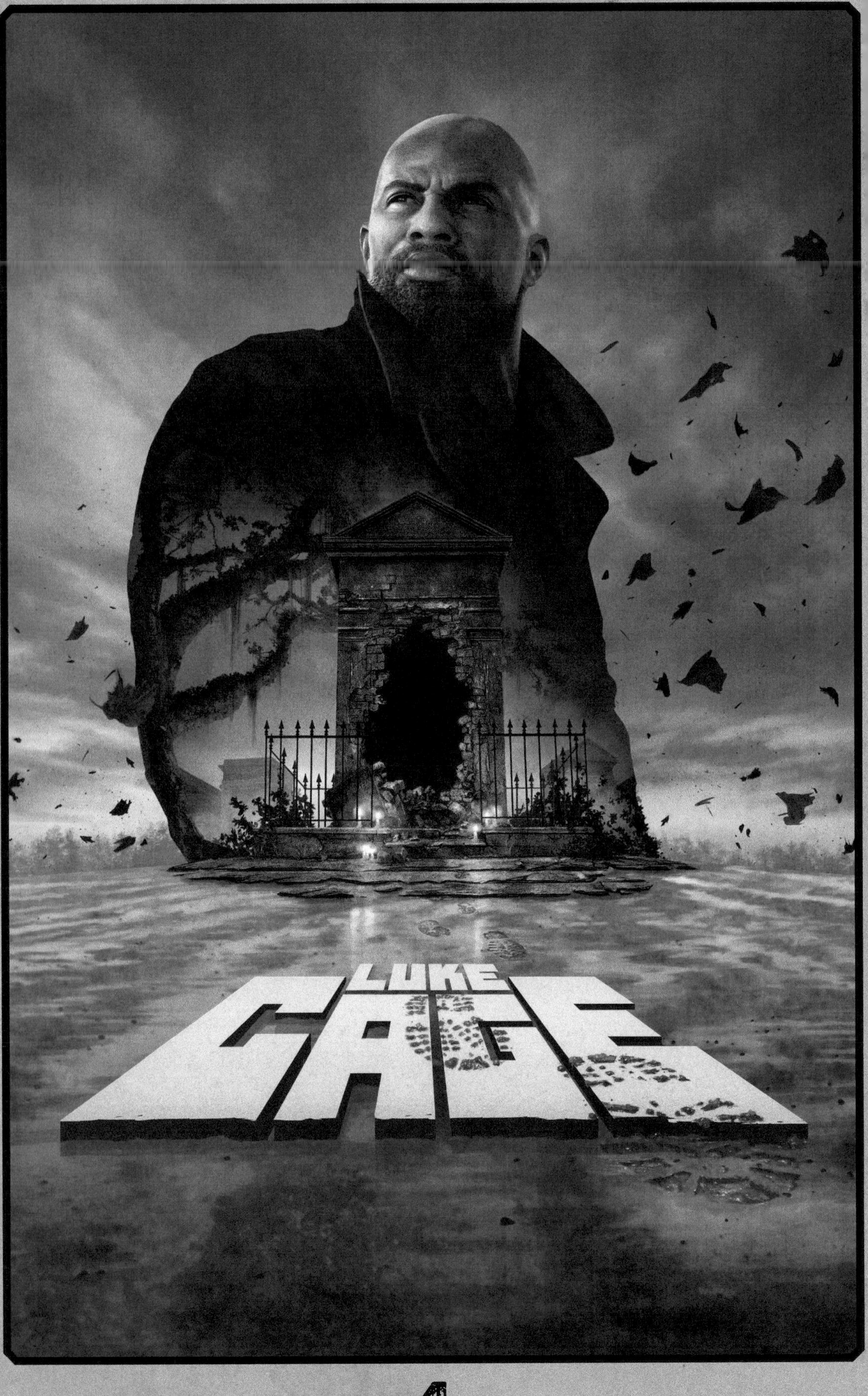
LUKE
CAGE

4

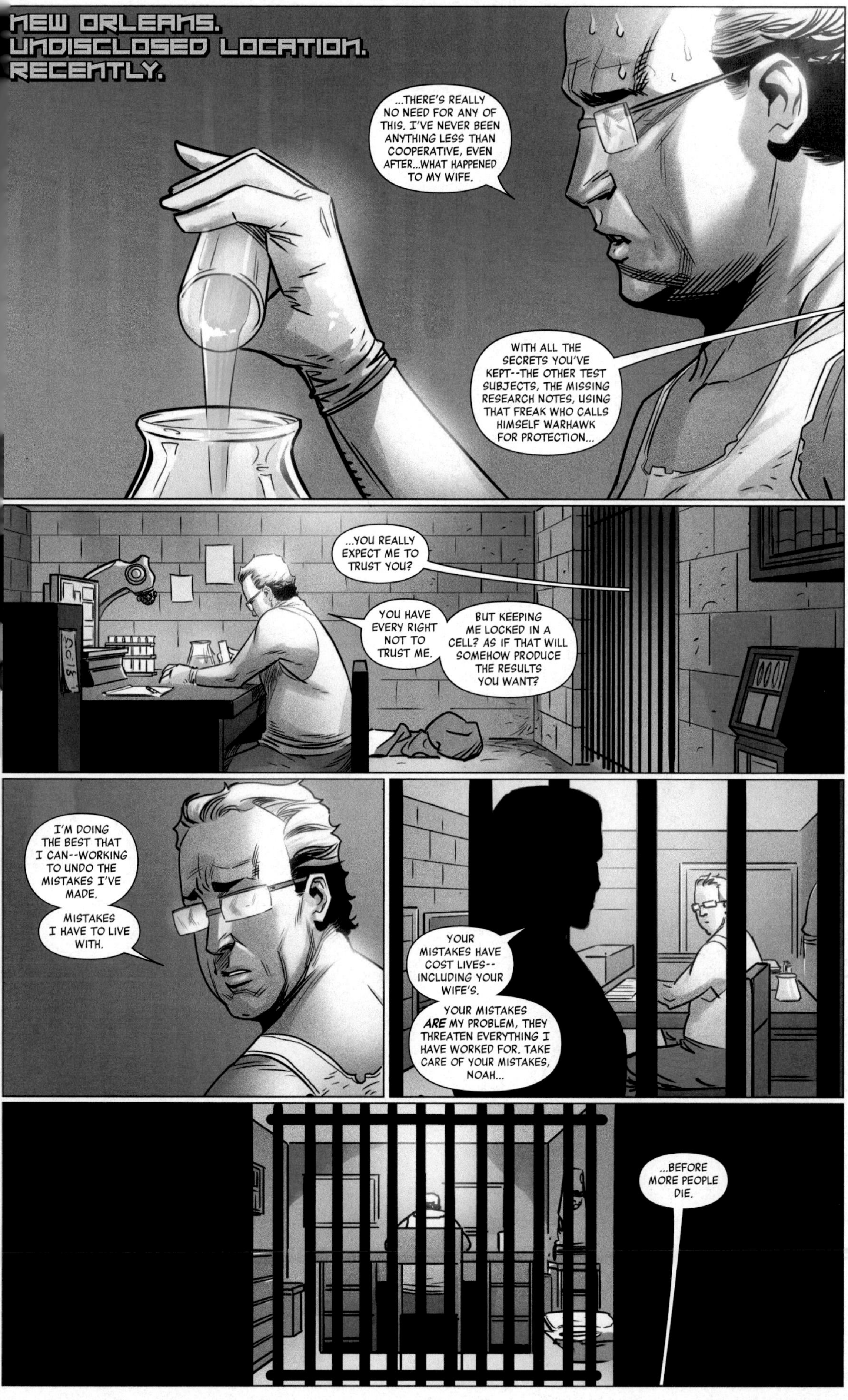
NEW ORLEANS. UNDISCLOSED LOCATION. RECENTLY.
...THERE'S REALLY NO NEED FOR ANY OF THIS. I'VE NEVER BEEN ANYTHING LESS THAN COOPERATIVE, EVEN AFTER...WHAT HAPPENED TO MY WIFE.
WITH ALL THE SECRETS YOU'VE KEPT--THE OTHER TEST SUBJECTS, THE MISSING RESEARCH NOTES, USING THAT FREAK WHO CALLS HIMSELF WARHAWK FOR PROTECTION...
...YOU REALLY EXPECT ME TO TRUST YOU?
YOU HAVE EVERY RIGHT NOT TO TRUST ME.
BUT KEEPING ME LOCKED IN A CELL? AS IF THAT WILL SOMEHOW PRODUCE THE RESULTS YOU WANT?
I'M DOING THE BEST THAT I CAN--WORKING TO UNDO THE MISTAKES I'VE MADE.
MISTAKES I HAVE TO LIVE WITH.
YOUR MISTAKES HAVE COST LIVES--INCLUDING YOUR WIFE'S.
YOUR MISTAKES *ARE* MY PROBLEM, THEY THREATEN EVERYTHING I HAVE WORKED FOR. TAKE CARE OF YOUR MISTAKES, NOAH...
...BEFORE MORE PEOPLE DIE.

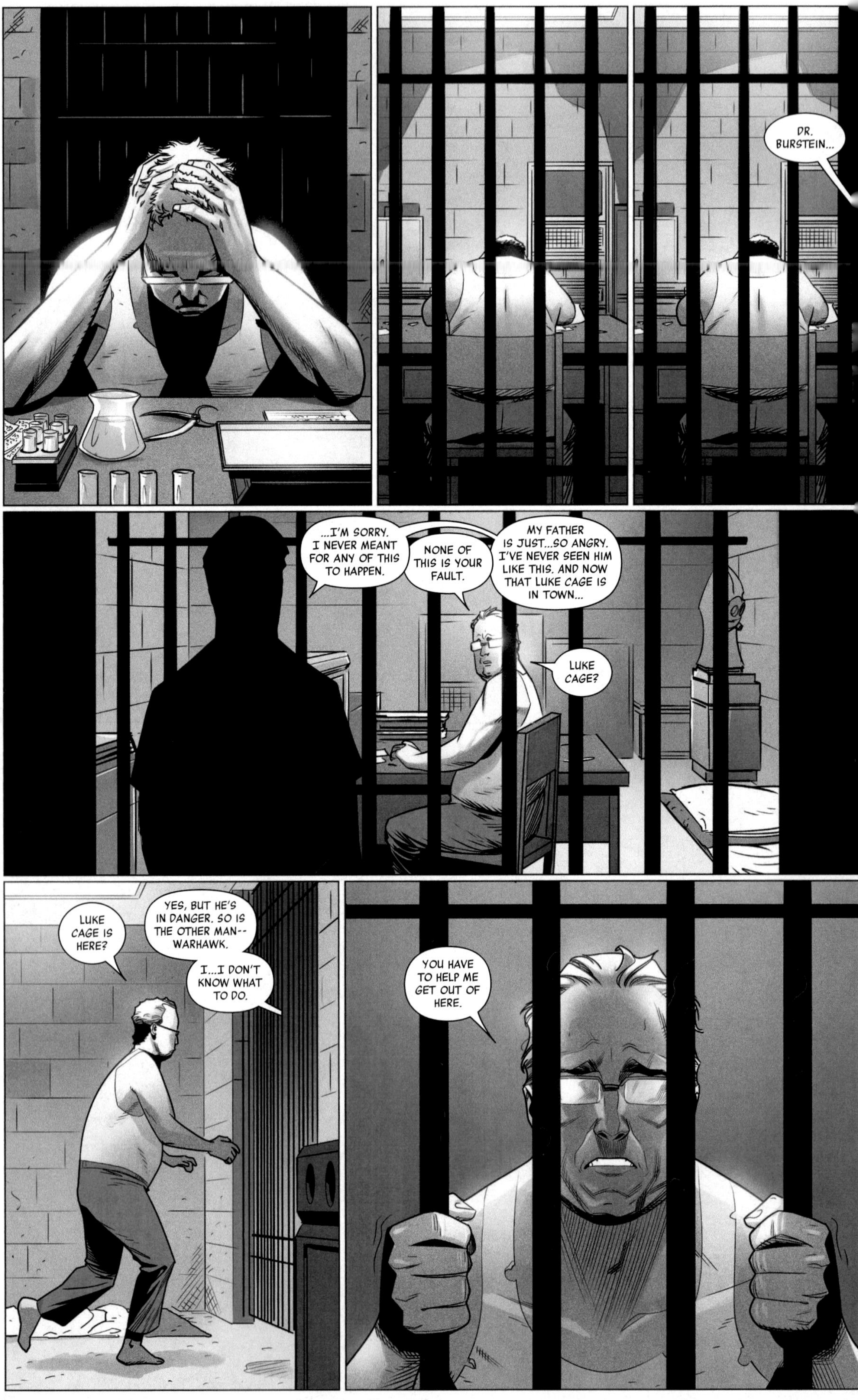
DR. BURSTEIN...
...I'M SORRY. I NEVER MEANT FOR ANY OF THIS TO HAPPEN.
NONE OF THIS IS YOUR FAULT.
MY FATHER IS JUST...SO ANGRY. I'VE NEVER SEEN HIM LIKE THIS. AND NOW THAT LUKE CAGE IS IN TOWN...
LUKE CAGE?
LUKE CAGE IS HERE?
YES, BUT HE'S IN DANGER. SO IS THE OTHER MAN-- WARHAWK.
I...I DON'T KNOW WHAT TO DO.
YOU HAVE TO HELP ME GET OUT OF HERE.

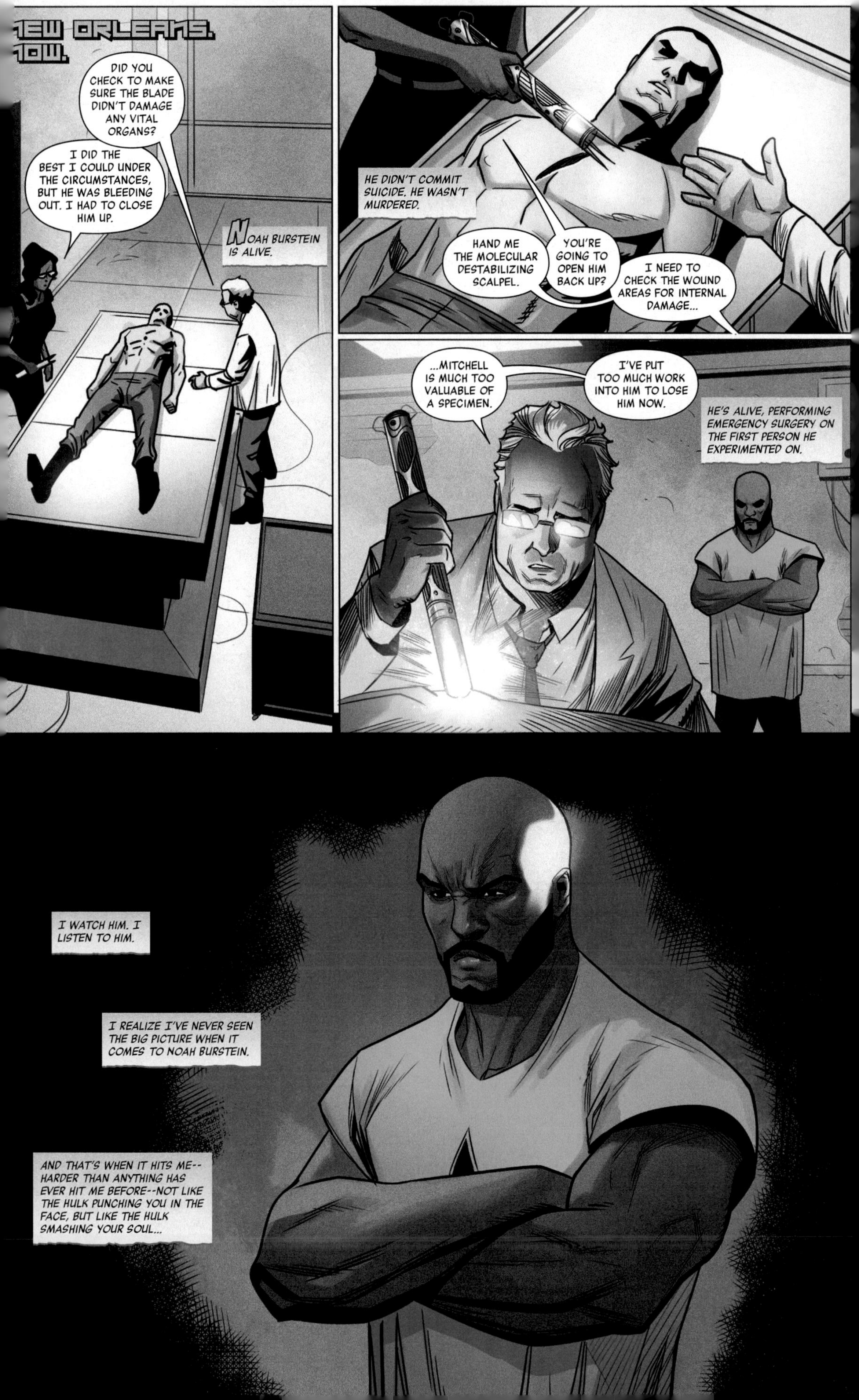
NEW ORLEANS.
NOW.
DID YOU CHECK TO MAKE SURE THE BLADE DIDN'T DAMAGE ANY VITAL ORGANS?
I DID THE BEST I COULD UNDER THE CIRCUMSTANCES, BUT HE WAS BLEEDING OUT. I HAD TO CLOSE HIM UP.
NOAH BURSTEIN IS ALIVE.
HE DIDN'T COMMIT SUICIDE. HE WASN'T MURDERED.
HAND ME THE MOLECULAR DESTABILIZING SCALPEL.
YOU'RE GOING TO OPEN HIM BACK UP?
I NEED TO CHECK THE WOUND AREAS FOR INTERNAL DAMAGE...
...MITCHELL IS MUCH TOO VALUABLE OF A SPECIMEN.
I'VE PUT TOO MUCH WORK INTO HIM TO LOSE HIM NOW.
HE'S ALIVE, PERFORMING EMERGENCY SURGERY ON THE FIRST PERSON HE EXPERIMENTED ON.
I WATCH HIM. I LISTEN TO HIM.
I REALIZE I'VE NEVER SEEN THE BIG PICTURE WHEN IT COMES TO NOAH BURSTEIN.
AND THAT'S WHEN IT HITS ME--HARDER THAN ANYTHING HAS EVER HIT ME BEFORE--NOT LIKE THE HULK PUNCHING YOU IN THE FACE, BUT LIKE THE HULK SMASHING YOUR SOUL...

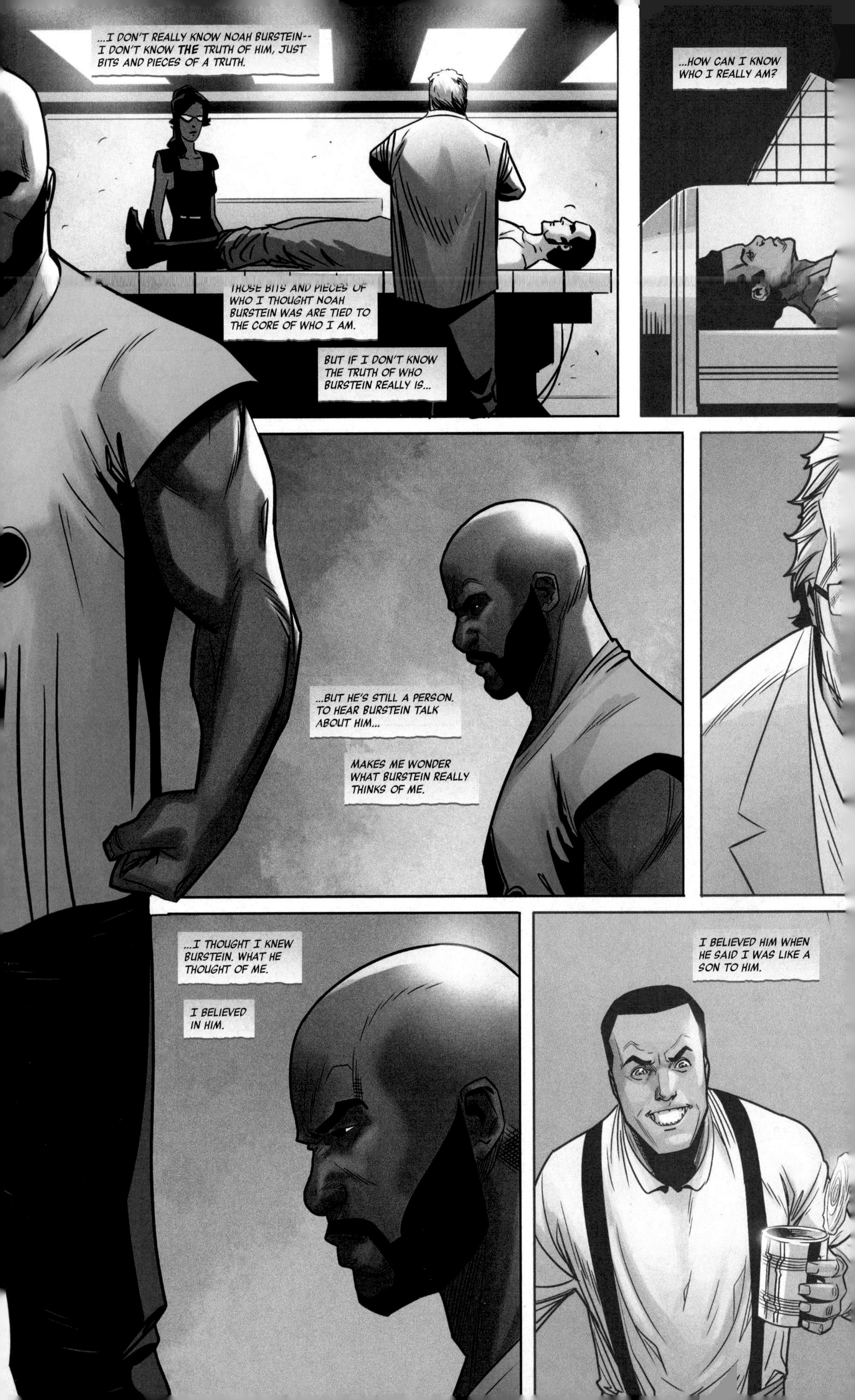
...I DON'T REALLY KNOW NOAH BURSTEIN-- I DON'T KNOW THE TRUTH OF HIM, JUST BITS AND PIECES OF A TRUTH.
THOSE BITS AND PIECES OF WHO I THOUGHT NOAH BURSTEIN WAS ARE TIED TO THE CORE OF WHO I AM.
BUT IF I DON'T KNOW THE TRUTH OF WHO BURSTEIN REALLY IS...
...HOW CAN I KNOW WHO I REALLY AM?
...BUT HE'S STILL A PERSON. TO HEAR BURSTEIN TALK ABOUT HIM...
MAKES ME WONDER WHAT BURSTEIN REALLY THINKS OF ME.
...I THOUGHT I KNEW BURSTEIN. WHAT HE THOUGHT OF ME.
I BELIEVED IN HIM.
I BELIEVED HIM WHEN HE SAID I WAS LIKE A SON TO HIM.

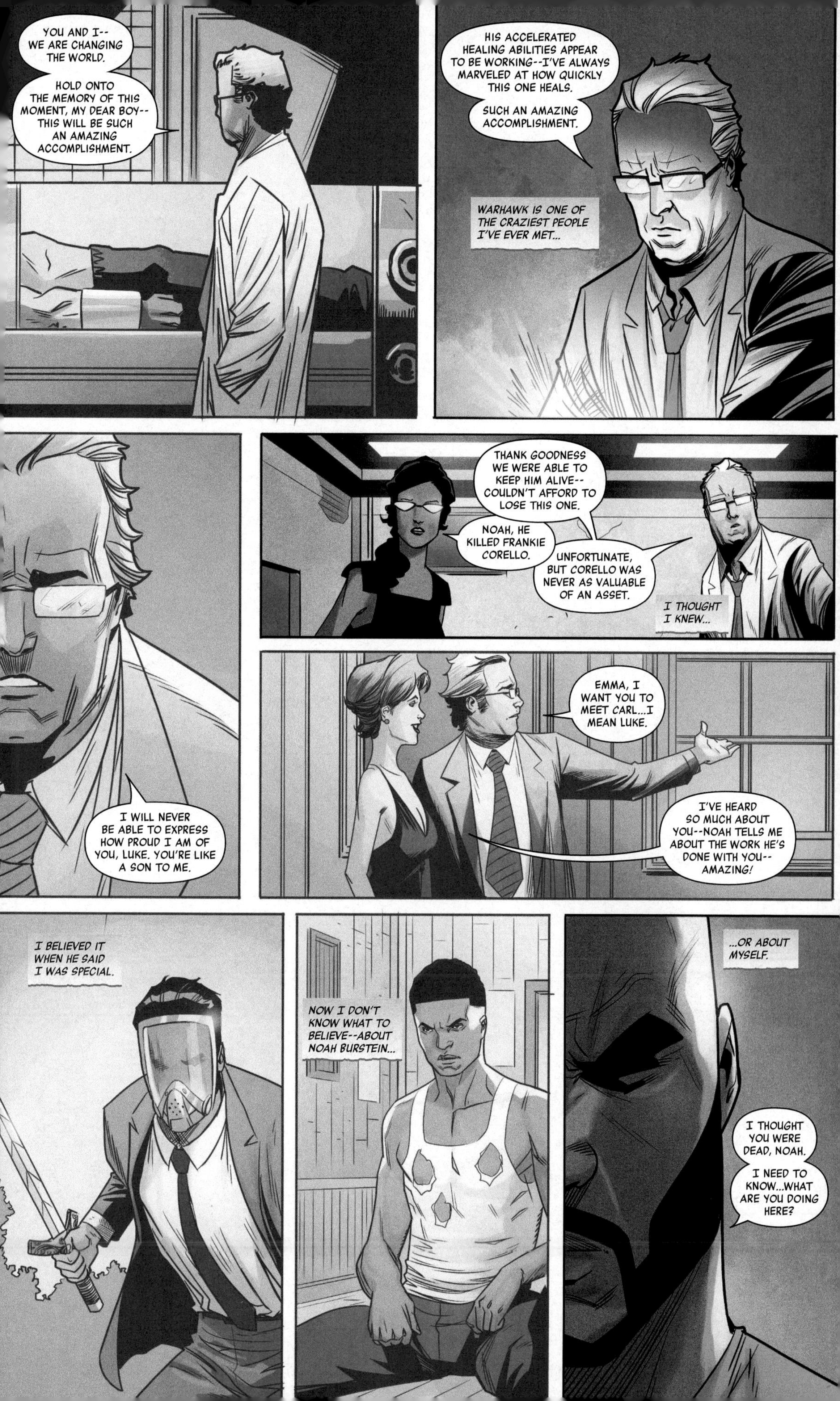
YOU AND I-- WE ARE CHANGING THE WORLD.
HOLD ONTO THE MEMORY OF THIS MOMENT, MY DEAR BOY-- THIS WILL BE SUCH AN AMAZING ACCOMPLISHMENT.
HIS ACCELERATED HEALING ABILITIES APPEAR TO BE WORKING--I'VE ALWAYS MARVELED AT HOW QUICKLY THIS ONE HEALS.
SUCH AN AMAZING ACCOMPLISHMENT.
WARHAWK IS ONE OF THE CRAZIEST PEOPLE I'VE EVER MET...
I WILL NEVER BE ABLE TO EXPRESS HOW PROUD I AM OF YOU, LUKE. YOU'RE LIKE A SON TO ME.
THANK GOODNESS WE WERE ABLE TO KEEP HIM ALIVE-- COULDN'T AFFORD TO LOSE THIS ONE.
NOAH, HE KILLED FRANKIE CORELLO.
UNFORTUNATE, BUT CORELLO WAS NEVER AS VALUABLE OF AN ASSET.
I THOUGHT I KNEW...
EMMA, I WANT YOU TO MEET CARL...I MEAN LUKE.
I'VE HEARD SO MUCH ABOUT YOU--NOAH TELLS ME ABOUT THE WORK HE'S DONE WITH YOU-- AMAZING!
I BELIEVED IT WHEN HE SAID I WAS SPECIAL.
NOW I DON'T KNOW WHAT TO BELIEVE--ABOUT NOAH BURSTEIN...
...OR ABOUT MYSELF.
I THOUGHT YOU WERE DEAD, NOAH.
I NEED TO KNOW...WHAT ARE YOU DOING HERE?

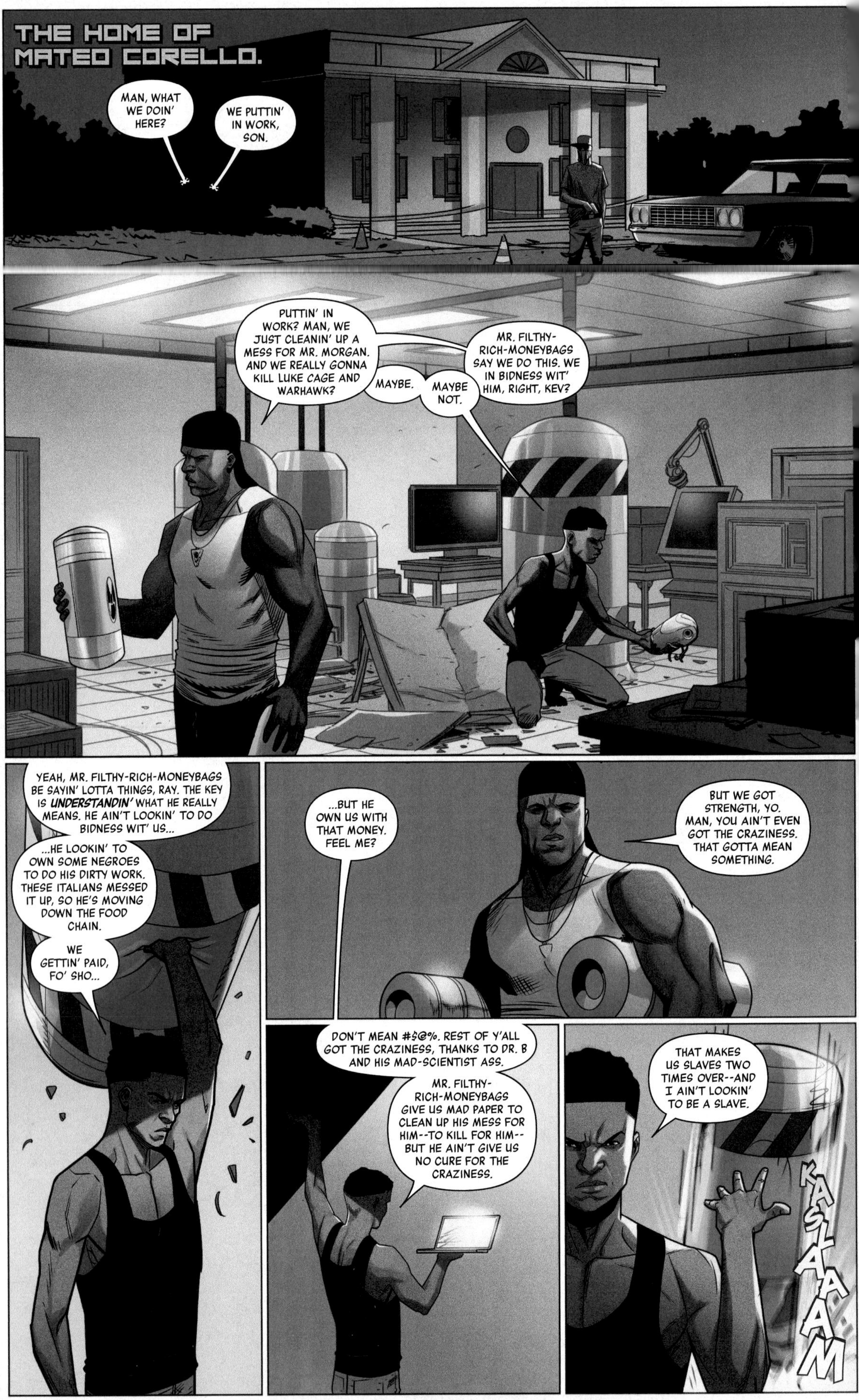
THE HOME OF MATEO CORELLO.
MAN, WHAT WE DOIN' HERE?
WE PUTTIN' IN WORK, SON.
PUTTIN' IN WORK? MAN, WE JUST CLEANIN' UP A MESS FOR MR. MORGAN. AND WE REALLY GONNA KILL LUKE CAGE AND WARHAWK?
MR. FILTHY-RICH-MONEYBAGS SAY WE DO THIS. WE IN BIDNESS WIT' HIM, RIGHT, KEV?
MAYBE.
MAYBE NOT.
YEAH, MR. FILTHY-RICH-MONEYBAGS BE SAYIN' LOTTA THINGS, RAY. THE KEY IS UNDERSTANDIN' WHAT HE REALLY MEANS. HE AIN'T LOOKIN' TO DO BIDNESS WIT' US...
...HE LOOKIN' TO OWN SOME NEGROES TO DO HIS DIRTY WORK. THESE ITALIANS MESSED IT UP, SO HE'S MOVING DOWN THE FOOD CHAIN.
WE GETTIN' PAID, FO' SHO...
...BUT HE OWN US WITH THAT MONEY. FEEL ME?
BUT WE GOT STRENGTH, YO. MAN, YOU AIN'T EVEN GOT THE CRAZINESS. THAT GOTTA MEAN SOMETHING.
DON'T MEAN #$@%. REST OF Y'ALL GOT THE CRAZINESS, THANKS TO DR. B AND HIS MAD-SCIENTIST ASS.
MR. FILTHY-RICH-MONEYBAGS GIVE US MAD PAPER TO CLEAN UP HIS MESS FOR HIM--TO KILL FOR HIM--BUT HE AIN'T GIVE US NO CURE FOR THE CRAZINESS.
THAT MAKES US SLAVES TWO TIMES OVER--AND I AIN'T LOOKIN' TO BE A SLAVE.
KASLAAAM

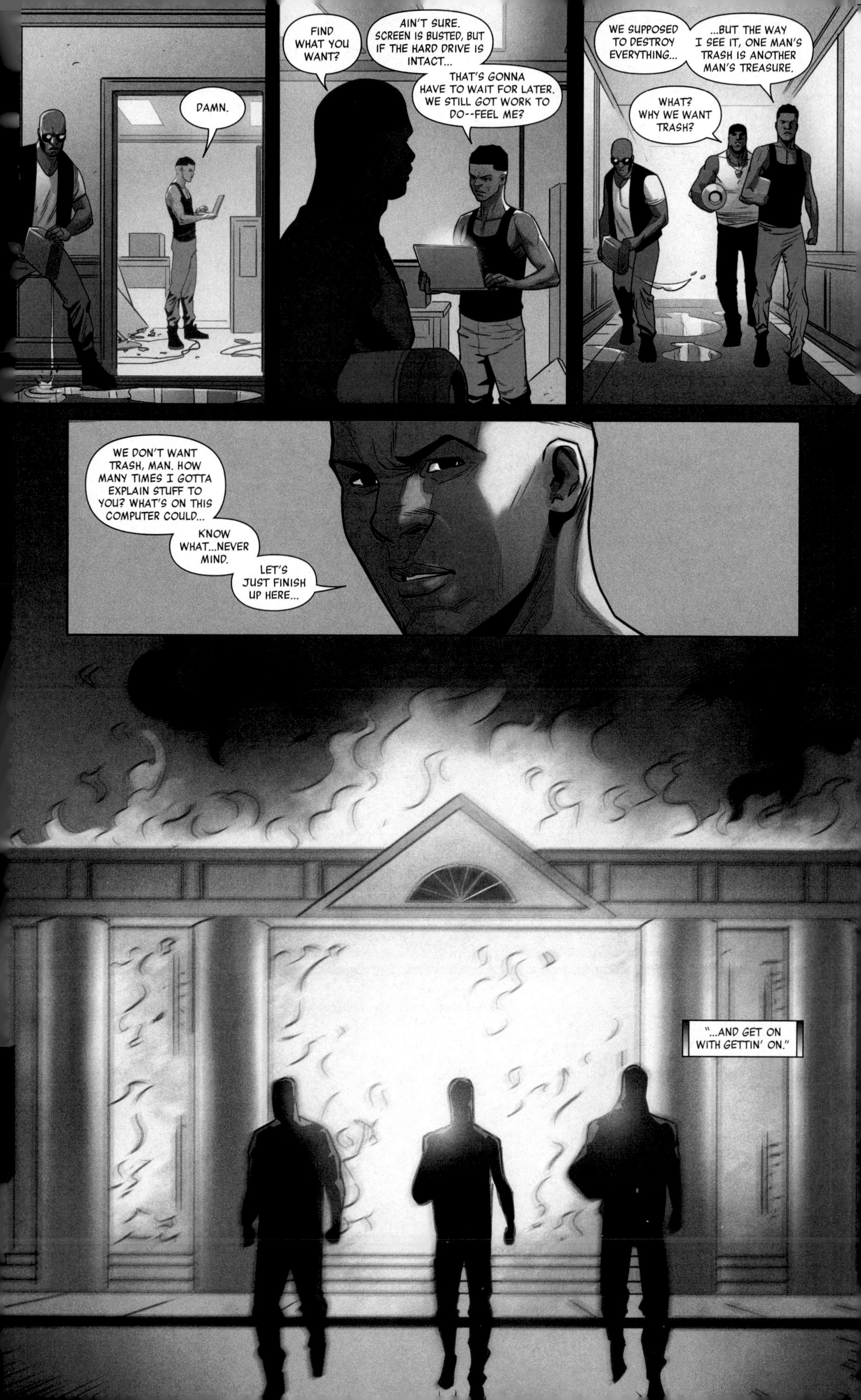
DAMN.
FIND WHAT YOU WANT?
AIN'T SURE. SCREEN IS BUSTED, BUT IF THE HARD DRIVE IS INTACT...
THAT'S GONNA HAVE TO WAIT FOR LATER. WE STILL GOT WORK TO DO--FEEL ME?
WE SUPPOSED TO DESTROY EVERYTHING...
...BUT THE WAY I SEE IT, ONE MAN'S TRASH IS ANOTHER MAN'S TREASURE.
WHAT? WHY WE WANT TRASH?
WE DON'T WANT TRASH, MAN. HOW MANY TIMES I GOTTA EXPLAIN STUFF TO YOU? WHAT'S ON THIS COMPUTER COULD...
KNOW WHAT...NEVER MIND.
LET'S JUST FINISH UP HERE...
"...AND GET ON WITH GETTIN' ON."

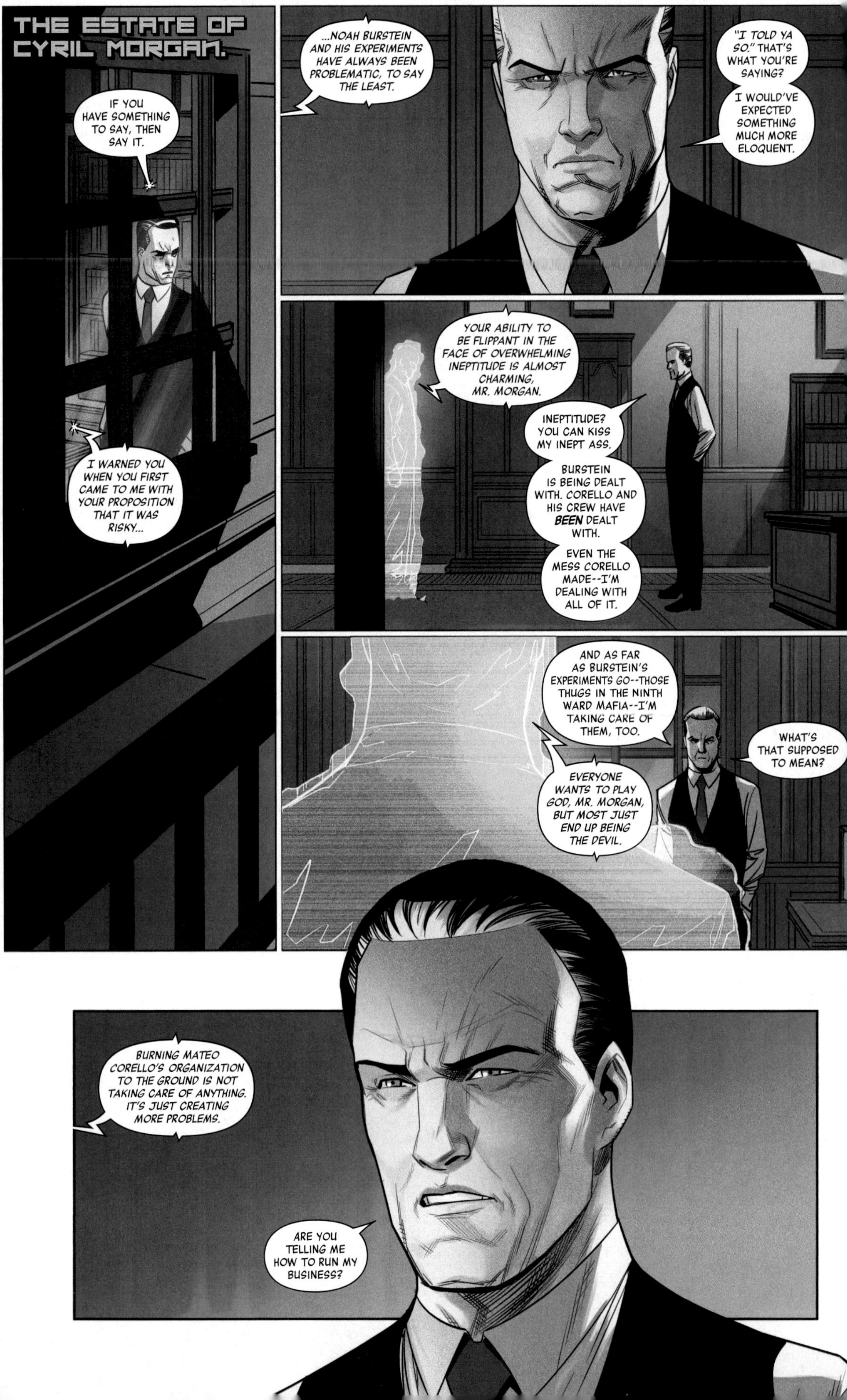
THE ESTATE OF CYRIL MORGAN.
IF YOU HAVE SOMETHING TO SAY, THEN SAY IT.
I WARNED YOU WHEN YOU FIRST CAME TO ME WITH YOUR PROPOSITION THAT IT WAS RISKY...
...NOAH BURSTEIN AND HIS EXPERIMENTS HAVE ALWAYS BEEN PROBLEMATIC, TO SAY THE LEAST.
"I TOLD YA SO." THAT'S WHAT YOU'RE SAYING?
I WOULD'VE EXPECTED SOMETHING MUCH MORE ELOQUENT.
YOUR ABILITY TO BE FLIPPANT IN THE FACE OF OVERWHELMING INEPTITUDE IS ALMOST CHARMING, MR. MORGAN.
INEPTITUDE? YOU CAN KISS MY INEPT ASS.
BURSTEIN IS BEING DEALT WITH. CORELLO AND HIS CREW HAVE BEEN DEALT WITH.
EVEN THE MESS CORELLO MADE--I'M DEALING WITH ALL OF IT.
AND AS FAR AS BURSTEIN'S EXPERIMENTS GO--THOSE THUGS IN THE NINTH WARD MAFIA--I'M TAKING CARE OF THEM, TOO.
EVERYONE WANTS TO PLAY GOD, MR. MORGAN, BUT MOST JUST END UP BEING THE DEVIL.
WHAT'S THAT SUPPOSED TO MEAN?
BURNING MATEO CORELLO'S ORGANIZATION TO THE GROUND IS NOT TAKING CARE OF ANYTHING. IT'S JUST CREATING MORE PROBLEMS.
ARE YOU TELLING ME HOW TO RUN MY BUSINESS?

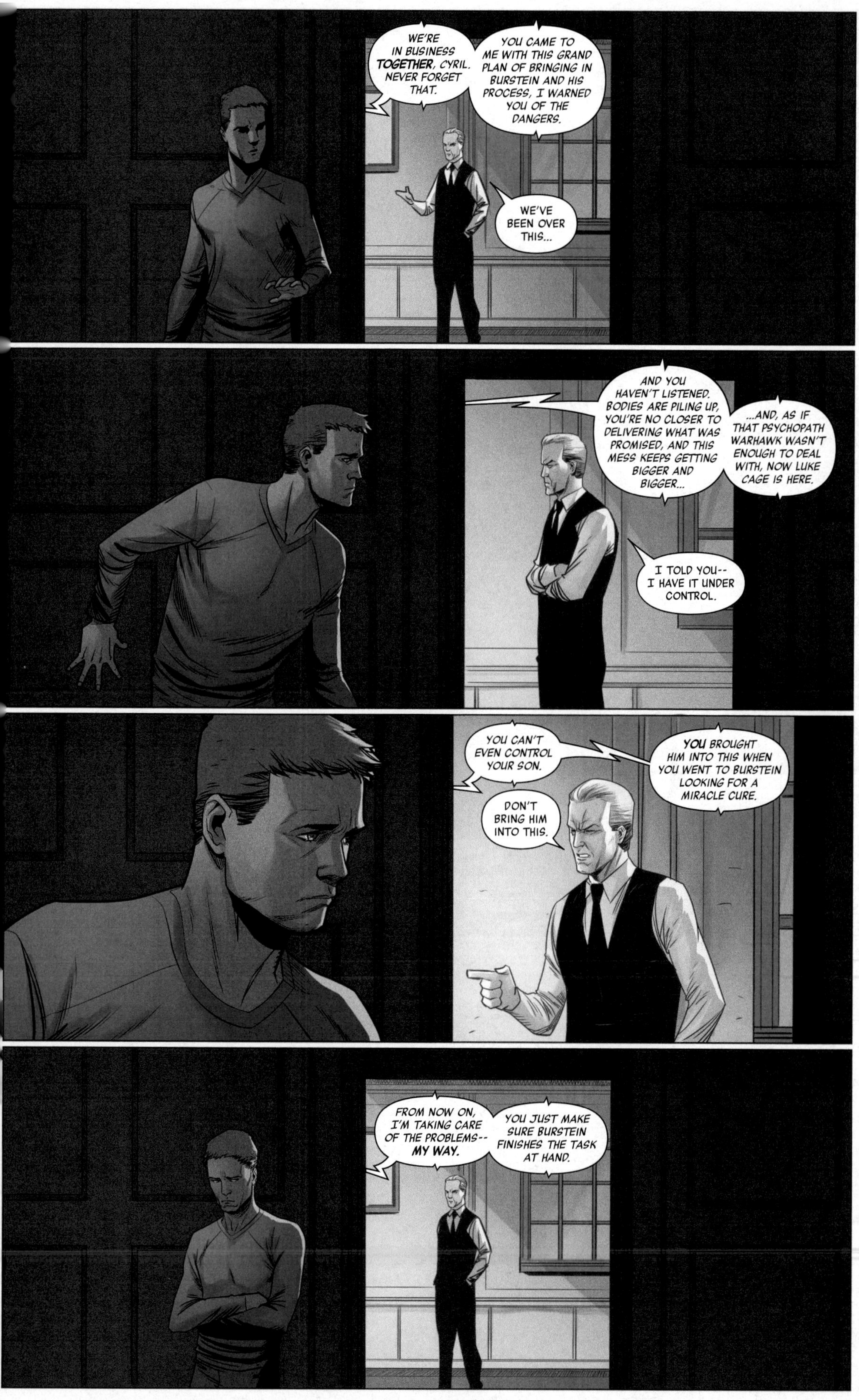
WE'RE IN BUSINESS TOGETHER, CYRIL. NEVER FORGET THAT.
YOU CAME TO ME WITH THIS GRAND PLAN OF BRINGING IN BURSTEIN AND HIS PROCESS, I WARNED YOU OF THE DANGERS.
WE'VE BEEN OVER THIS...
AND YOU HAVEN'T LISTENED. BODIES ARE PILING UP, YOU'RE NO CLOSER TO DELIVERING WHAT WAS PROMISED, AND THIS MESS KEEPS GETTING BIGGER AND BIGGER...
...AND, AS IF THAT PSYCHOPATH WARHAWK WASN'T ENOUGH TO DEAL WITH, NOW LUKE CAGE IS HERE.
I TOLD YOU-- I HAVE IT UNDER CONTROL.
YOU CAN'T EVEN CONTROL YOUR SON.
YOU BROUGHT HIM INTO THIS WHEN YOU WENT TO BURSTEIN LOOKING FOR A MIRACLE CURE.
DON'T BRING HIM INTO THIS.
FROM NOW ON, I'M TAKING CARE OF THE PROBLEMS-- MY WAY.
YOU JUST MAKE SURE BURSTEIN FINISHES THE TASK AT HAND.

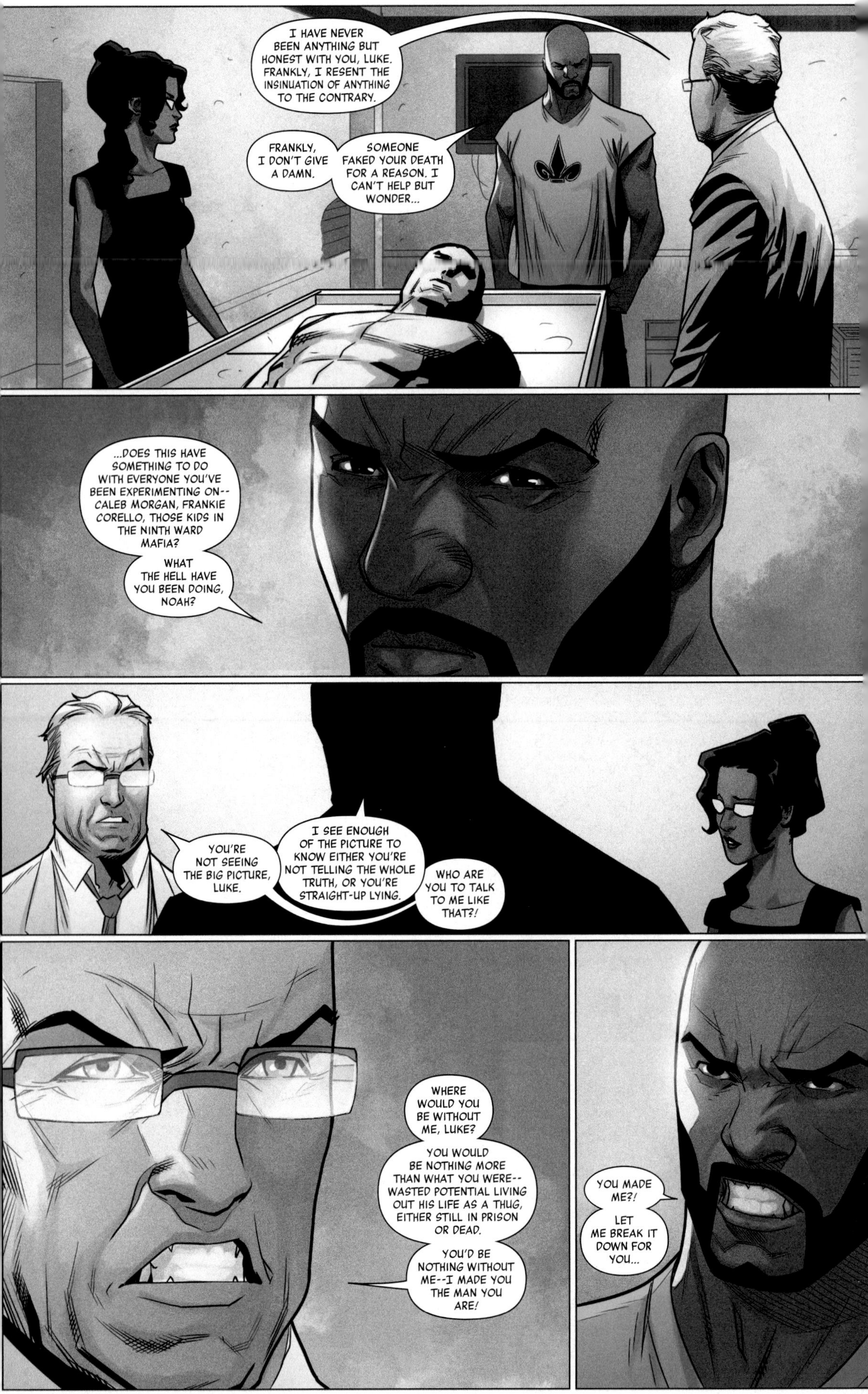
I HAVE NEVER BEEN ANYTHING BUT HONEST WITH YOU, LUKE. FRANKLY, I RESENT THE INSINUATION OF ANYTHING TO THE CONTRARY.
FRANKLY, I DON'T GIVE A DAMN.
SOMEONE FAKED YOUR DEATH FOR A REASON. I CAN'T HELP BUT WONDER...
...DOES THIS HAVE SOMETHING TO DO WITH EVERYONE YOU'VE BEEN EXPERIMENTING ON--CALEB MORGAN, FRANKIE CORELLO, THOSE KIDS IN THE NINTH WARD MAFIA?
WHAT THE HELL HAVE YOU BEEN DOING, NOAH?
YOU'RE NOT SEEING THE BIG PICTURE, LUKE.
I SEE ENOUGH OF THE PICTURE TO KNOW EITHER YOU'RE NOT TELLING THE WHOLE TRUTH, OR YOU'RE STRAIGHT-UP LYING.
WHO ARE YOU TO TALK TO ME LIKE THAT?!
WHERE WOULD YOU BE WITHOUT ME, LUKE?
YOU WOULD BE NOTHING MORE THAN WHAT YOU WERE--WASTED POTENTIAL LIVING OUT HIS LIFE AS A THUG, EITHER STILL IN PRISON OR DEAD.
YOU'D BE NOTHING WITHOUT ME--I MADE YOU THE MAN YOU ARE!
YOU MADE ME?!
LET ME BREAK IT DOWN FOR YOU...

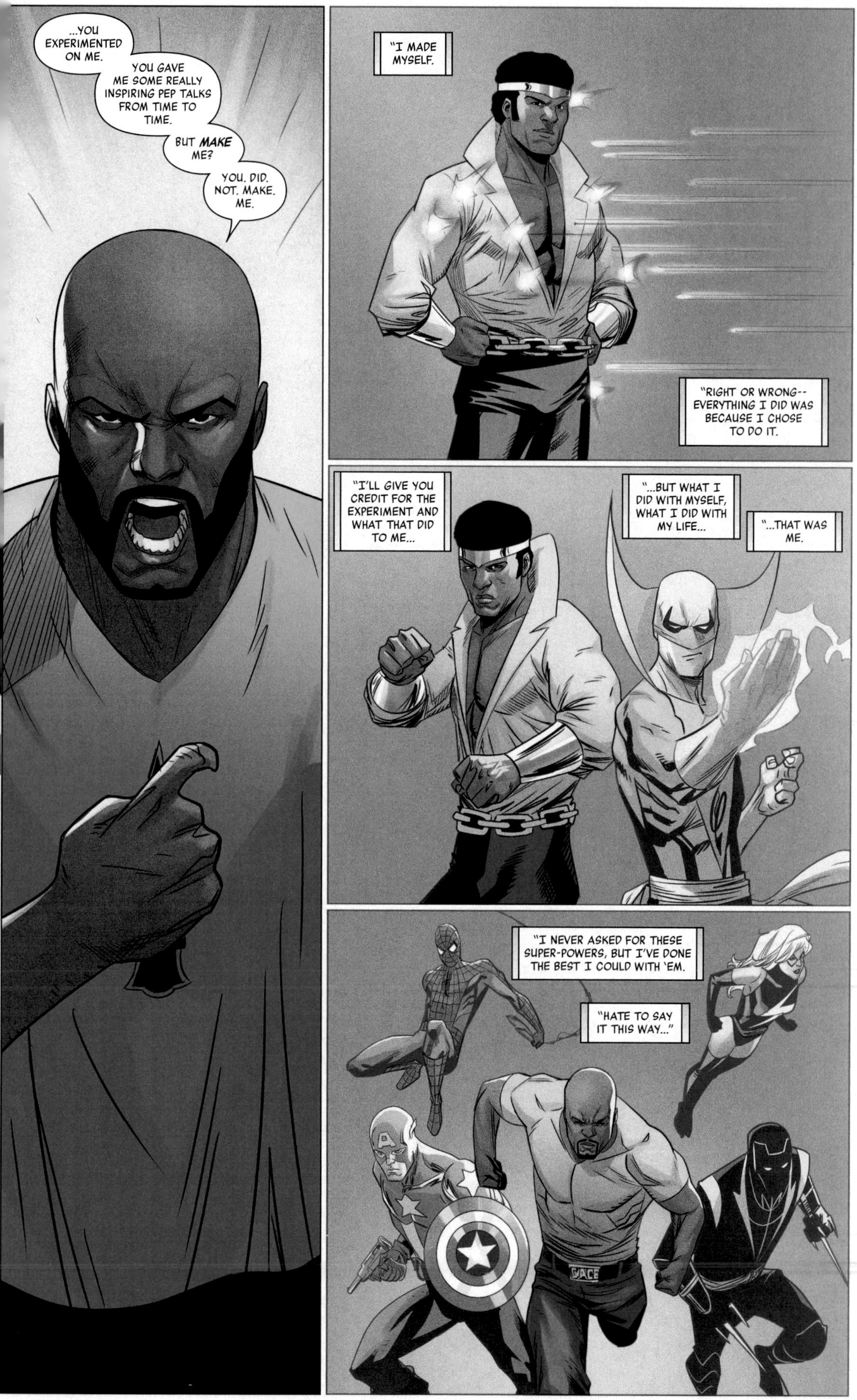
...YOU EXPERIMENTED ON ME.
YOU GAVE ME SOME REALLY INSPIRING PEP TALKS FROM TIME TO TIME.
BUT MAKE ME?
YOU. DID. NOT. MAKE. ME.
"I MADE MYSELF.
"RIGHT OR WRONG-- EVERYTHING I DID WAS BECAUSE I CHOSE TO DO IT.
"I'LL GIVE YOU CREDIT FOR THE EXPERIMENT AND WHAT THAT DID TO ME...
"...BUT WHAT I DID WITH MYSELF, WHAT I DID WITH MY LIFE...
"...THAT WAS ME.
"I NEVER ASKED FOR THESE SUPER-POWERS, BUT I'VE DONE THE BEST I COULD WITH 'EM.
"HATE TO SAY IT THIS WAY..."

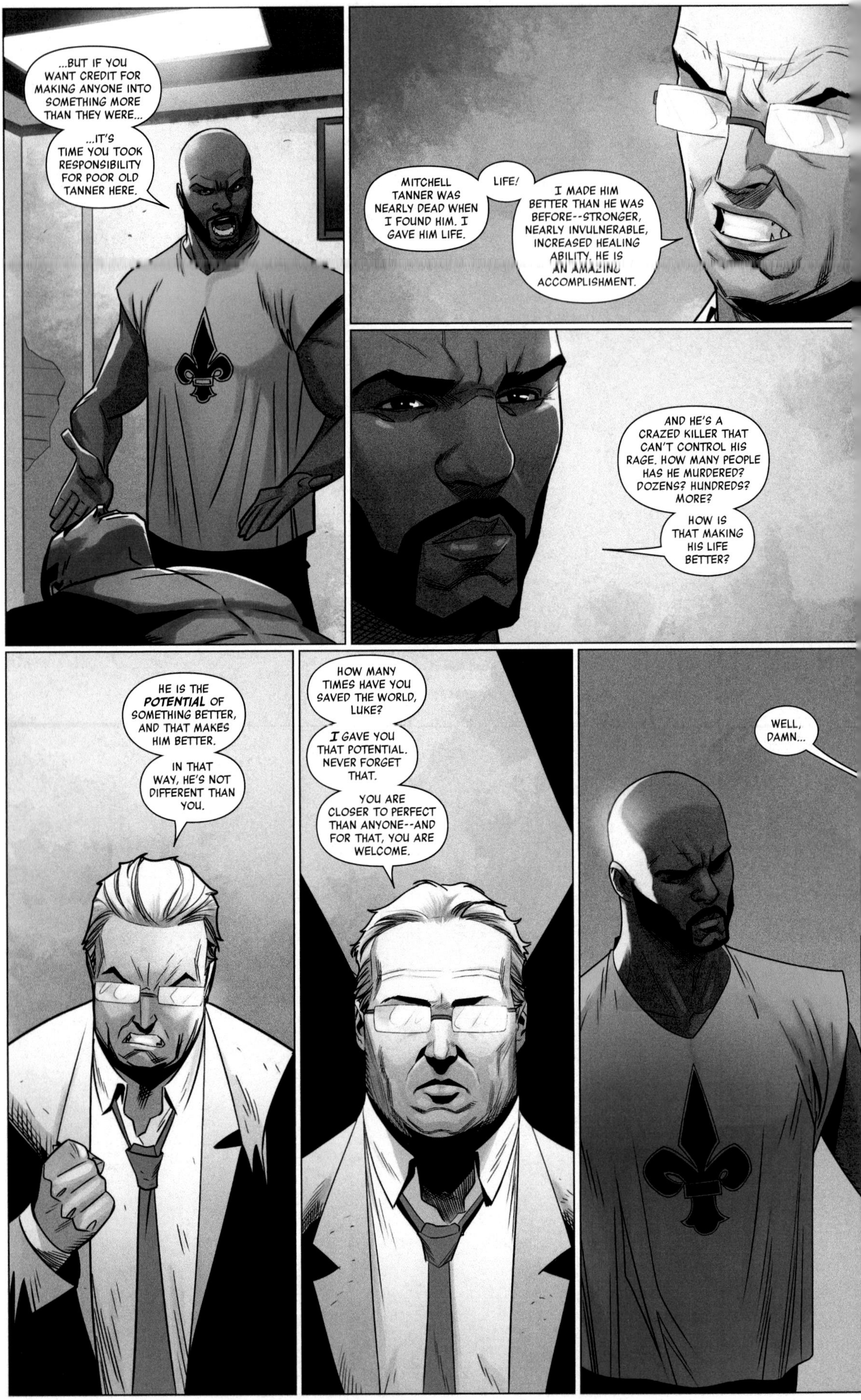
...BUT IF YOU WANT CREDIT FOR MAKING ANYONE INTO SOMETHING MORE THAN THEY WERE...
...IT'S TIME YOU TOOK RESPONSIBILITY FOR POOR OLD TANNER HERE.
MITCHELL TANNER WAS NEARLY DEAD WHEN I FOUND HIM. I GAVE HIM LIFE.
LIFE!
I MADE HIM BETTER THAN HE WAS BEFORE--STRONGER, NEARLY INVULNERABLE, INCREASED HEALING ABILITY. HE IS AN AMAZING ACCOMPLISHMENT.
AND HE'S A CRAZED KILLER THAT CAN'T CONTROL HIS RAGE. HOW MANY PEOPLE HAS HE MURDERED? DOZENS? HUNDREDS? MORE?
HOW IS THAT MAKING HIS LIFE BETTER?
HE IS THE ***POTENTIAL*** OF SOMETHING BETTER, AND THAT MAKES HIM BETTER.
IN THAT WAY, HE'S NOT DIFFERENT THAN YOU.
HOW MANY TIMES HAVE YOU SAVED THE WORLD, LUKE?
I GAVE YOU THAT POTENTIAL. NEVER FORGET THAT.
YOU ARE CLOSER TO PERFECT THAN ANYONE--AND FOR THAT, YOU ARE WELCOME.
WELL, DAMN...

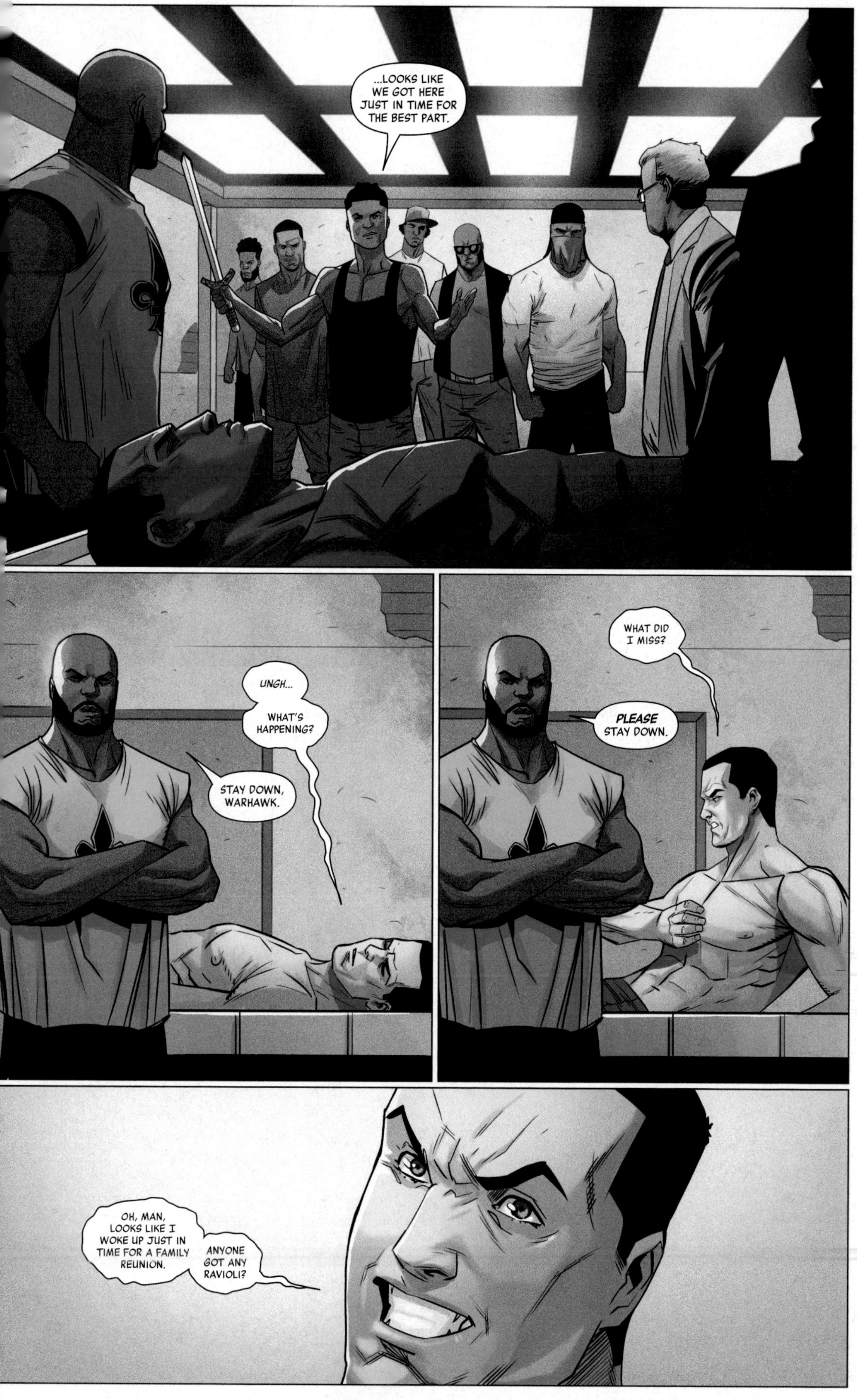
...LOOKS LIKE WE GOT HERE JUST IN TIME FOR THE BEST PART.
UNGH...
WHAT'S HAPPENING?
STAY DOWN, WARHAWK.
WHAT DID I MISS?
PLEASE STAY DOWN.
OH, MAN, LOOKS LIKE I WOKE UP JUST IN TIME FOR A FAMILY REUNION.
ANYONE GOT ANY RAVIOLI?

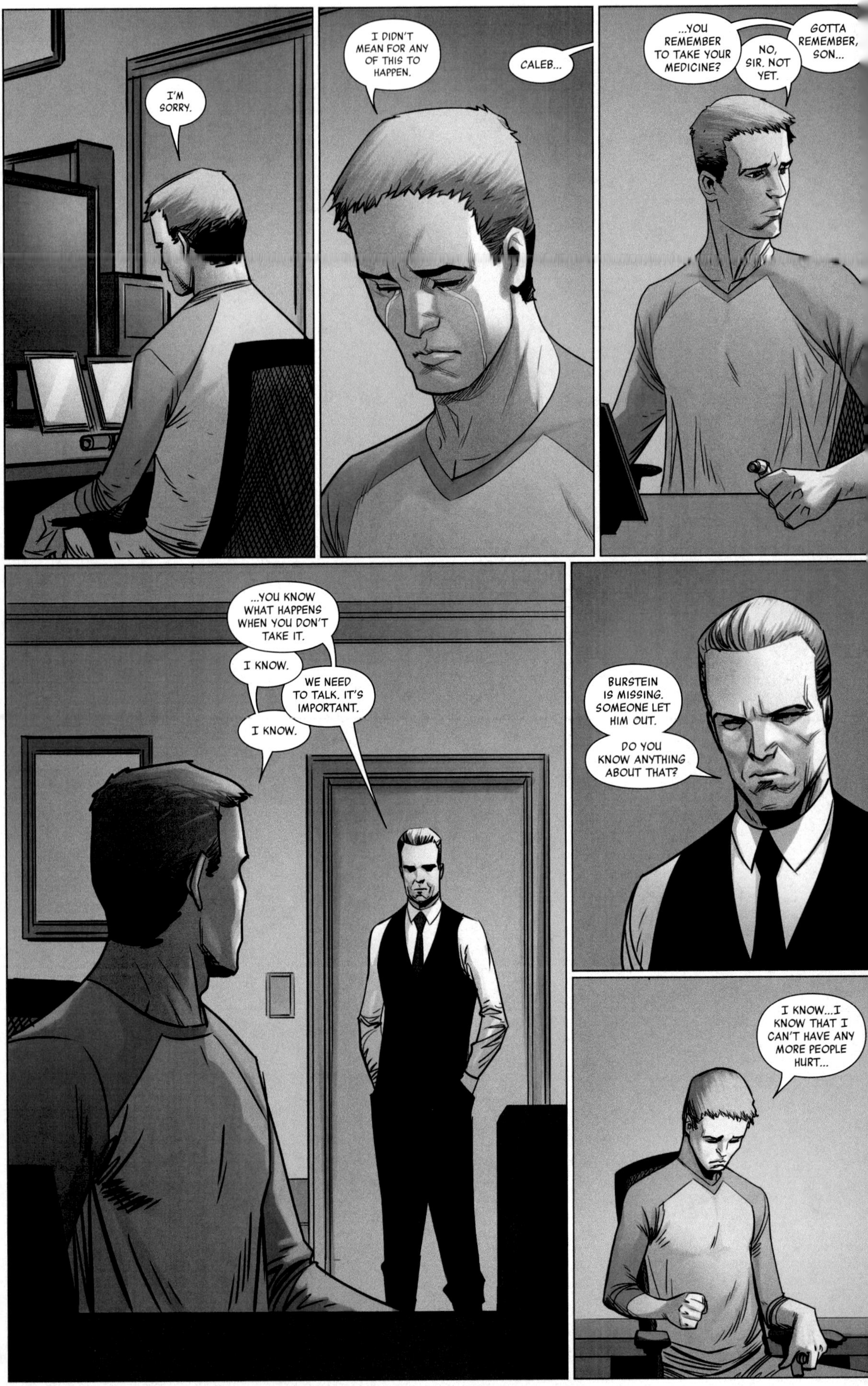
I'M SORRY.
I DIDN'T MEAN FOR ANY OF THIS TO HAPPEN.
CALEB...
GOTTA REMEMBER, SON...
...YOU REMEMBER TO TAKE YOUR MEDICINE?
NO, SIR. NOT YET.
...YOU KNOW WHAT HAPPENS WHEN YOU DON'T TAKE IT.
I KNOW.
WE NEED TO TALK. IT'S IMPORTANT.
I KNOW.
BURSTEIN IS MISSING. SOMEONE LET HIM OUT.
DO YOU KNOW ANYTHING ABOUT THAT?
I KNOW...I KNOW THAT I CAN'T HAVE ANY MORE PEOPLE HURT...

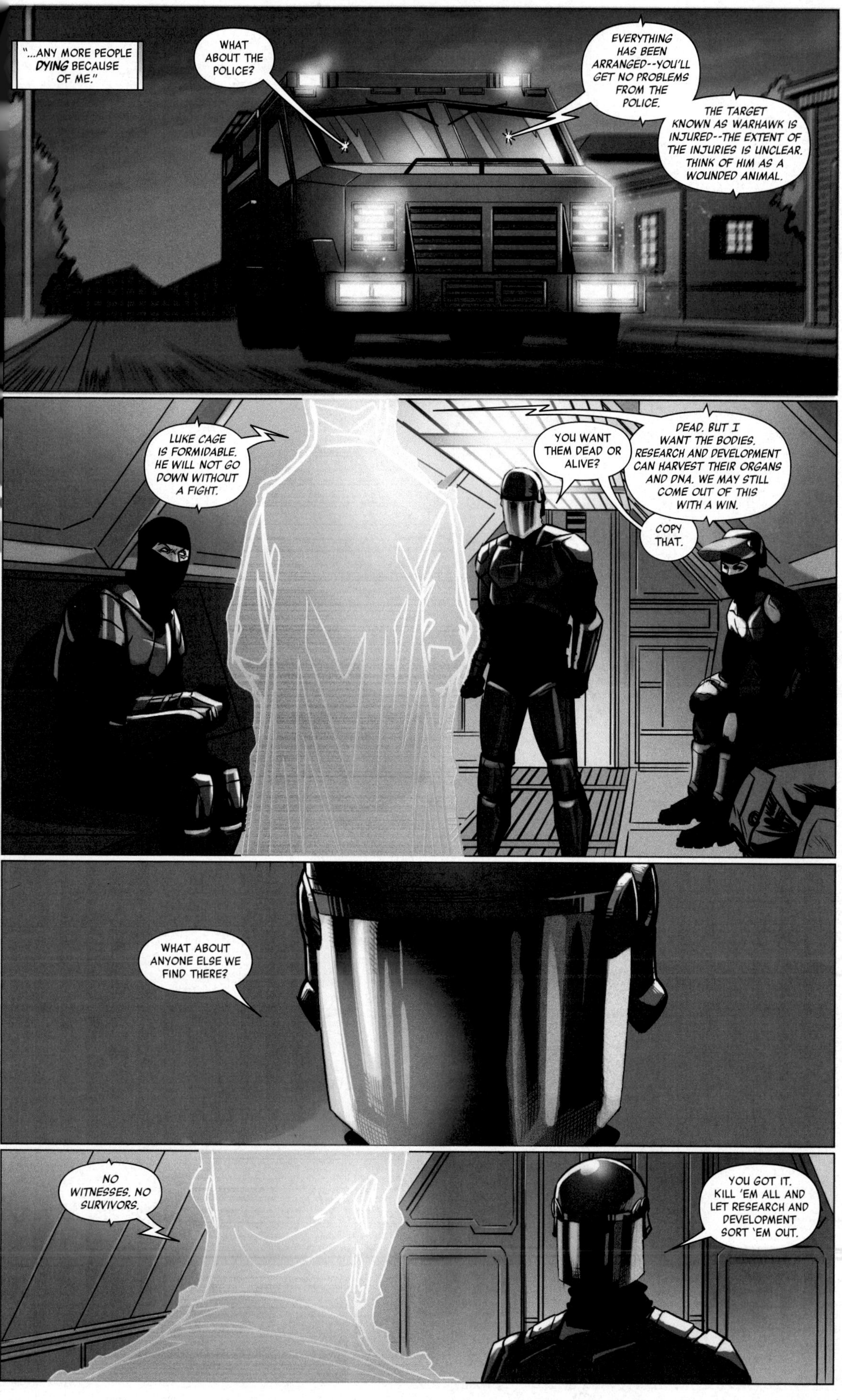
"...ANY MORE PEOPLE DYING BECAUSE OF ME."
WHAT ABOUT THE POLICE?
EVERYTHING HAS BEEN ARRANGED--YOU'LL GET NO PROBLEMS FROM THE POLICE.
THE TARGET KNOWN AS WARHAWK IS INJURED--THE EXTENT OF THE INJURIES IS UNCLEAR. THINK OF HIM AS A WOUNDED ANIMAL.
LUKE CAGE IS FORMIDABLE. HE WILL NOT GO DOWN WITHOUT A FIGHT.
YOU WANT THEM DEAD OR ALIVE?
DEAD. BUT I WANT THE BODIES. RESEARCH AND DEVELOPMENT CAN HARVEST THEIR ORGANS AND DNA. WE MAY STILL COME OUT OF THIS WITH A WIN.
COPY THAT.
WHAT ABOUT ANYONE ELSE WE FIND THERE?
NO WITNESSES. NO SURVIVORS.
YOU GOT IT. KILL 'EM ALL AND LET RESEARCH AND DEVELOPMENT SORT 'EM OUT.

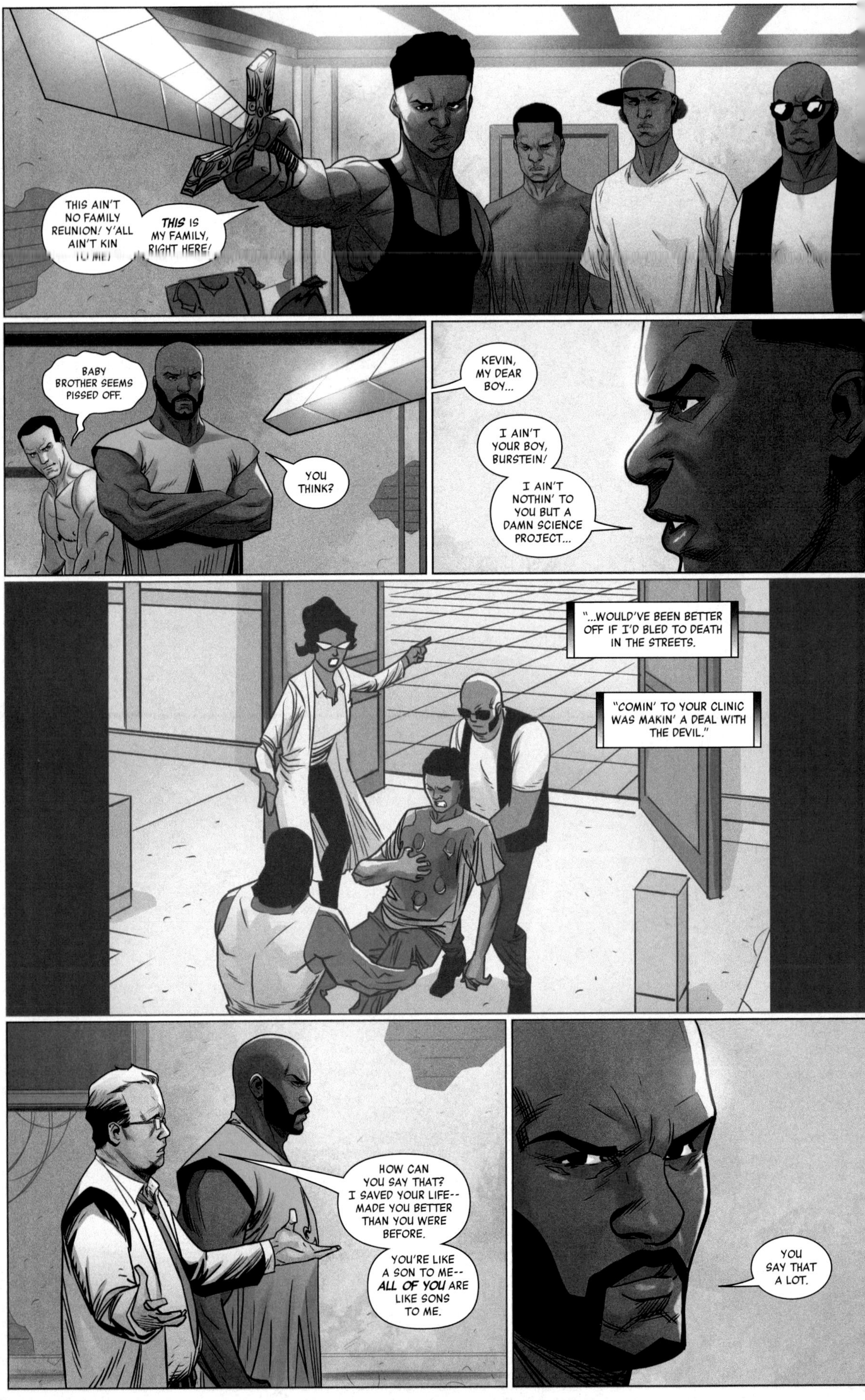

THIS AIN'T NO FAMILY REUNION! Y'ALL AIN'T KIN
THIS IS MY FAMILY, RIGHT HERE!
BABY BROTHER SEEMS PISSED OFF.
YOU THINK?
KEVIN, MY DEAR BOY...
I AIN'T YOUR BOY, BURSTEIN!
I AIN'T NOTHIN' TO YOU BUT A DAMN SCIENCE PROJECT...
"...WOULD'VE BEEN BETTER OFF IF I'D BLED TO DEATH IN THE STREETS.
"COMIN' TO YOUR CLINIC WAS MAKIN' A DEAL WITH THE DEVIL."
HOW CAN YOU SAY THAT? I SAVED YOUR LIFE-- MADE YOU BETTER THAN YOU WERE BEFORE.
YOU'RE LIKE A SON TO ME-- ALL OF YOU ARE LIKE SONS TO ME.
YOU SAY THAT A LOT.

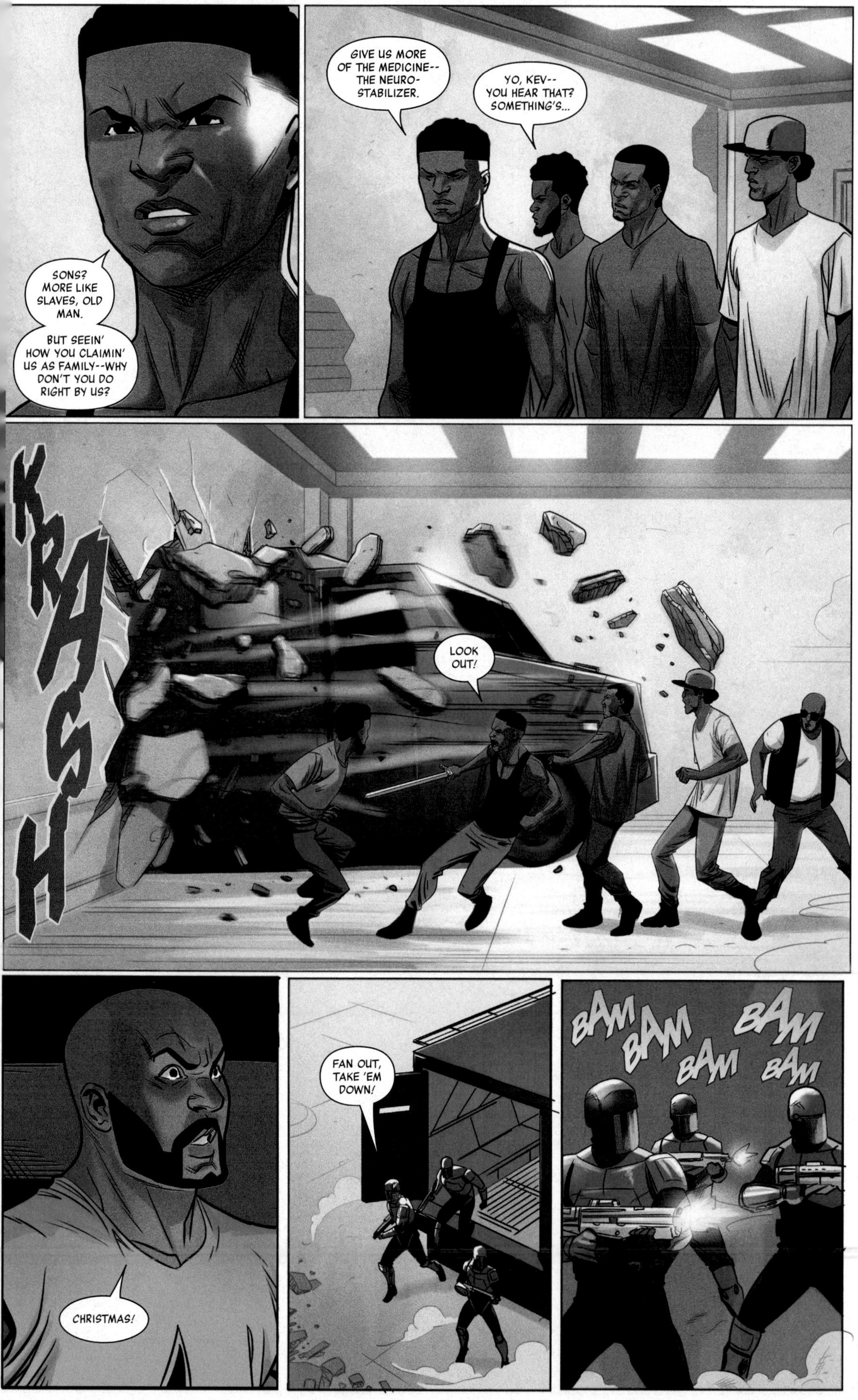
SONS? MORE LIKE SLAVES, OLD MAN.
BUT SEEIN' HOW YOU CLAIMIN' US AS FAMILY--WHY DON'T YOU DO RIGHT BY US?
GIVE US MORE OF THE MEDICINE--THE NEURO-STABILIZER.
YO, KEV--YOU HEAR THAT? SOMETHING'S...
KRASH
LOOK OUT!
CHRISTMAS!
FAN OUT, TAKE 'EM DOWN!
BAM BAM BAM BAM BAM BAM

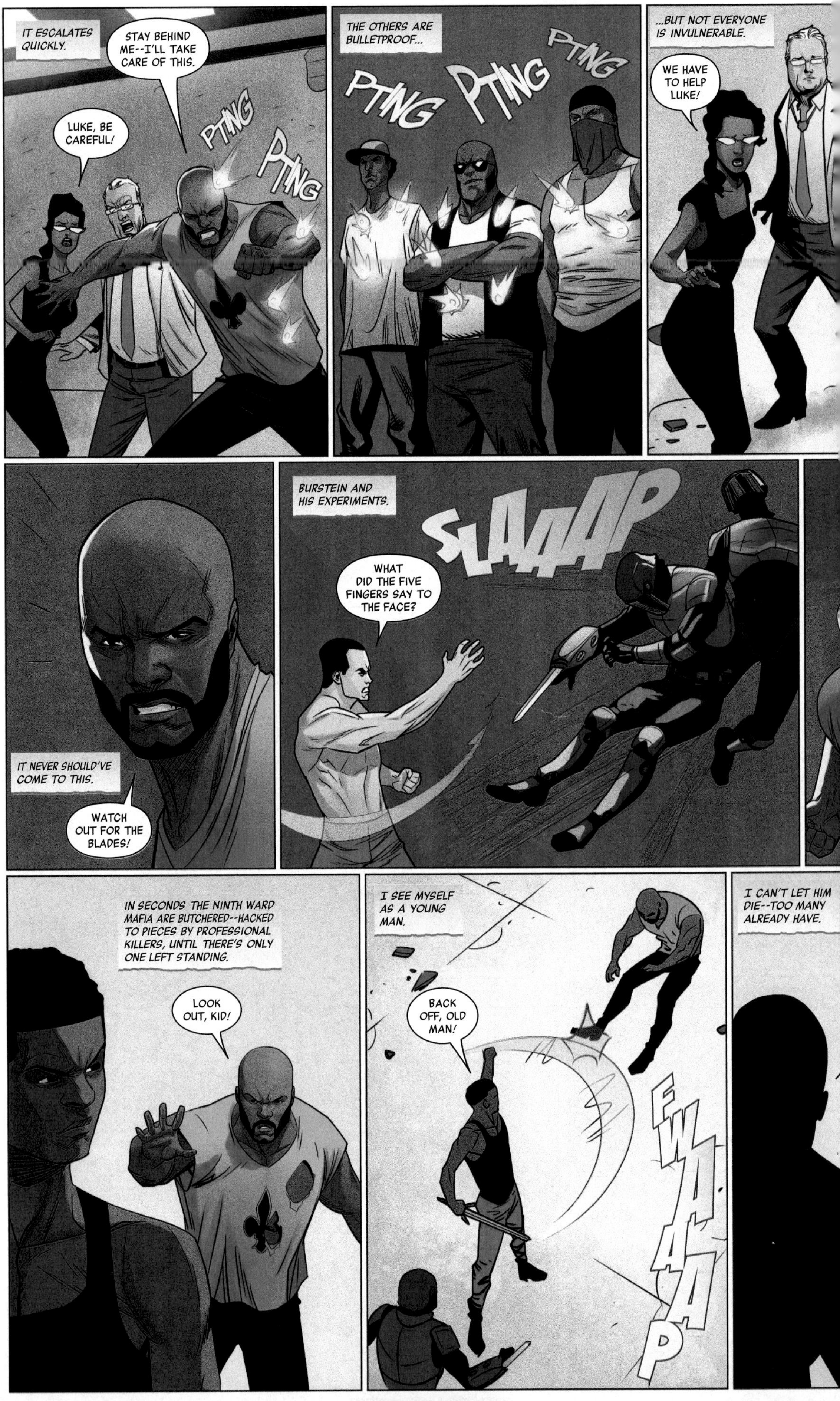
IT ESCALATES QUICKLY.
STAY BEHIND ME--I'LL TAKE CARE OF THIS.
LUKE, BE CAREFUL!
PTING
PTING
THE OTHERS ARE BULLETPROOF...
PTING
PTING
PTING
...BUT NOT EVERYONE IS INVULNERABLE.
WE HAVE TO HELP LUKE!
IT NEVER SHOULD'VE COME TO THIS.
WATCH OUT FOR THE BLADES!
BURSTEIN AND HIS EXPERIMENTS.
SLAAAP
WHAT DID THE FIVE FINGERS SAY TO THE FACE?
IN SECONDS THE NINTH WARD MAFIA ARE BUTCHERED--HACKED TO PIECES BY PROFESSIONAL KILLERS, UNTIL THERE'S ONLY ONE LEFT STANDING.
LOOK OUT, KID!
I SEE MYSELF AS A YOUNG MAN.
BACK OFF, OLD MAN!
FWAAAAP
I CAN'T LET HIM DIE--TOO MANY ALREADY HAVE.

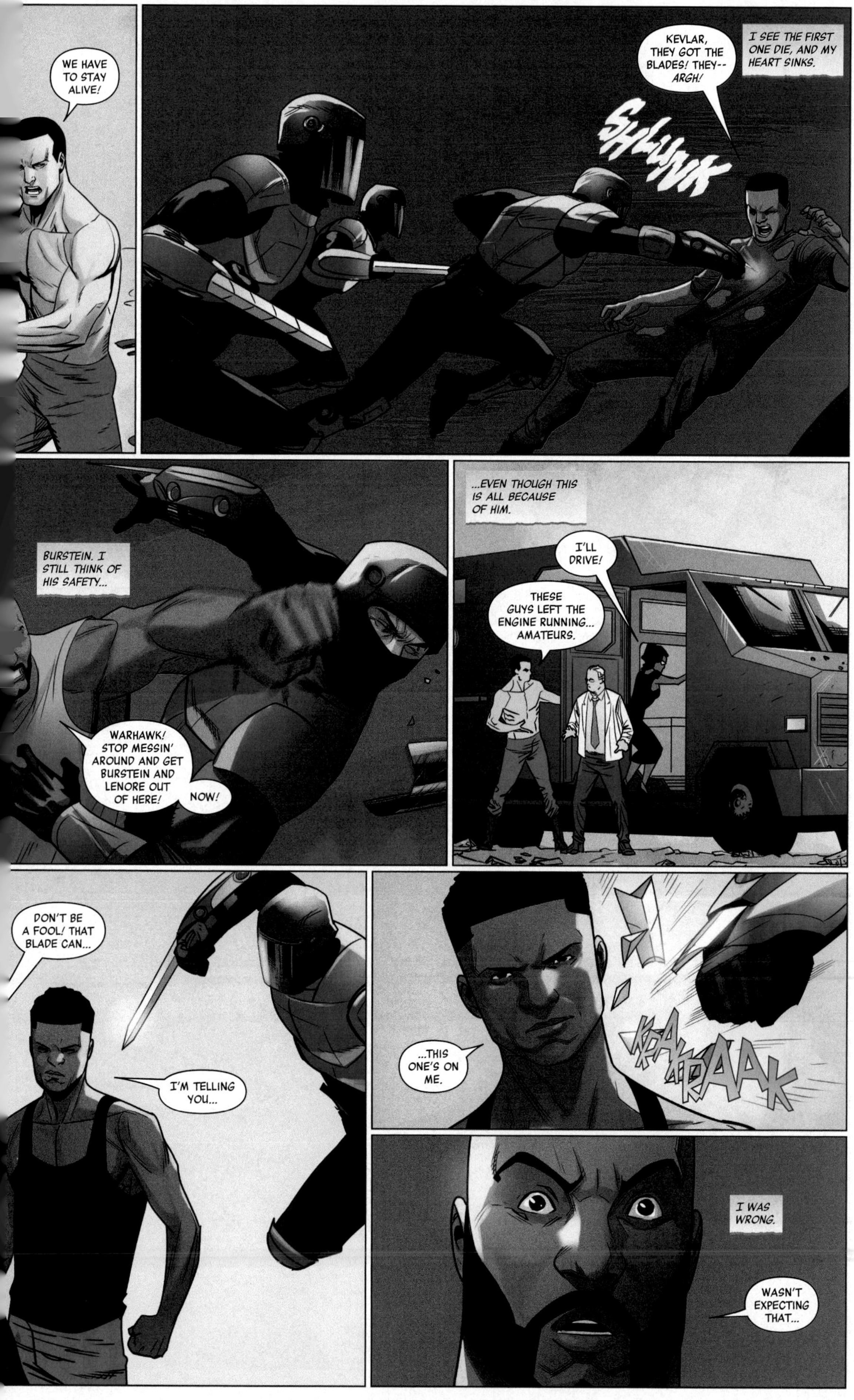
WE HAVE TO STAY ALIVE!
I SEE THE FIRST ONE DIE, AND MY HEART SINKS.
KEVLAR, THEY GOT THE BLADES! THEY-- ARGH!
SHLUNK
BURSTEIN. I STILL THINK OF HIS SAFETY...
WARHAWK! STOP MESSIN' AROUND AND GET BURSTEIN AND LENORE OUT OF HERE!
NOW!
...EVEN THOUGH THIS IS ALL BECAUSE OF HIM.
I'LL DRIVE!
THESE GUYS LEFT THE ENGINE RUNNING... AMATEURS.
DON'T BE A FOOL! THAT BLADE CAN...
I'M TELLING YOU...
...THIS ONE'S ON ME.
KRAKRAAK
I WAS WRONG.
WASN'T EXPECTING THAT...

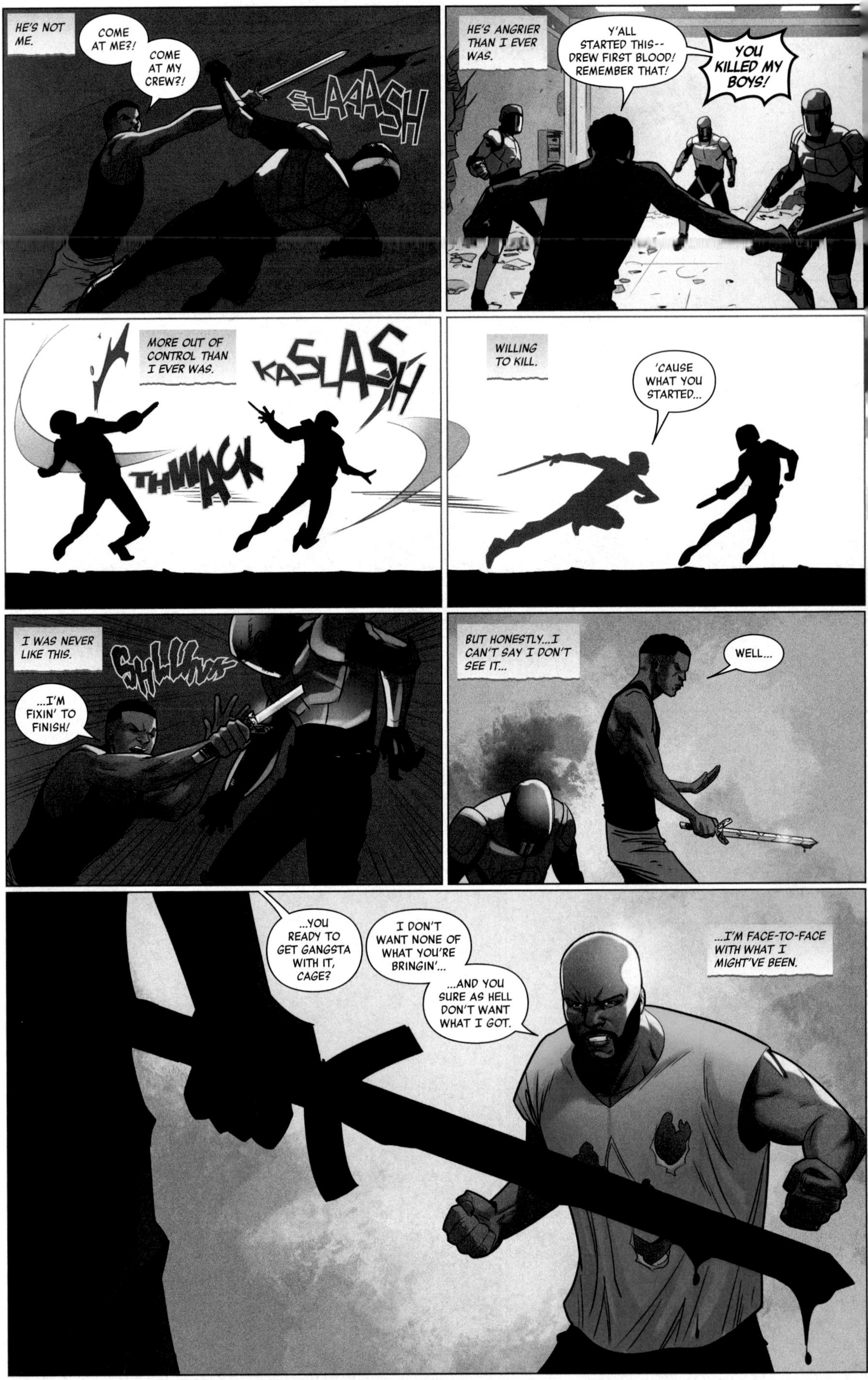
HE'S NOT ME.
COME AT ME?!
COME AT MY CREW?!
SLAAASH
HE'S ANGRIER THAN I EVER WAS.
Y'ALL STARTED THIS-- DREW FIRST BLOOD! REMEMBER THAT!
YOU KILLED MY BOYS!
MORE OUT OF CONTROL THAN I EVER WAS.
KASLASH
THWACK
WILLING TO KILL.
'CAUSE WHAT YOU STARTED...
I WAS NEVER LIKE THIS.
SHLUNK
...I'M FIXIN' TO FINISH!
BUT HONESTLY...I CAN'T SAY I DON'T SEE IT...
WELL...
...YOU READY TO GET GANGSTA WITH IT, CAGE?
I DON'T WANT NONE OF WHAT YOU'RE BRINGIN'...
...AND YOU SURE AS HELL DON'T WANT WHAT I GOT.
...I'M FACE-TO-FACE WITH WHAT I MIGHT'VE BEEN.

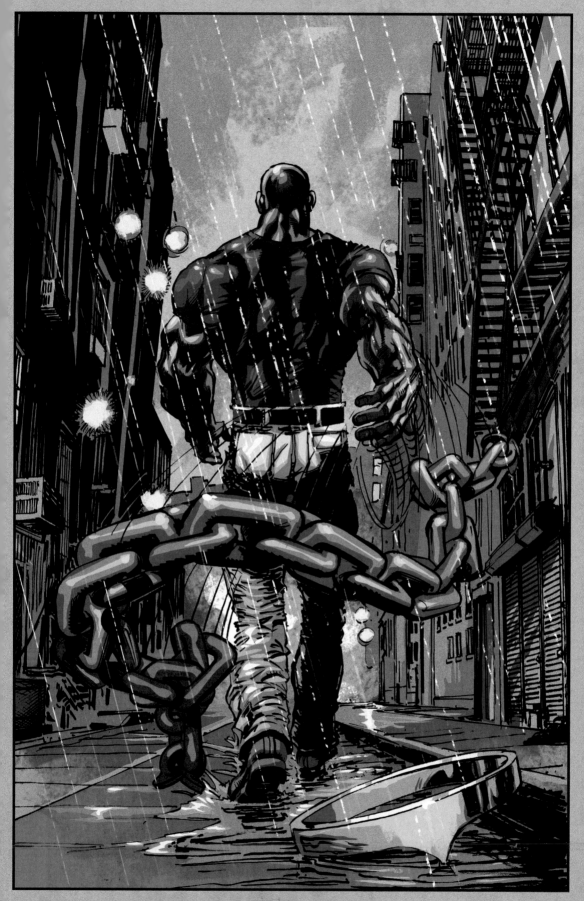

#1 VARIANT BY
NEAL ADAMS & **DAVE McCAIG**

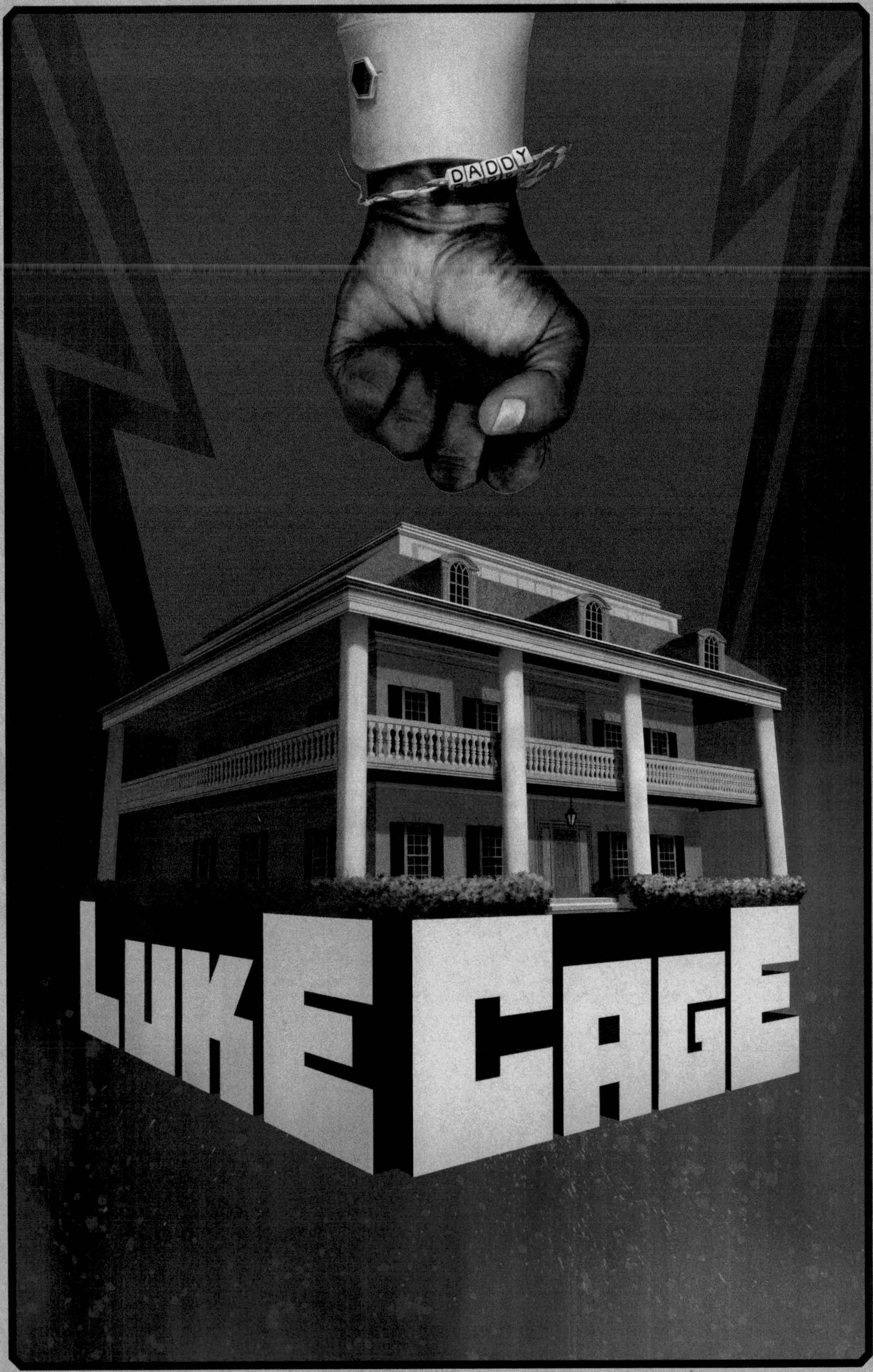
DADDY
LUKE CAGE

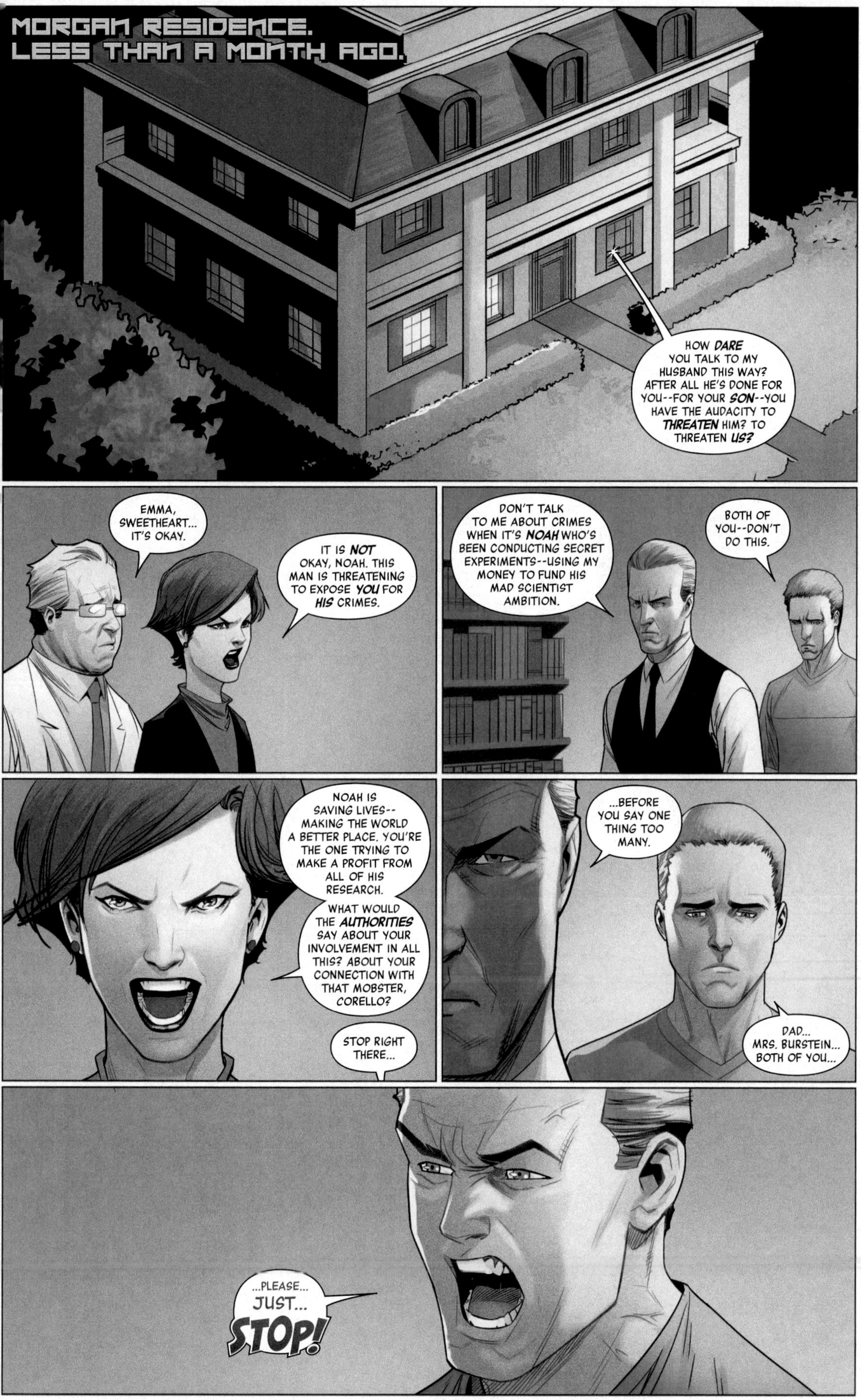
MORGAN RESIDENCE.
LESS THAN A MONTH AGO.
HOW DARE YOU TALK TO MY HUSBAND THIS WAY? AFTER ALL HE'S DONE FOR YOU--FOR YOUR SON--YOU HAVE THE AUDACITY TO THREATEN HIM? TO THREATEN US?
EMMA, SWEETHEART... IT'S OKAY.
IT IS NOT OKAY, NOAH. THIS MAN IS THREATENING TO EXPOSE YOU FOR HIS CRIMES.
DON'T TALK TO ME ABOUT CRIMES WHEN IT'S NOAH WHO'S BEEN CONDUCTING SECRET EXPERIMENTS--USING MY MONEY TO FUND HIS MAD SCIENTIST AMBITION.
BOTH OF YOU--DON'T DO THIS.
NOAH IS SAVING LIVES--MAKING THE WORLD A BETTER PLACE. YOU'RE THE ONE TRYING TO MAKE A PROFIT FROM ALL OF HIS RESEARCH.
WHAT WOULD THE AUTHORITIES SAY ABOUT YOUR INVOLVEMENT IN ALL THIS? ABOUT YOUR CONNECTION WITH THAT MOBSTER, CORELLO?
STOP RIGHT THERE...
...BEFORE YOU SAY ONE THING TOO MANY.
DAD... MRS. BURSTEIN... BOTH OF YOU...
...PLEASE... JUST... STOP!

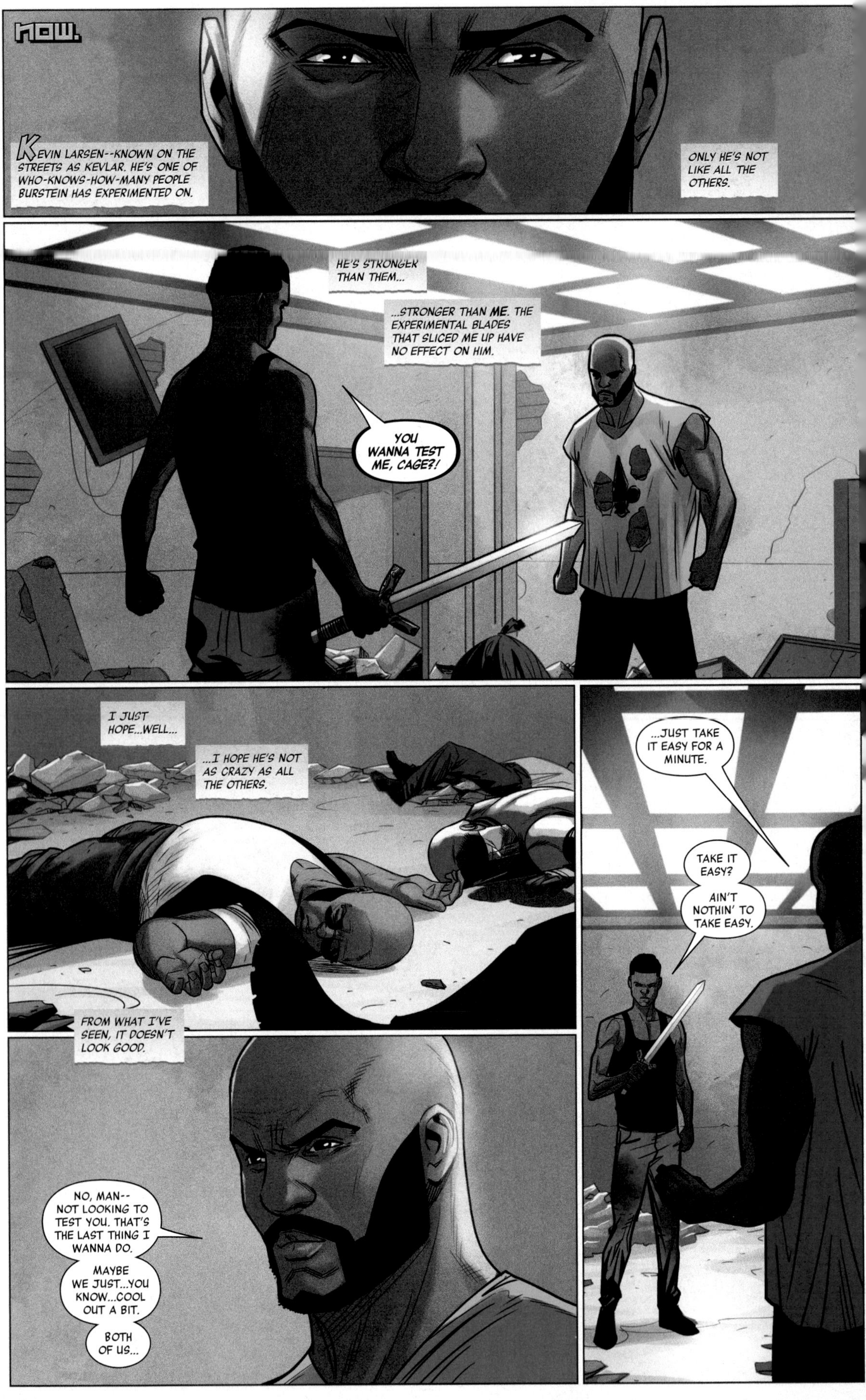
NOW.
KEVIN LARSEN--KNOWN ON THE STREETS AS KEVLAR. HE'S ONE OF WHO-KNOWS-HOW-MANY PEOPLE BURSTEIN HAS EXPERIMENTED ON.
ONLY HE'S NOT LIKE ALL THE OTHERS.
HE'S STRONGER THAN THEM...
...STRONGER THAN ME. THE EXPERIMENTAL BLADES THAT SLICED ME UP HAVE NO EFFECT ON HIM.
YOU WANNA TEST ME, CAGE?!
I JUST HOPE...WELL...
...I HOPE HE'S NOT AS CRAZY AS ALL THE OTHERS.
FROM WHAT I'VE SEEN, IT DOESN'T LOOK GOOD.
NO, MAN--NOT LOOKING TO TEST YOU. THAT'S THE LAST THING I WANNA DO.
MAYBE WE JUST...YOU KNOW...COOL OUT A BIT.
BOTH OF US...
...JUST TAKE IT EASY FOR A MINUTE.
TAKE IT EASY?
AIN'T NOTHIN' TO TAKE EASY.

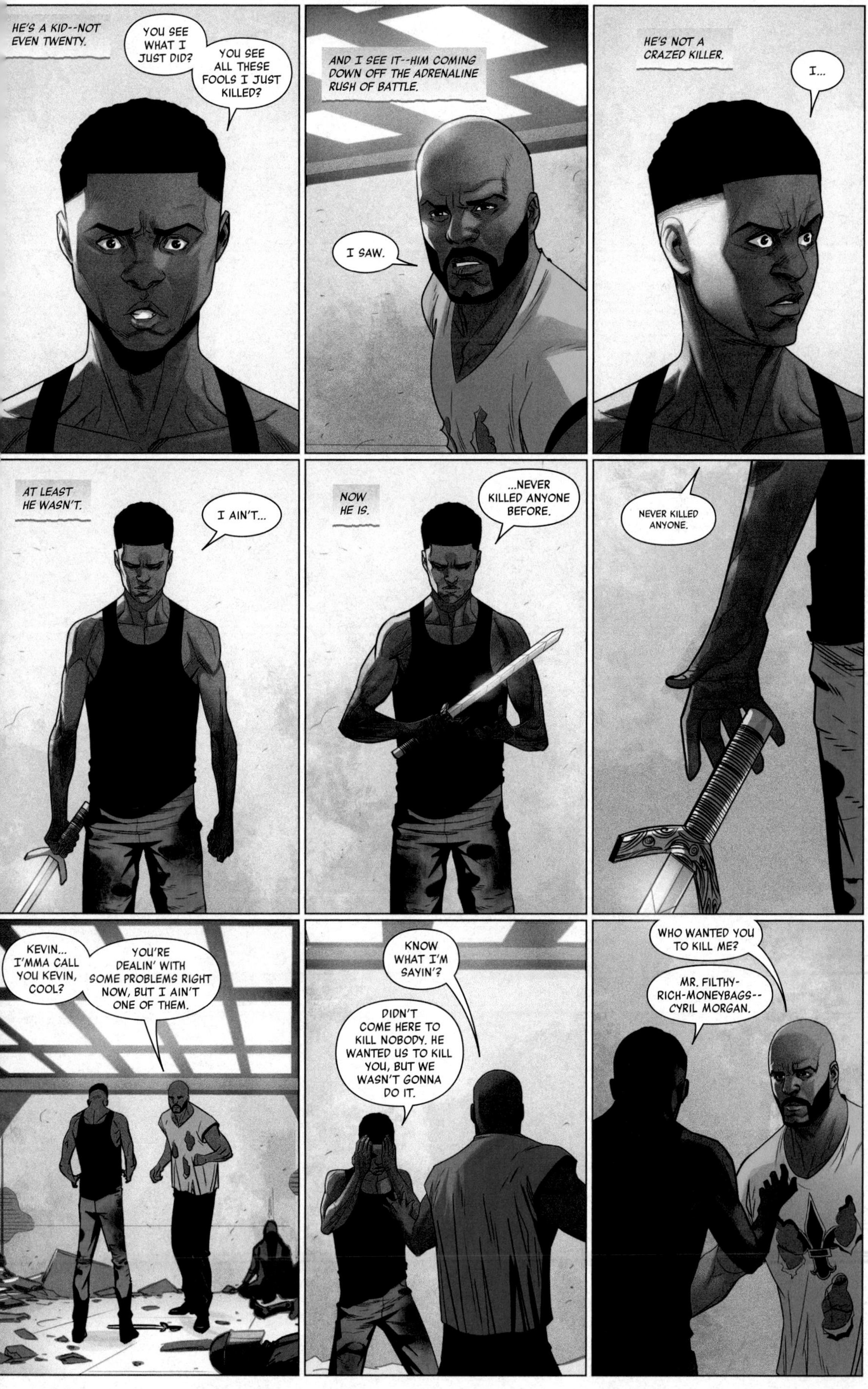
HE'S A KID--NOT EVEN TWENTY.
YOU SEE WHAT I JUST DID?
YOU SEE ALL THESE FOOLS I JUST KILLED?
AND I SEE IT--HIM COMING DOWN OFF THE ADRENALINE RUSH OF BATTLE.
I SAW.
HE'S NOT A CRAZED KILLER.
I...
AT LEAST HE WASN'T.
I AIN'T...
NOW HE IS.
...NEVER KILLED ANYONE BEFORE.
NEVER KILLED ANYONE.
KEVIN... I'MMA CALL YOU KEVIN, COOL?
YOU'RE DEALIN' WITH SOME PROBLEMS RIGHT NOW, BUT I AIN'T ONE OF THEM.
KNOW WHAT I'M SAYIN'?
DIDN'T COME HERE TO KILL NOBODY. HE WANTED US TO KILL YOU, BUT WE WASN'T GONNA DO IT.
WHO WANTED YOU TO KILL ME?
MR. FILTHY-RICH-MONEYBAGS--CYRIL MORGAN.

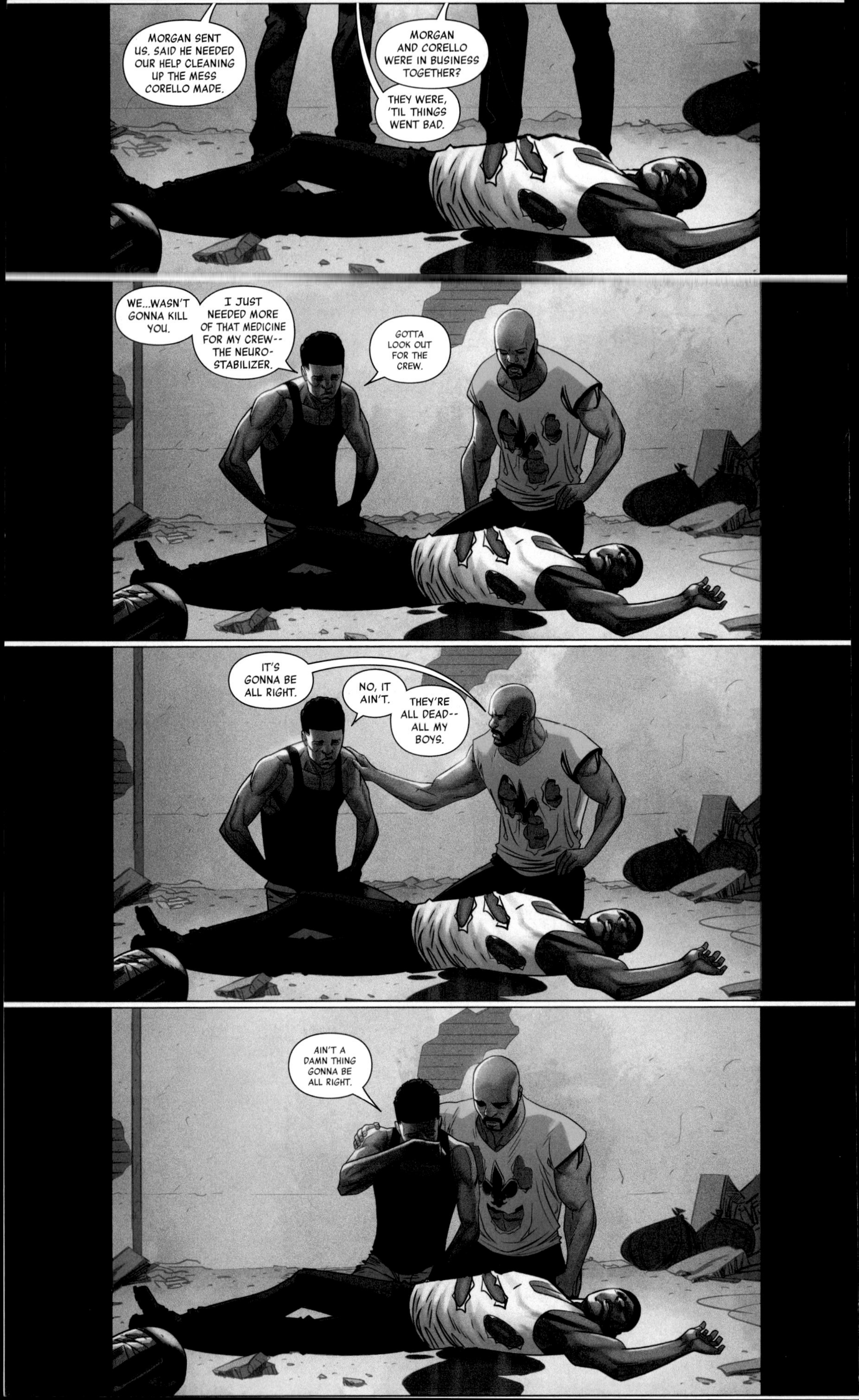
MORGAN SENT US. SAID HE NEEDED OUR HELP CLEANING UP THE MESS CORELLO MADE.
MORGAN AND CORELLO WERE IN BUSINESS TOGETHER?
THEY WERE, 'TIL THINGS WENT BAD.
WE...WASN'T GONNA KILL YOU.
I JUST NEEDED MORE OF THAT MEDICINE FOR MY CREW-- THE NEURO-STABILIZER.
GOTTA LOOK OUT FOR THE CREW.
IT'S GONNA BE ALL RIGHT.
NO, IT AIN'T.
THEY'RE ALL DEAD-- ALL MY BOYS.
AIN'T A DAMN THING GONNA BE ALL RIGHT.

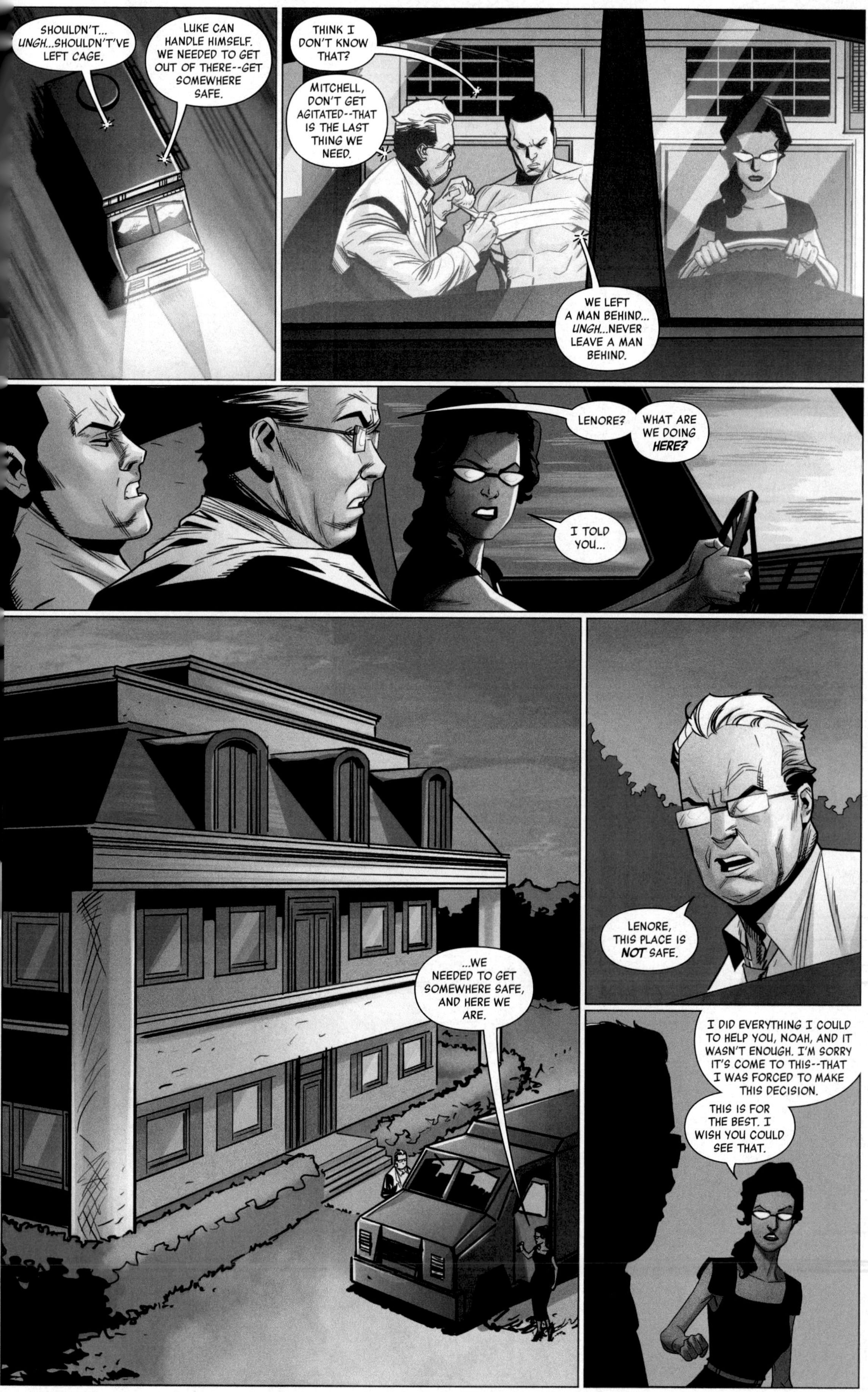
SHOULDN'T... UNGH...SHOULDN'T'VE LEFT CAGE.
LUKE CAN HANDLE HIMSELF. WE NEEDED TO GET OUT OF THERE--GET SOMEWHERE SAFE.
THINK I DON'T KNOW THAT?
MITCHELL, DON'T GET AGITATED--THAT IS THE LAST THING WE NEED.
WE LEFT A MAN BEHIND... UNGH...NEVER LEAVE A MAN BEHIND.
LENORE?
WHAT ARE WE DOING HERE?
I TOLD YOU...
...WE NEEDED TO GET SOMEWHERE SAFE, AND HERE WE ARE.
LENORE, THIS PLACE IS NOT SAFE.
I DID EVERYTHING I COULD TO HELP YOU, NOAH, AND IT WASN'T ENOUGH. I'M SORRY IT'S COME TO THIS--THAT I WAS FORCED TO MAKE THIS DECISION.
THIS IS FOR THE BEST. I WISH YOU COULD SEE THAT.

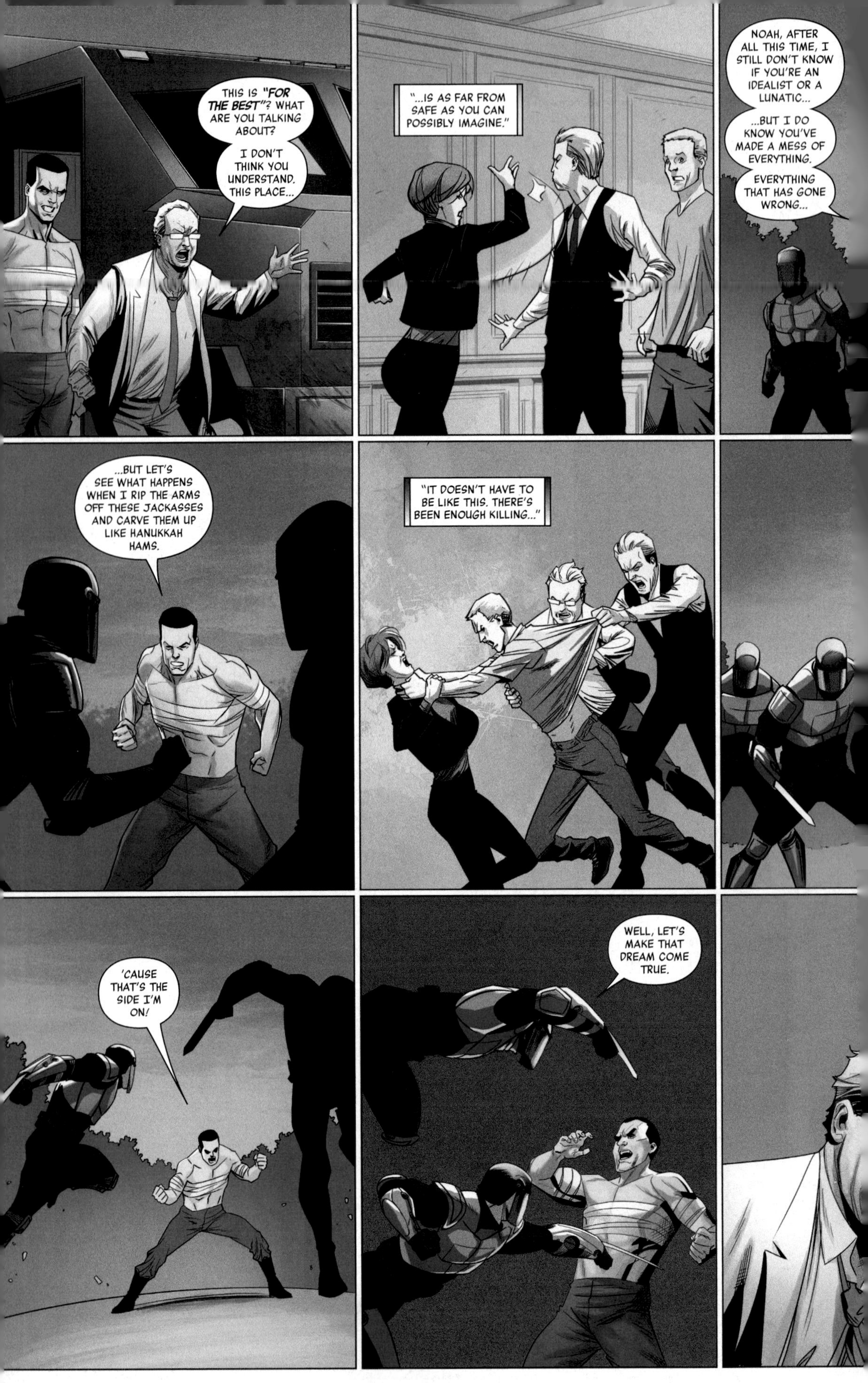
THIS IS "FOR THE BEST"? WHAT ARE YOU TALKING ABOUT?
I DON'T THINK YOU UNDERSTAND. THIS PLACE...
"...IS AS FAR FROM SAFE AS YOU CAN POSSIBLY IMAGINE."
NOAH, AFTER ALL THIS TIME, I STILL DON'T KNOW IF YOU'RE AN IDEALIST OR A LUNATIC...
...BUT I DO KNOW YOU'VE MADE A MESS OF EVERYTHING.
EVERYTHING THAT HAS GONE WRONG...
...BUT LET'S SEE WHAT HAPPENS WHEN I RIP THE ARMS OFF THESE JACKASSES AND CARVE THEM UP LIKE HANUKKAH HAMS.
"IT DOESN'T HAVE TO BE LIKE THIS. THERE'S BEEN ENOUGH KILLING..."
'CAUSE THAT'S THE SIDE I'M ON!
WELL, LET'S MAKE THAT DREAM COME TRUE.

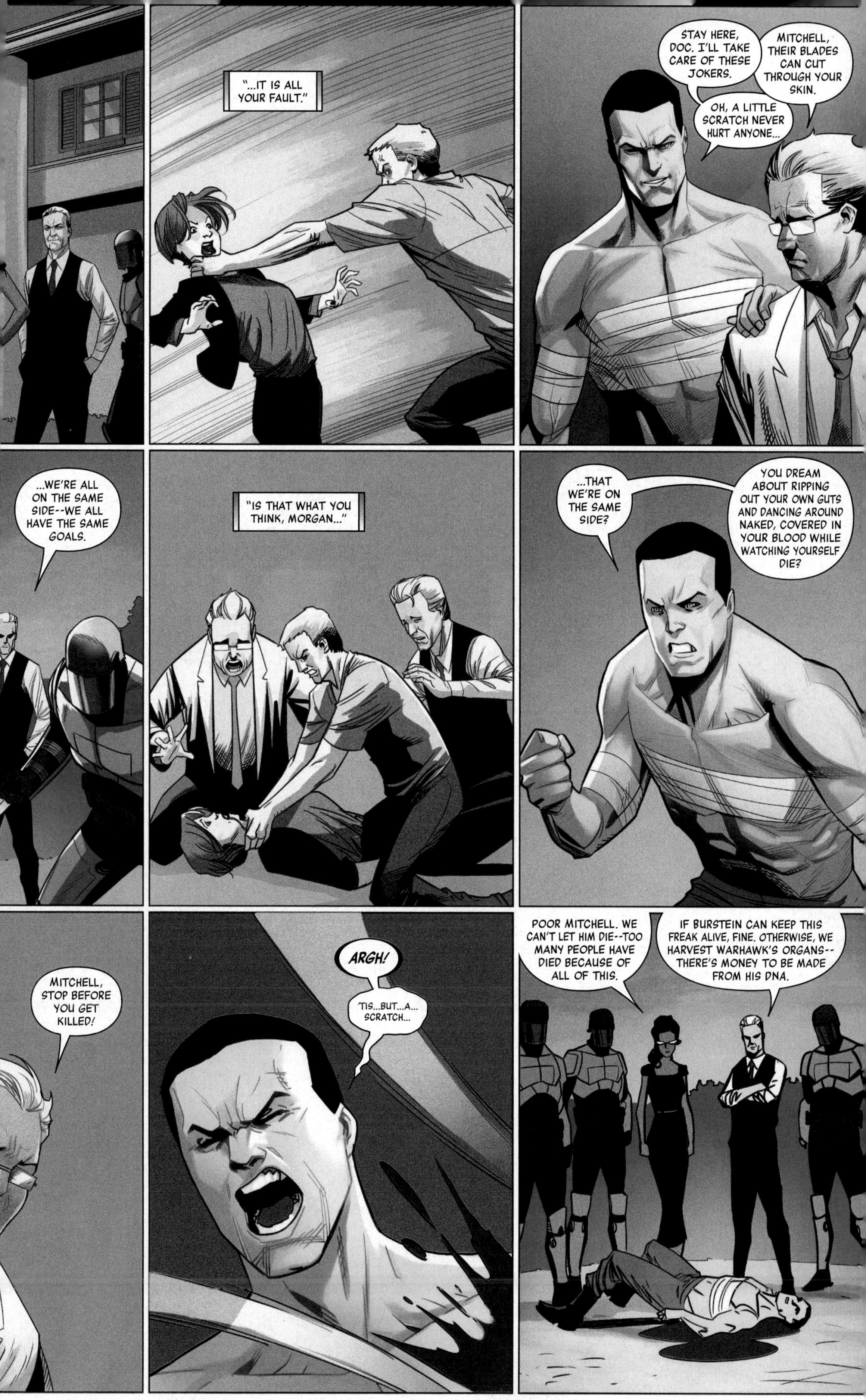
"...IT IS ALL YOUR FAULT."
STAY HERE, DOC. I'LL TAKE CARE OF THESE JOKERS.
MITCHELL, THEIR BLADES CAN CUT THROUGH YOUR SKIN.
OH, A LITTLE SCRATCH NEVER HURT ANYONE...
...WE'RE ALL ON THE SAME SIDE--WE ALL HAVE THE SAME GOALS.
"IS THAT WHAT YOU THINK, MORGAN..."
...THAT WE'RE ON THE SAME SIDE?
YOU DREAM ABOUT RIPPING OUT YOUR OWN GUTS AND DANCING AROUND NAKED, COVERED IN YOUR BLOOD WHILE WATCHING YOURSELF DIE?
MITCHELL, STOP BEFORE YOU GET KILLED!
ARGH!
'TIS...BUT...A... SCRATCH...
POOR MITCHELL. WE CAN'T LET HIM DIE--TOO MANY PEOPLE HAVE DIED BECAUSE OF ALL OF THIS.
IF BURSTEIN CAN KEEP THIS FREAK ALIVE, FINE. OTHERWISE, WE HARVEST WARHAWK'S ORGANS--THERE'S MONEY TO BE MADE FROM HIS DNA.

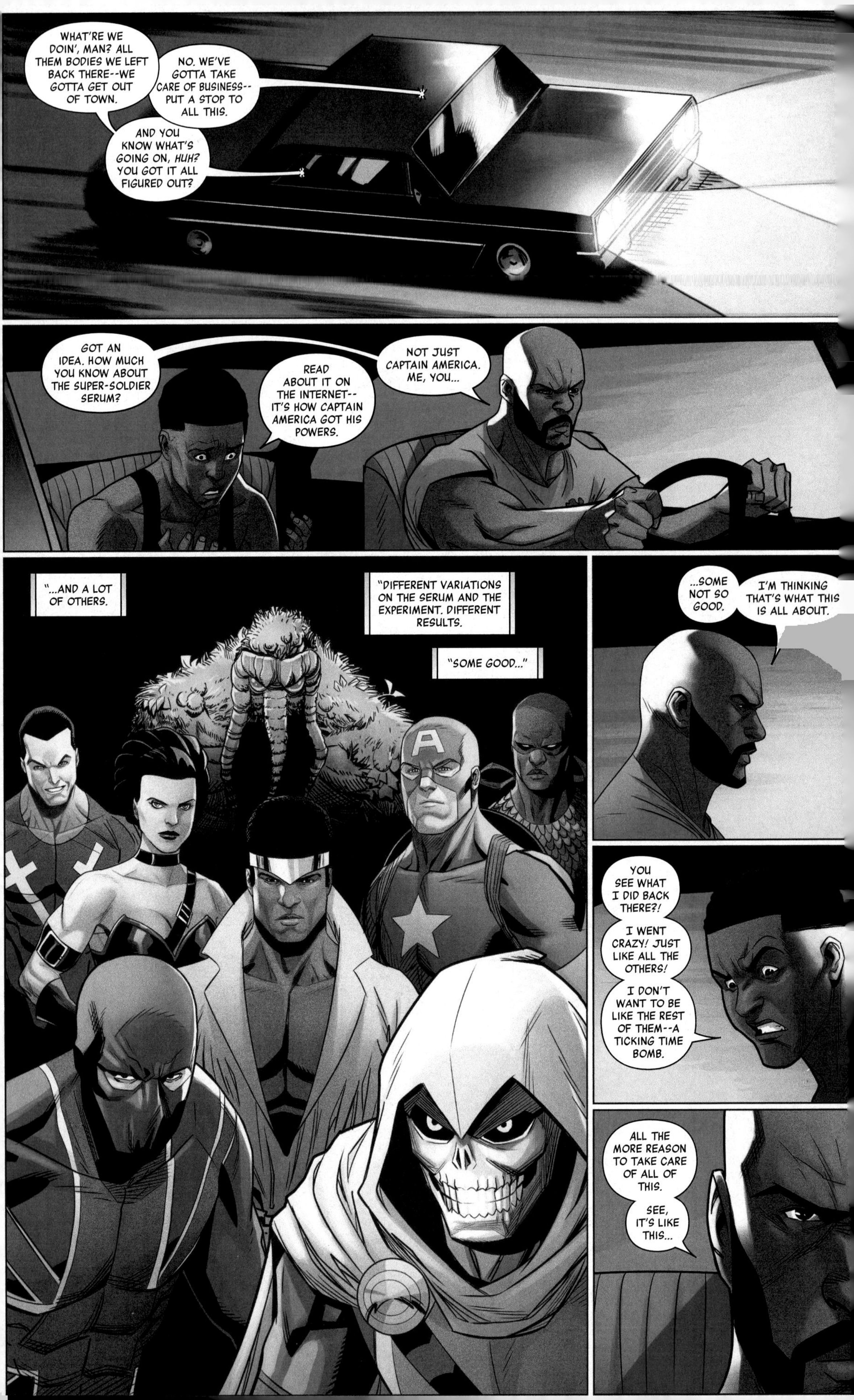
WHAT'RE WE DOIN', MAN? ALL THEM BODIES WE LEFT BACK THERE--WE GOTTA GET OUT OF TOWN.
NO. WE'VE GOTTA TAKE CARE OF BUSINESS--PUT A STOP TO ALL THIS.
AND YOU KNOW WHAT'S GOING ON, HUH? YOU GOT IT ALL FIGURED OUT?
GOT AN IDEA. HOW MUCH YOU KNOW ABOUT THE SUPER-SOLDIER SERUM?
READ ABOUT IT ON THE INTERNET--IT'S HOW CAPTAIN AMERICA GOT HIS POWERS.
NOT JUST CAPTAIN AMERICA. ME, YOU...
"...AND A LOT OF OTHERS.
"DIFFERENT VARIATIONS ON THE SERUM AND THE EXPERIMENT. DIFFERENT RESULTS.
"SOME GOOD..."
...SOME NOT SO GOOD.
I'M THINKING THAT'S WHAT THIS IS ALL ABOUT.
YOU SEE WHAT I DID BACK THERE?!
I WENT CRAZY! JUST LIKE ALL THE OTHERS!
I DON'T WANT TO BE LIKE THE REST OF THEM--A TICKING TIME BOMB.
ALL THE MORE REASON TO TAKE CARE OF ALL OF THIS.
SEE, IT'S LIKE THIS...

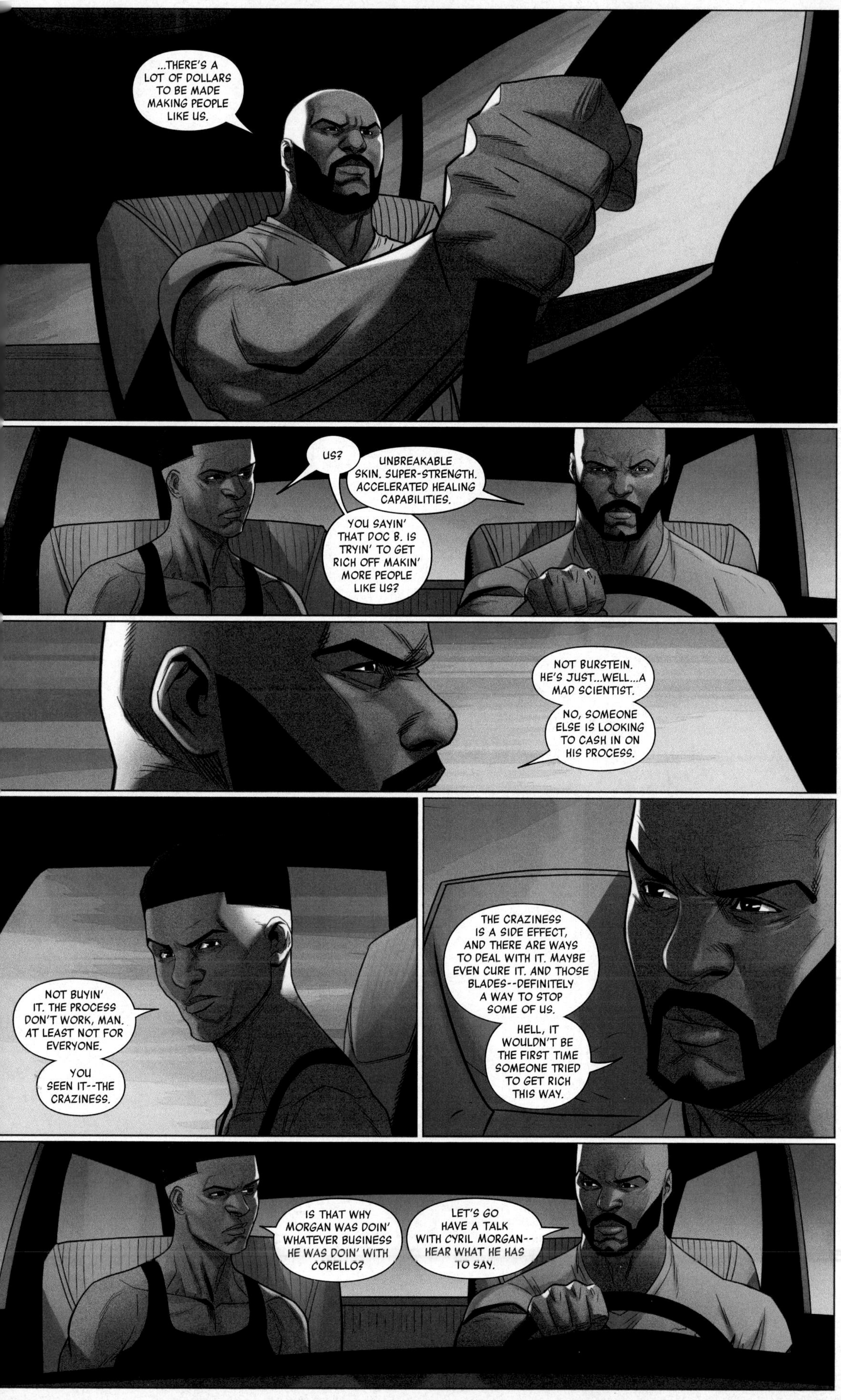
...THERE'S A LOT OF DOLLARS TO BE MADE MAKING PEOPLE LIKE US.
US?
UNBREAKABLE SKIN. SUPER-STRENGTH. ACCELERATED HEALING CAPABILITIES.
YOU SAYIN' THAT DOC B. IS TRYIN' TO GET RICH OFF MAKIN' MORE PEOPLE LIKE US?
NOT BURSTEIN. HE'S JUST...WELL...A MAD SCIENTIST.
NO, SOMEONE ELSE IS LOOKING TO CASH IN ON HIS PROCESS.
NOT BUYIN' IT. THE PROCESS DON'T WORK, MAN. AT LEAST NOT FOR EVERYONE.
YOU SEEN IT--THE CRAZINESS.
THE CRAZINESS IS A SIDE EFFECT, AND THERE ARE WAYS TO DEAL WITH IT. MAYBE EVEN CURE IT. AND THOSE BLADES--DEFINITELY A WAY TO STOP SOME OF US.
HELL, IT WOULDN'T BE THE FIRST TIME SOMEONE TRIED TO GET RICH THIS WAY.
IS THAT WHY MORGAN WAS DOIN' WHATEVER BUSINESS HE WAS DOIN' WITH CORELLO?
LET'S GO HAVE A TALK WITH CYRIL MORGAN--HEAR WHAT HE HAS TO SAY.

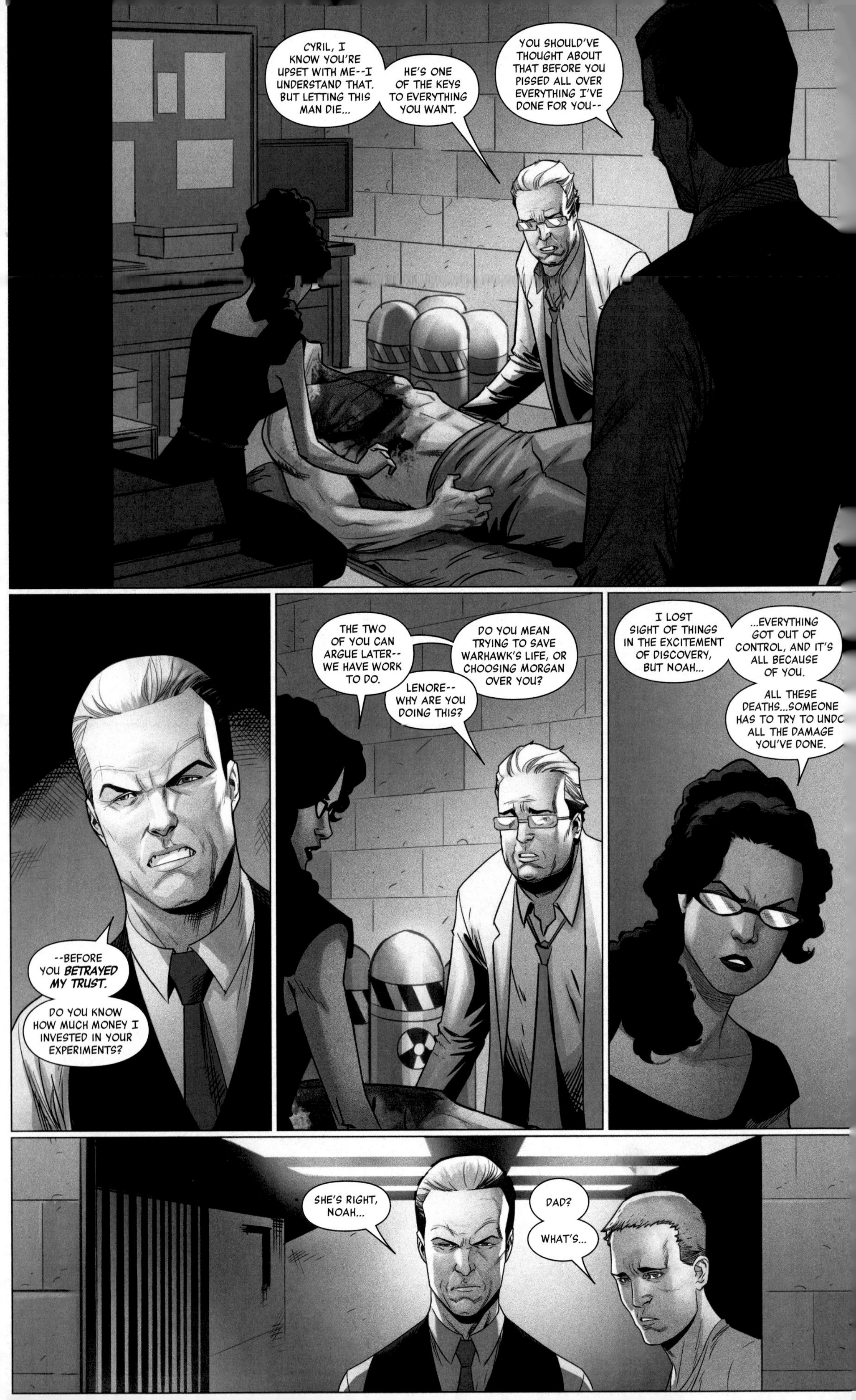
CYRIL, I KNOW YOU'RE UPSET WITH ME--I UNDERSTAND THAT. BUT LETTING THIS MAN DIE...
HE'S ONE OF THE KEYS TO EVERYTHING YOU WANT.
YOU SHOULD'VE THOUGHT ABOUT THAT BEFORE YOU PISSED ALL OVER EVERYTHING I'VE DONE FOR YOU--
--BEFORE YOU **BETRAYED MY TRUST.**
DO YOU KNOW HOW MUCH MONEY I INVESTED IN YOUR EXPERIMENTS?
THE TWO OF YOU CAN ARGUE LATER--WE HAVE WORK TO DO.
DO YOU MEAN TRYING TO SAVE WARHAWK'S LIFE, OR CHOOSING MORGAN OVER YOU?
LENORE--WHY ARE YOU DOING THIS?
I LOST SIGHT OF THINGS IN THE EXCITEMENT OF DISCOVERY, BUT NOAH...
...EVERYTHING GOT OUT OF CONTROL, AND IT'S ALL BECAUSE OF YOU.
ALL THESE DEATHS...SOMEONE HAS TO TRY TO UNDO ALL THE DAMAGE YOU'VE DONE.
SHE'S RIGHT, NOAH...
DAD?
WHAT'S...

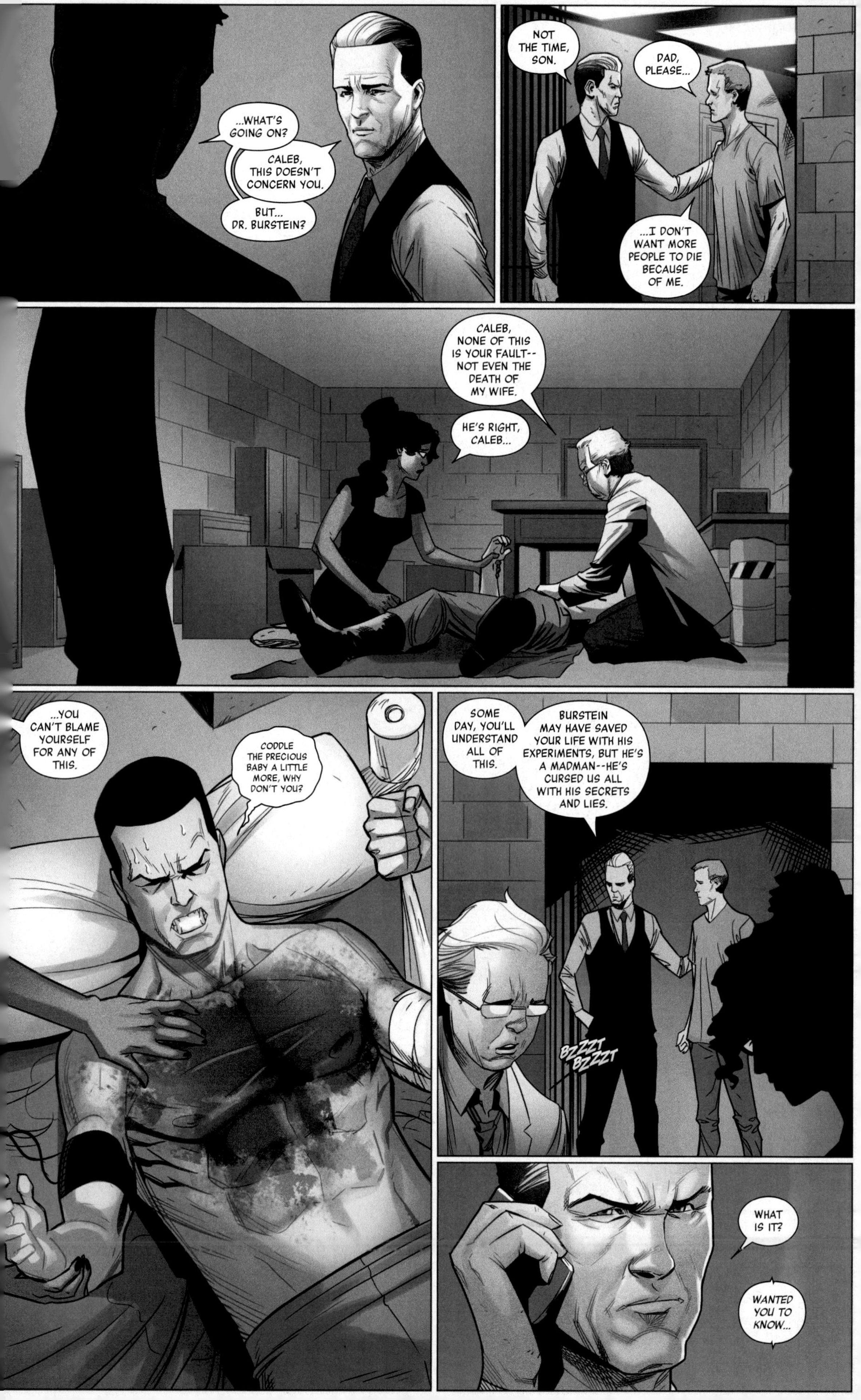
...WHAT'S GOING ON?
CALEB, THIS DOESN'T CONCERN YOU.
BUT... DR. BURSTEIN?
NOT THE TIME, SON.
DAD, PLEASE...
...I DON'T WANT MORE PEOPLE TO DIE BECAUSE OF ME.
CALEB, NONE OF THIS IS YOUR FAULT--NOT EVEN THE DEATH OF MY WIFE.
HE'S RIGHT, CALEB...
...YOU CAN'T BLAME YOURSELF FOR ANY OF THIS.
CODDLE THE PRECIOUS BABY A LITTLE MORE, WHY DON'T YOU?
SOME DAY, YOU'LL UNDERSTAND ALL OF THIS.
BURSTEIN MAY HAVE SAVED YOUR LIFE WITH HIS EXPERIMENTS, BUT HE'S A MADMAN--HE'S CURSED US ALL WITH HIS SECRETS AND LIES.
BZZZT BZZZT
WHAT IS IT?
WANTED YOU TO KNOW...

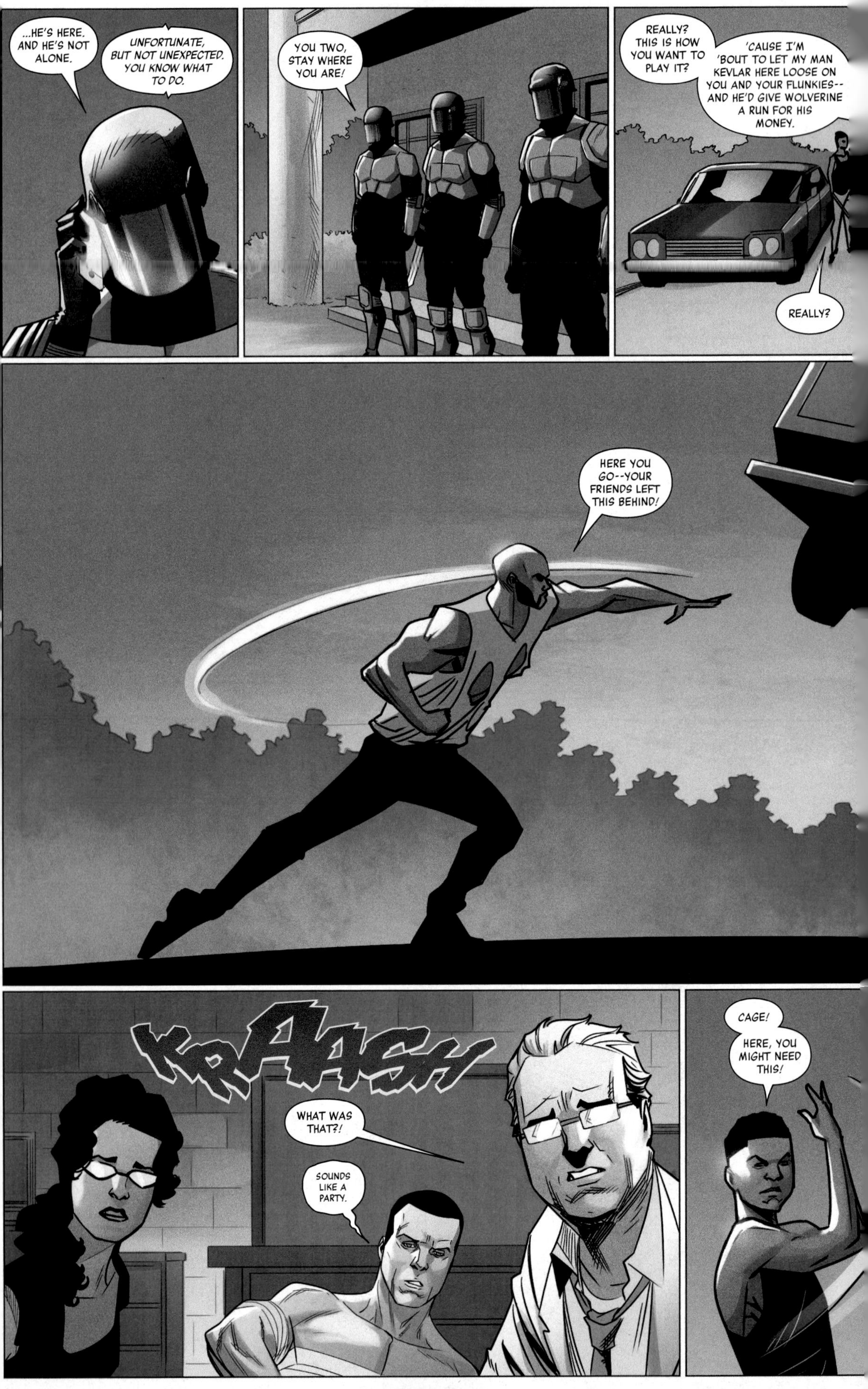
...HE'S HERE. AND HE'S NOT ALONE.
UNFORTUNATE, BUT NOT UNEXPECTED. YOU KNOW WHAT TO DO.
YOU TWO, STAY WHERE YOU ARE!
REALLY? THIS IS HOW YOU WANT TO PLAY IT?
'CAUSE I'M 'BOUT TO LET MY MAN KEVLAR HERE LOOSE ON YOU AND YOUR FLUNKIES--AND HE'D GIVE WOLVERINE A RUN FOR HIS MONEY.
REALLY?
HERE YOU GO--YOUR FRIENDS LEFT THIS BEHIND!
KRAASH
WHAT WAS THAT?!
SOUNDS LIKE A PARTY.
CAGE!
HERE, YOU MIGHT NEED THIS!

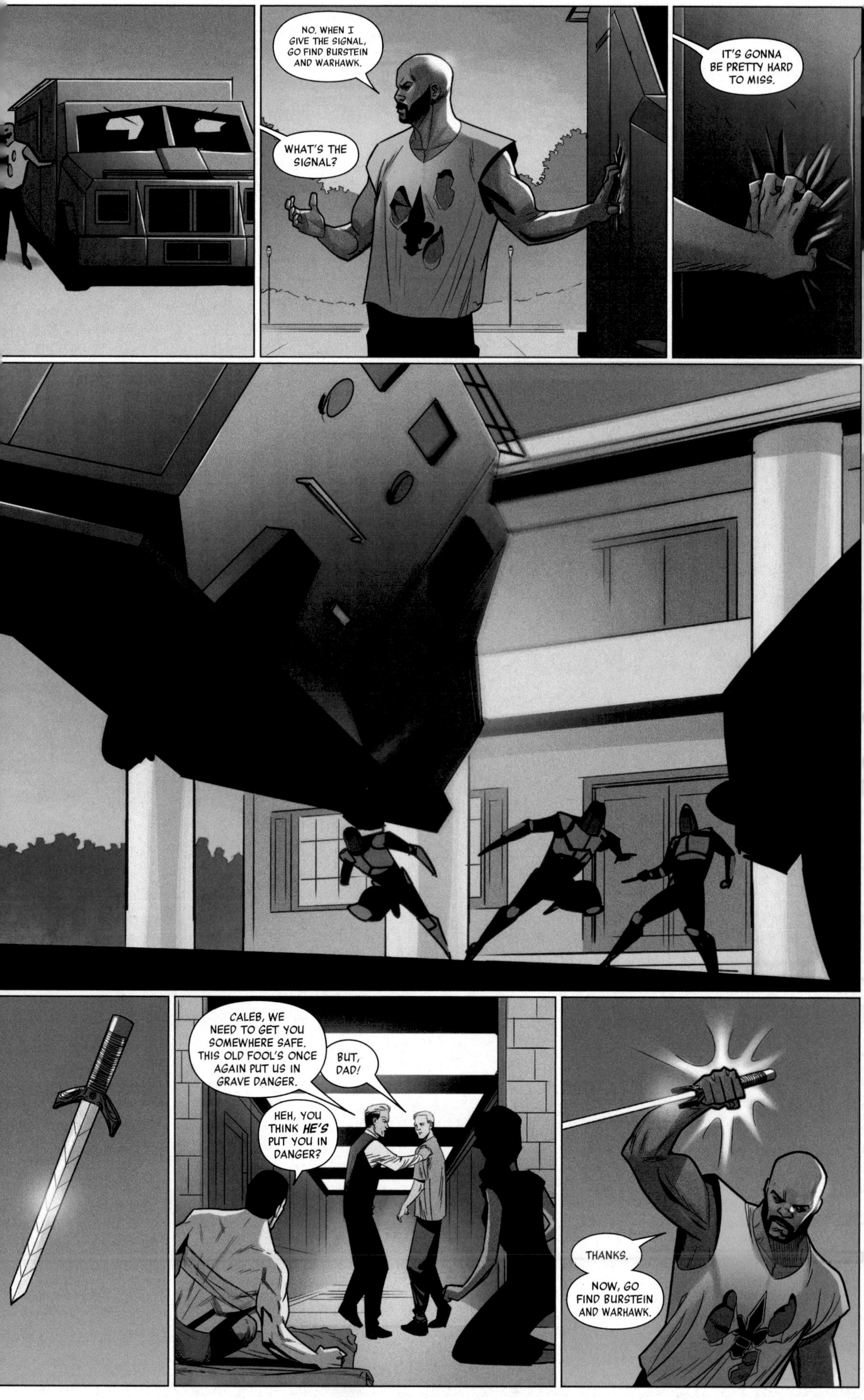
NO. WHEN I GIVE THE SIGNAL, GO FIND BURSTEIN AND WARHAWK.
WHAT'S THE SIGNAL?
IT'S GONNA BE PRETTY HARD TO MISS.
CALEB, WE NEED TO GET YOU SOMEWHERE SAFE. THIS OLD FOOL'S ONCE AGAIN PUT US IN GRAVE DANGER.
BUT, DAD!
HEH, YOU THINK *HE'S* PUT YOU IN DANGER?
THANKS.
NOW, GO FIND BURSTEIN AND WARHAWK.

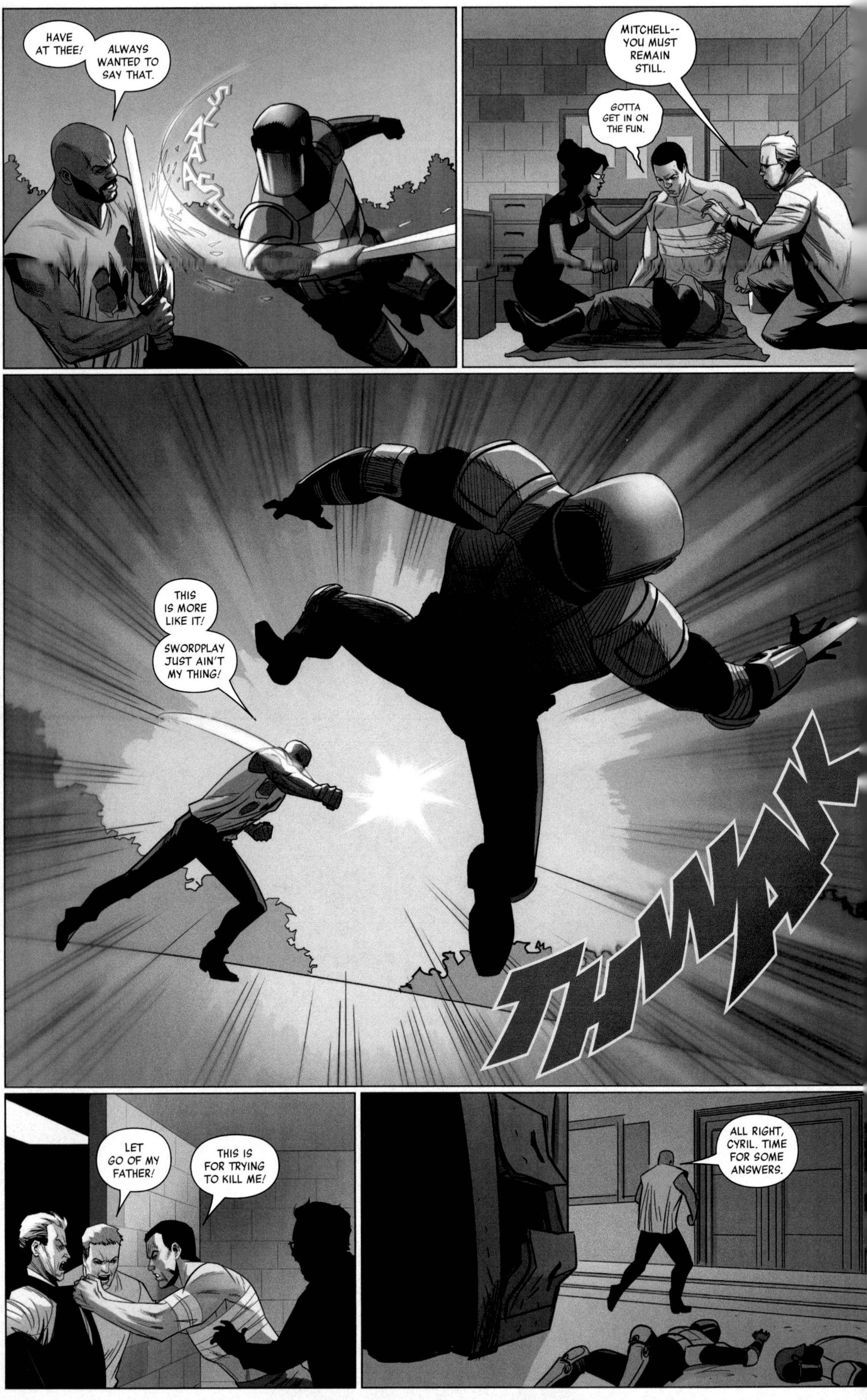
HAVE AT THEE!
ALWAYS WANTED TO SAY THAT.
SLAAASH
MITCHELL-- YOU MUST REMAIN STILL.
GOTTA GET IN ON THE FUN.
THIS IS MORE LIKE IT!
SWORDPLAY JUST AIN'T MY THING!
THWAK
LET GO OF MY FATHER!
THIS IS FOR TRYING TO KILL ME!
ALL RIGHT, CYRIL. TIME FOR SOME ANSWERS.

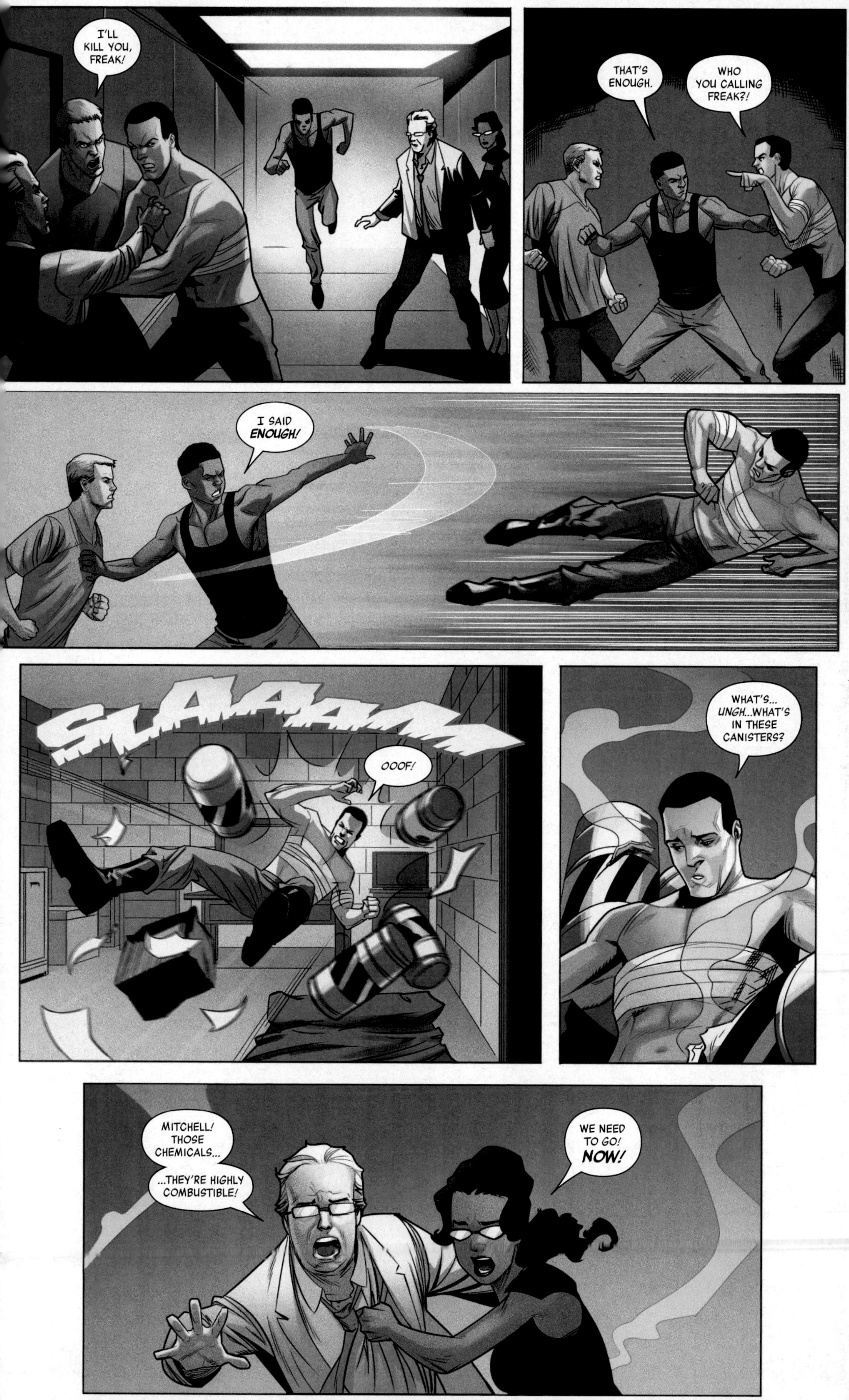

I'LL KILL YOU, FREAK!
THAT'S ENOUGH.
WHO YOU CALLING FREAK?!
I SAID *ENOUGH!*
SLAAAM
OOOF!
WHAT'S... *UNGH*...WHAT'S IN THESE CANISTERS?
MITCHELL! THOSE CHEMICALS...
...THEY'RE HIGHLY COMBUSTIBLE!
WE NEED TO GO! **NOW!**

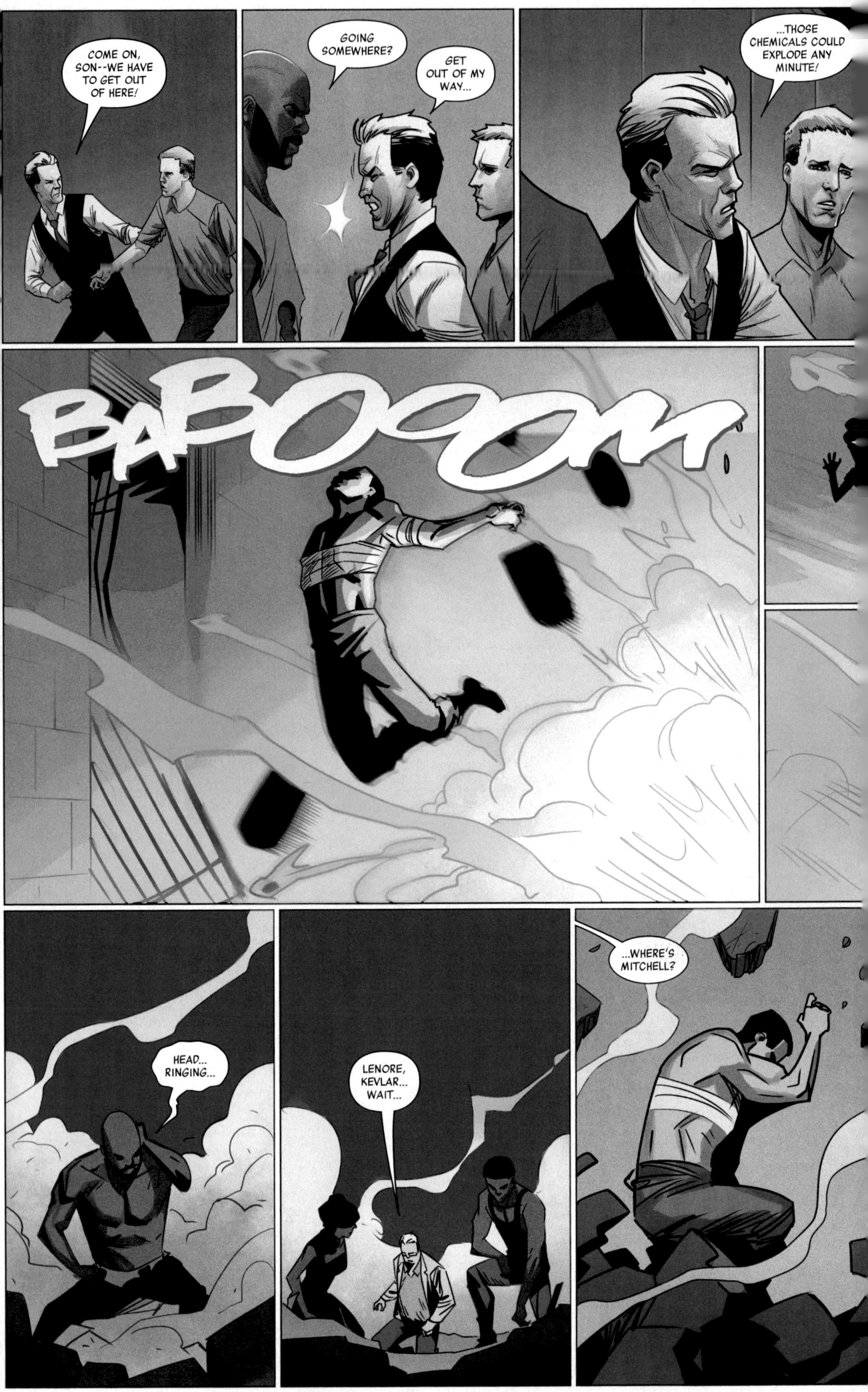
COME ON, SON--WE HAVE TO GET OUT OF HERE!
GOING SOMEWHERE?
GET OUT OF MY WAY...
...THOSE CHEMICALS COULD EXPLODE ANY MINUTE!
BABOOOM
HEAD... RINGING...
LENORE, KEVLAR... WAIT...
...WHERE'S MITCHELL?

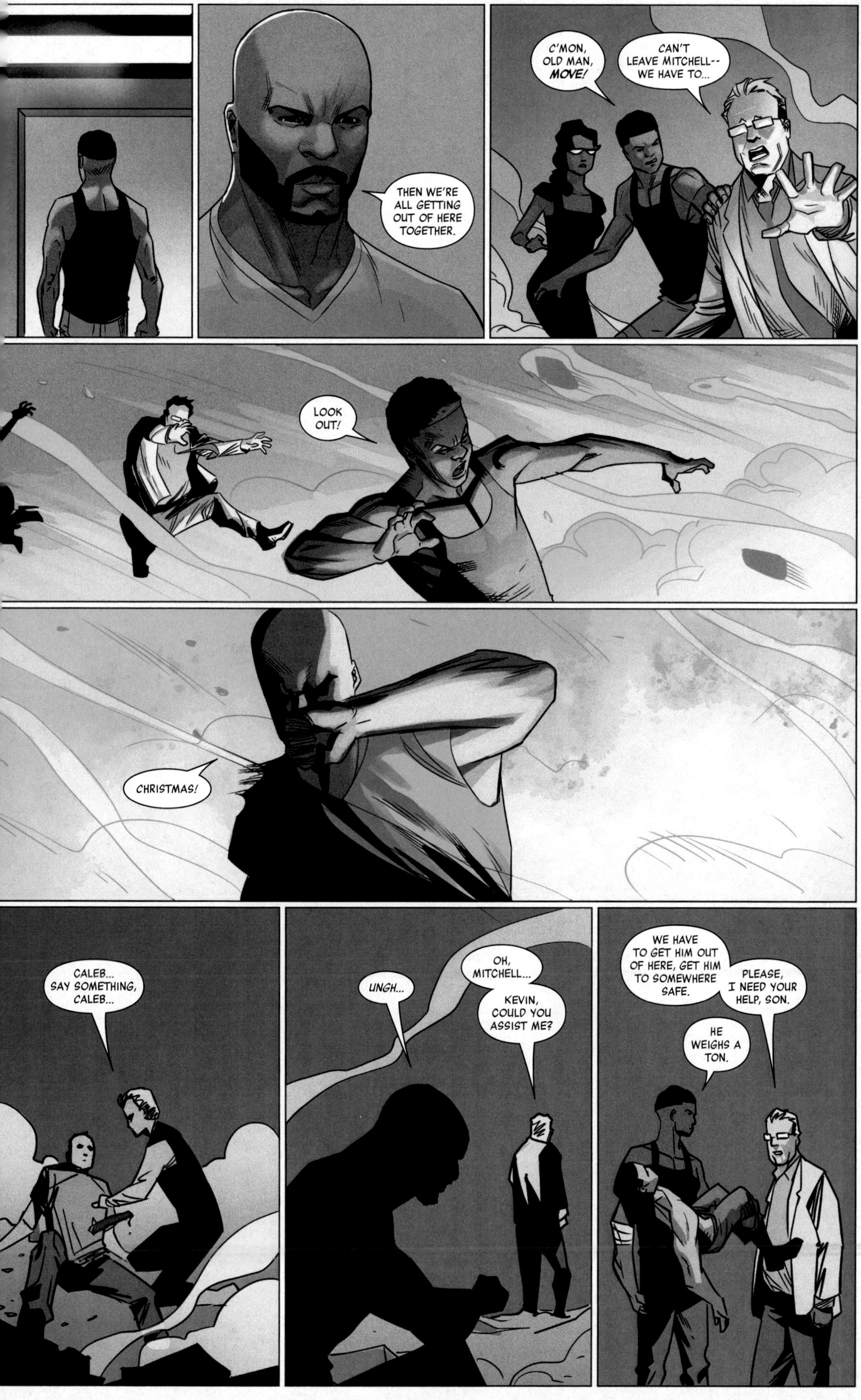

THEN WE'RE ALL GETTING OUT OF HERE TOGETHER.
C'MON, OLD MAN, MOVE!
CAN'T LEAVE MITCHELL-- WE HAVE TO...
LOOK OUT!
CHRISTMAS!
CALEB... SAY SOMETHING, CALEB...
UNGH...
OH, MITCHELL...
KEVIN, COULD YOU ASSIST ME?
WE HAVE TO GET HIM OUT OF HERE, GET HIM TO SOMEWHERE SAFE.
PLEASE, I NEED YOUR HELP, SON.
HE WEIGHS A TON.

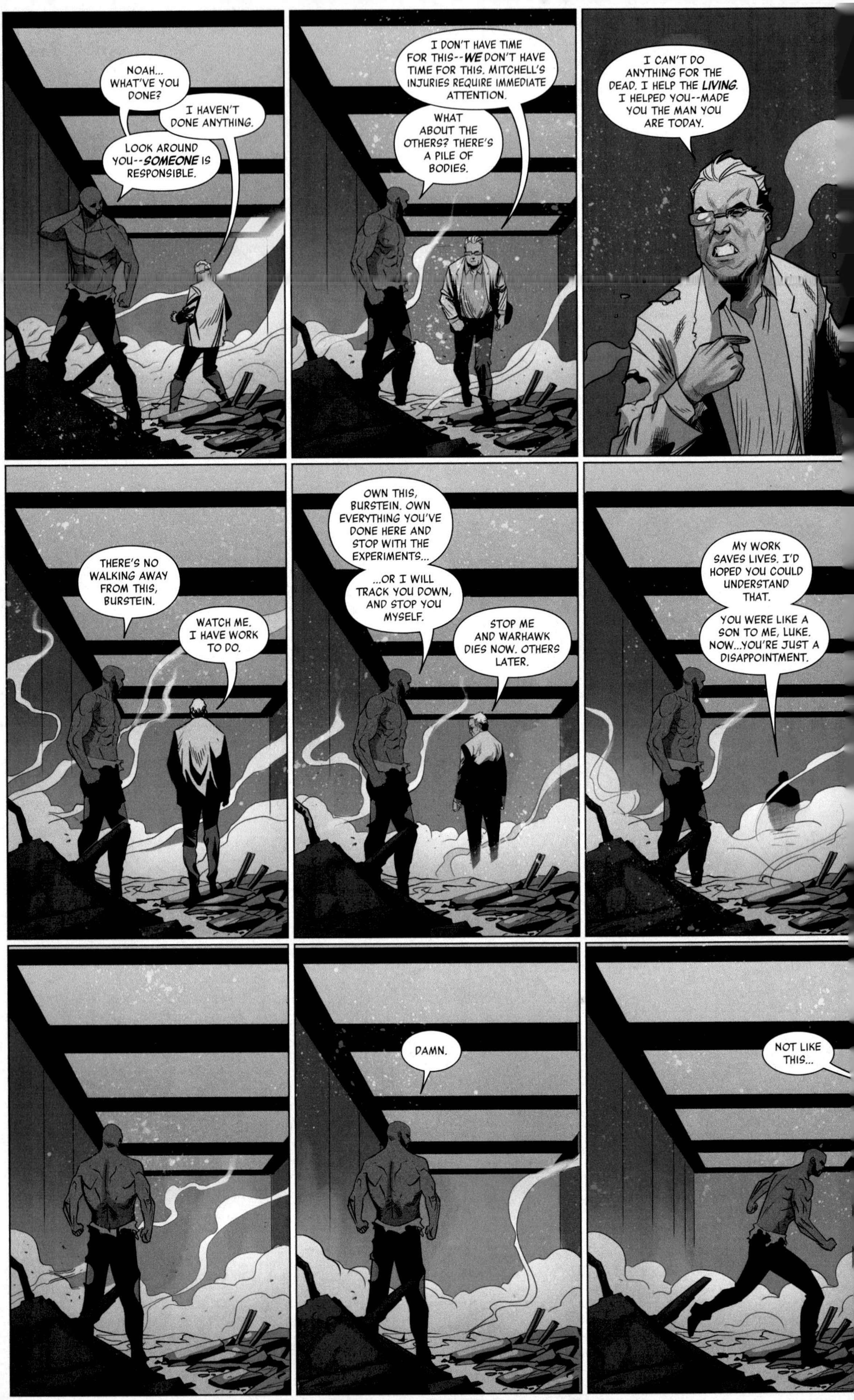
NOAH... WHAT'VE YOU DONE?
I HAVEN'T DONE ANYTHING.
LOOK AROUND YOU--SOMEONE IS RESPONSIBLE.
I DON'T HAVE TIME FOR THIS--WE DON'T HAVE TIME FOR THIS. MITCHELL'S INJURIES REQUIRE IMMEDIATE ATTENTION.
WHAT ABOUT THE OTHERS? THERE'S A PILE OF BODIES.
I CAN'T DO ANYTHING FOR THE DEAD. I HELP THE LIVING. I HELPED YOU--MADE YOU THE MAN YOU ARE TODAY.
THERE'S NO WALKING AWAY FROM THIS, BURSTEIN.
WATCH ME. I HAVE WORK TO DO.
OWN THIS, BURSTEIN. OWN EVERYTHING YOU'VE DONE HERE AND STOP WITH THE EXPERIMENTS...
...OR I WILL TRACK YOU DOWN, AND STOP YOU MYSELF.
STOP ME AND WARHAWK DIES NOW. OTHERS LATER.
MY WORK SAVES LIVES. I'D HOPED YOU COULD UNDERSTAND THAT.
YOU WERE LIKE A SON TO ME, LUKE. NOW...YOU'RE JUST A DISAPPOINTMENT.
DAMN.
NOT LIKE THIS...

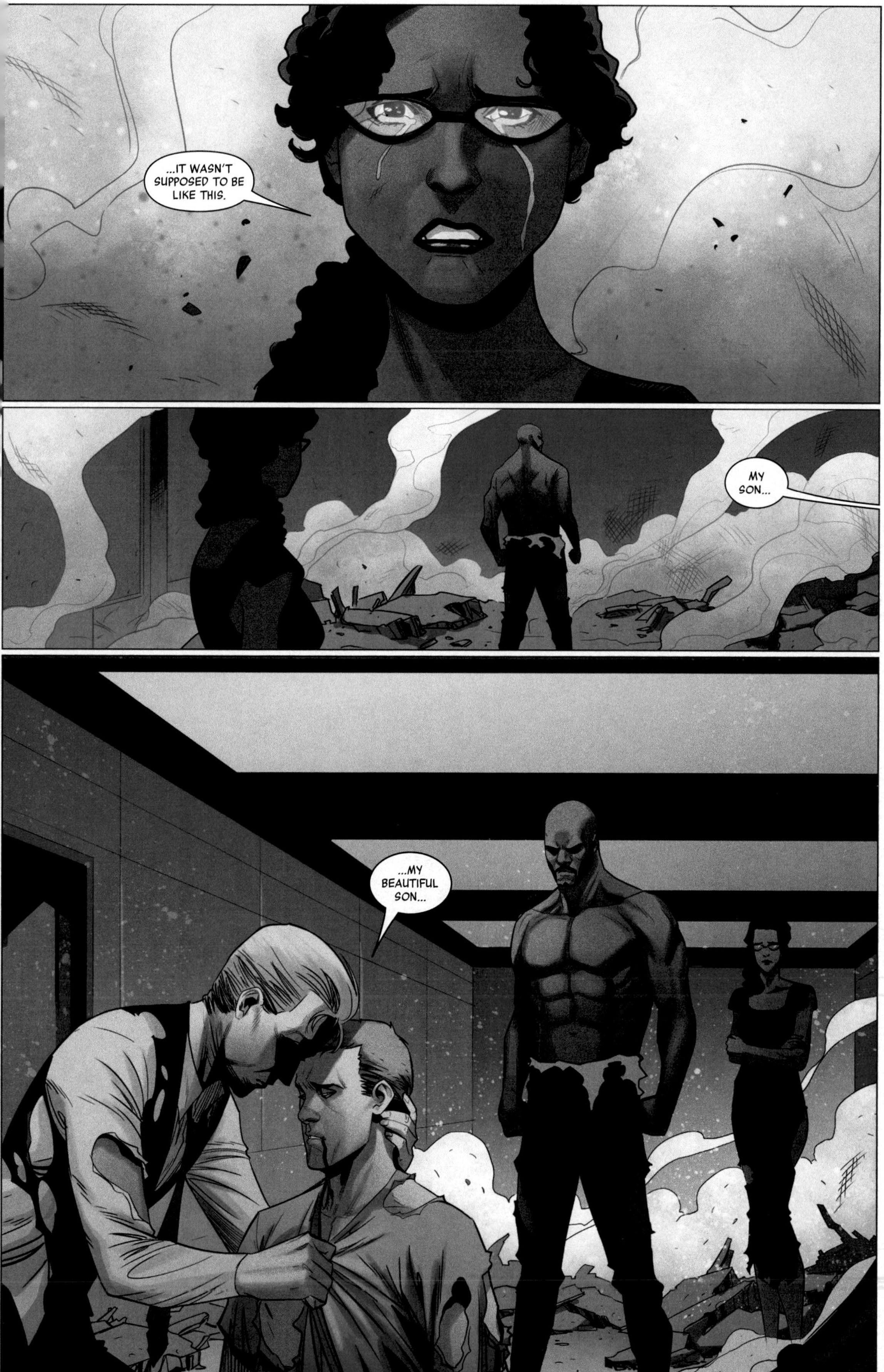

...IT WASN'T SUPPOSED TO BE LIKE THIS.
MY SON...
...MY BEAUTIFUL SON...

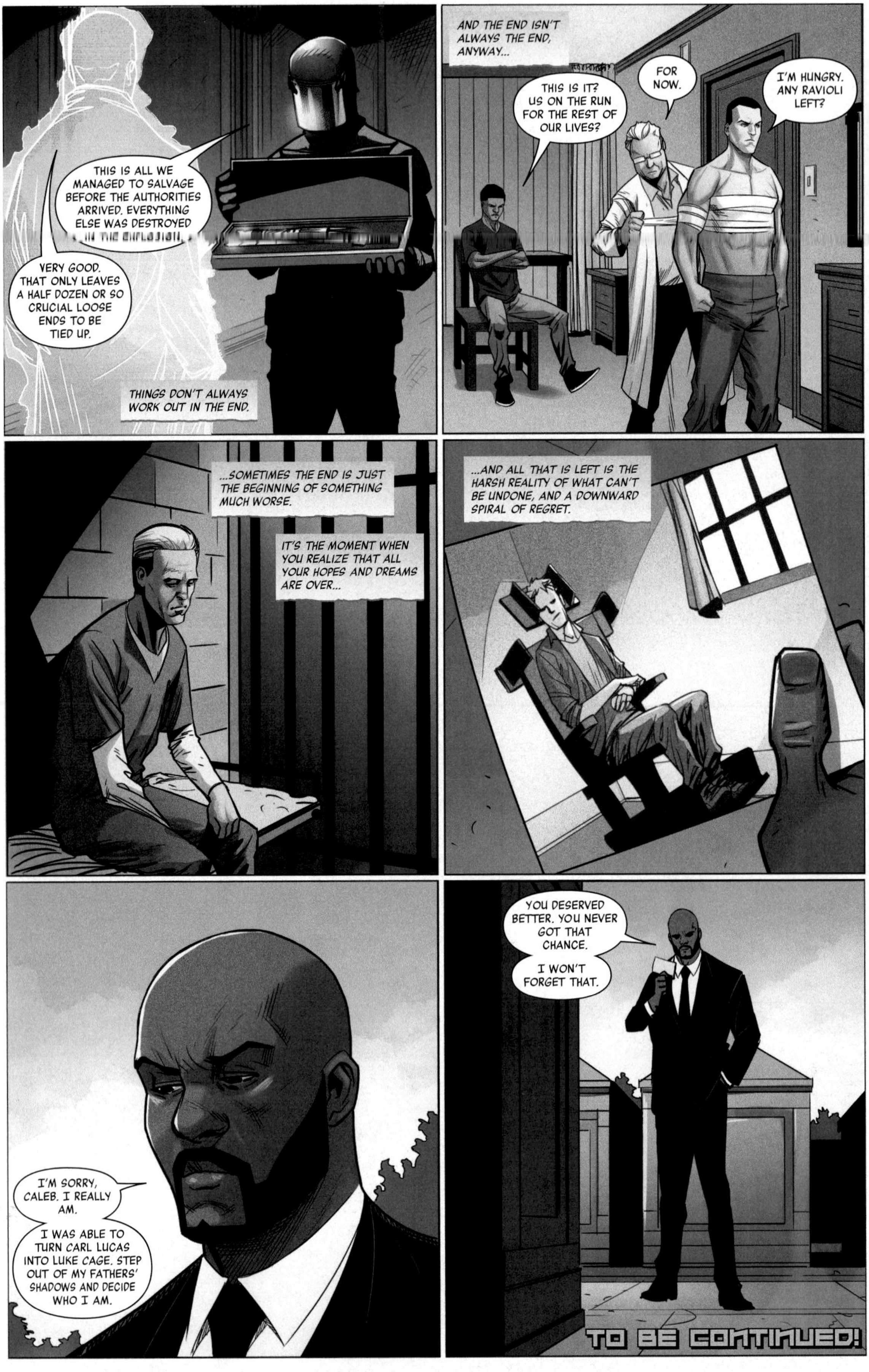
THIS IS ALL WE MANAGED TO SALVAGE BEFORE THE AUTHORITIES ARRIVED. EVERYTHING ELSE WAS DESTROYED
VERY GOOD. THAT ONLY LEAVES A HALF DOZEN OR SO CRUCIAL LOOSE ENDS TO BE TIED UP.
THINGS DON'T ALWAYS WORK OUT IN THE END.
AND THE END ISN'T ALWAYS THE END, ANYWAY...
THIS IS IT? US ON THE RUN FOR THE REST OF OUR LIVES?
FOR NOW.
I'M HUNGRY. ANY RAVIOLI LEFT?
...SOMETIMES THE END IS JUST THE BEGINNING OF SOMETHING MUCH WORSE.
IT'S THE MOMENT WHEN YOU REALIZE THAT ALL YOUR HOPES AND DREAMS ARE OVER...
...AND ALL THAT IS LEFT IS THE HARSH REALITY OF WHAT CAN'T BE UNDONE, AND A DOWNWARD SPIRAL OF REGRET.
I'M SORRY, CALEB. I REALLY AM.
I WAS ABLE TO TURN CARL LUCAS INTO LUKE CAGE. STEP OUT OF MY FATHERS' SHADOWS AND DECIDE WHO I AM.
YOU DESERVED BETTER. YOU NEVER GOT THAT CHANCE.
I WON'T FORGET THAT.
TO BE CONTINUED!

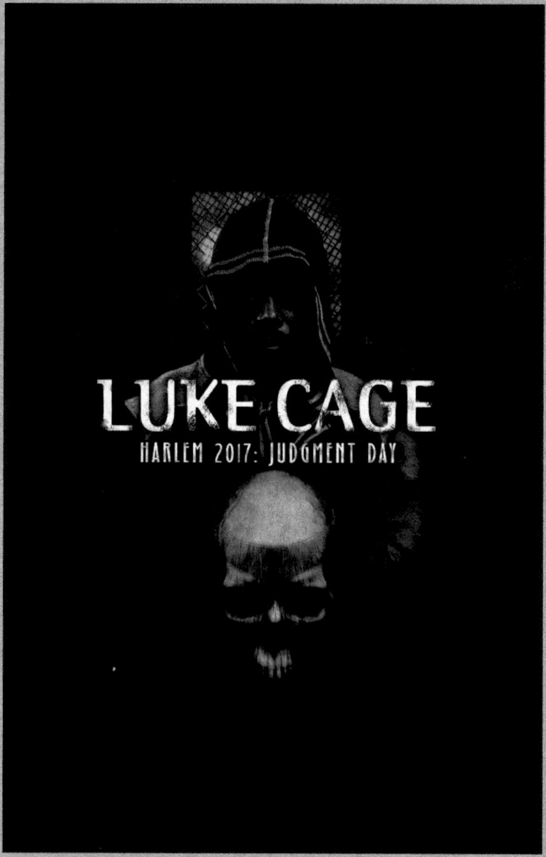
LUKE CAGE
HARLEM 2017: JUDGMENT DAY

#1 HIP-HOP VARIANT BY
TIM BRADSTREET

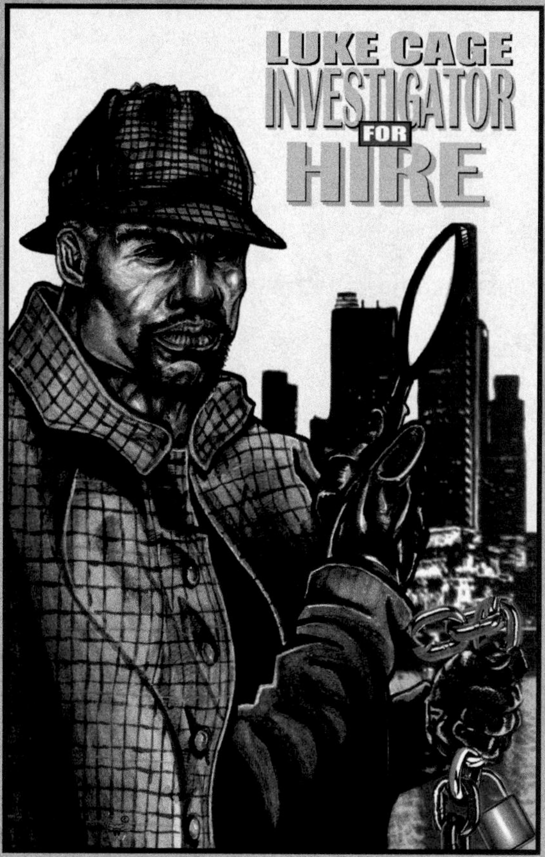
LUKE CAGE
INVESTIGATOR
FOR
HIRE

#1 VARIANT BY
ANDRÉ LEROY DAVIS

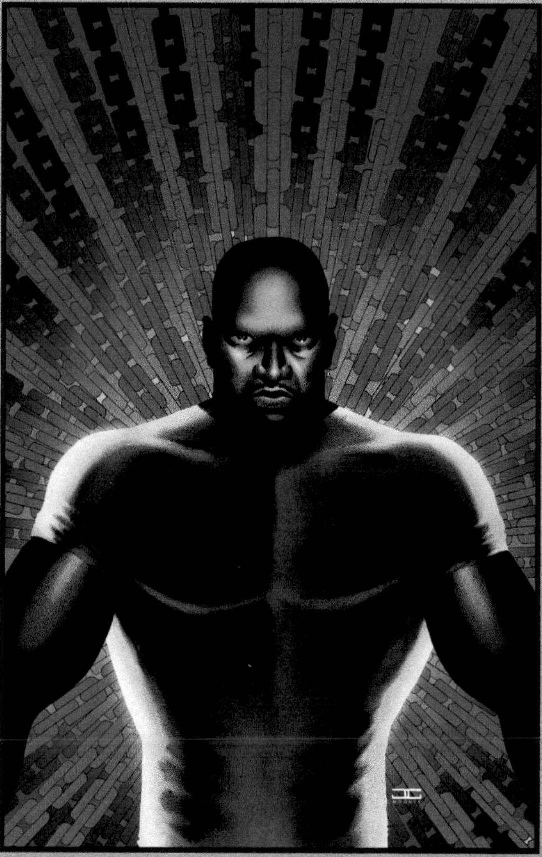

#2 VARIANT BY
JOHN CASSADAY & PAUL MOUNTS

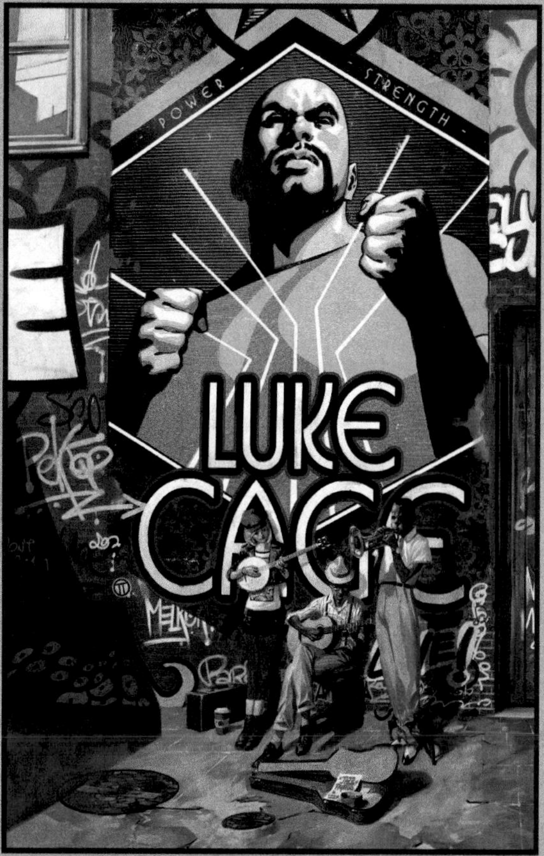
POWER
STRENGTH
LUKE

#3 VARIANT BY
JULIAN TOTINO TEDESCO

POWER MAIL

If memory serves me correctly, my introduction to Luke Cage came more than three years after his debut in the world of comics. My cousin Sean and I saw our first issue of LUKE CAGE, POWER MAN — issue #37, to be exact — on the comic rack at a 7-Eleven in Virginia. This was in 1976, and Sean will back me up when I say that this particular comic book changed our lives.

For two black kids growing up in the 1970s, Luke was unlike anything we had ever seen. Sure, we liked Falcon, but he didn't have his own series — it was Captain America AND Falcon. But this Luke Cage guy? He had his own comic! He didn't have to share it with anyone, and, more important, he wasn't the sidekick. And even though neither of us actually knew any black people that talked like Luke Cage, Sean and I accepted him for who he was — OUR hero. The very existence of Luke meant that we could be more than just the sidekick — the spotlight could shine on someone who looked a bit like us.

More than 40 years later, I find myself in a place I only dreamed of as a kid — I'm actually writing the solo adventures of Luke Cage. I can't tell you how lucky I am. I hope this chapter of Luke's life means as much to others as it did to Sean and me, so many years ago. This series is dedicated to those two kids in 1976 who went into a 7-Eleven for comic books and Slurpees, and came out knowing that there was a super hero that spoke for them and to them (in a weird kind of jive-talk vernacular). At the same time, this series is for more than just my cousin and me; it is for everyone — old fans and new fans — all the people who know that Luke Cage is, quite simply, one of the greatest super heroes of all time. Thank you to the entire artistic and editorial team that is making this series come to life. Sweet Christmas.

DAVID F. WALKER